# Mysteria Magica

## About the Authors

Osborne Phillips is the pen name of Leon Barcynski. Leon is an internationally recognized authority on the mainstream Western mysteries and Grand Master of the International Order Aurum Solis. In addition to his lifelong practical involvement in the Western magickal arts, he has a consuming passion for the spiritual disciplines of Hinduism and Buddhism. He is particularly interested in the phenomena of psychism, to which he has devoted many years of research, and in the psychology of religious mystical experience. Among his other interests are caving, archaeology, astronomy, and science fiction. He currently lives in the United Kingdom where he shares his life and aspirations with his partner, Sandra.

Melita Denning was the pen name of the late Vivian Godfrey Barcynski. Vivian, who passed into the Greater Life in 1997, was for many years Grand Master of the Order Aurum Solis. Under her direction and with her encouragement, the Order's program of making public aspects of its rites and teachings was inaugurated; and she was the inspiring genius of *The Magical Philosophy*, to which she contributed much high wisdom and poetic beauty. In addition to her magickal research and writings, Vivian was a brilliant historian. Her research into medieval and Renaissance aspects of the Ogdoadic Tradition was extensive and profound; and for her study of the history and ritual of the Knights Templar she was invested Dame d'Honneur by the Sovereign Military Order of the Temple of Jerusalem in 1967.

## To Write to the Author

If you wish to contact the author or would like more information about this book, please write to the author in care of Llewellyn Worldwide and we will forward your request. Both the author and publisher appreciate hearing from you and learning of your enjoyment of this book and how it has helped you. Llewellyn Worldwide cannot guarantee that every letter written to the author can be answered, but all will be forwarded. Please write to:

Osborne Phillips
℅ Llewellyn Worldwide
P.O. Box 64383, Dept. 0-7387-0169-6
St. Paul, MN 55164-0383, U.S.A.

Please enclose a self-addressed stamped envelope for reply,
or $1.00 to cover costs. If outside U.S.A., enclose
international postal reply coupon.

Many of Llewellyn's authors have websites with additional information and resources. For more information, please visit our website at http://www.llewellyn.com

# Mysteria Magica

## Fundamental Techniques of High Magick

# DENNING & PHILLIPS

2004
Llewellyn Publications
St. Paul, Minnesota 55164-0383, U.S.A.

THIRD EDITION, 2004
Second printing, 2004

FIRST EDITION, 1981. SECOND EDITION, 1986, three printings.


Cover design by Lisa Novak




Library of Congress Cataloging-in-Publication Data
Denning, Melita.
    Mysteria magica : fundamental techniques of high magick / Melita Denning & Osborne Phillips.—3rd ed.
        p. cm. — (Llewellyn's aurum solis series) (the magical philosophy ; v. 3, bk. 5)
    Includes bibliographical references.
    ISBN 0-7387-0169-6
        1. Magic.  I. Phillips, Osborne. II. Title. III. Series.

BF1611.D395 2004
133.4'—dc22                                                    2003066120

Llewellyn Worldwide does not participate in, endorse, or have any authority or responsibility concerning private business transactions between our authors and the public.
    All mail addressed to the author is forwarded but the publisher cannot, unless specifically instructed by the author, give out an address or phone number.
    Any Internet references contained in this work are current at publication time, but the publisher cannot guarantee that a specific location will continue to be maintained. Please refer to the publisher's website for links to authors' websites and other sources.

Llewellyn Publications
A Division of Llewellyn Worldwide, Ltd.
P.O. Box 64383, Dept. 0-7387-0169-6
St. Paul, MN 55164-0383, U.S.A.
www.llewellyn.com

Printed in the United States of America

# Other Books by the Authors

*Voudon Fire: The Living Reality of Mystical Religion*, 1979
*The Inner World of Fitness* (by Melita Denning), 1986

The Practical Guide Series
  *Practical Guide to Astral Projection*, 1979
  *Practical Guide to Creative Visualization*, 1980
  *Practical Guide to the Development of Psychic Powers*, 1981
  *Practical Guide to the Magick of Sex*, 1982
  *Practical Guide to the Magick of Tarot*, 1983
  *Practical Guide to Creative Moneymaking*, 1992

The Aurum Solis Series
  *Magical States of Consciousness*, 1985
  *The Magical Philosophy: The Foundations of High Magick* (Volume 1), 1991, and *The Sword and Serpent* (Volume 2), 1988
  *Planetary Magick*, 1989
  *Entrance to the Magical Qabalah* (Thoth Publications, UK), 1997

The Magical Philosophy
  (reprinted as part of the Aurum Solis Series [see above])
  Book I. *Robe and Ring*, 1974
  Book II. *The Apparel of High Magic*, 1975
  Book III. *The Sword and the Serpent*, 1975
  Book IV. *The Triumph of Light*, 1978
  Book V. *Mysteria Magica*, 1982

# Contents

*Tables of Correspondences*

# PART I

# FUNDAMENTAL TECHNIQUES

*I*

## POSTURE & BREATHING

The three established postures of the Western Tradition are:

A. The Sitting or *God-form Posture*
B. The Standing or *Wand Posture*
C. The Supine or *Earth Posture*

*A. The God-form Posture* is of ancient Egyptian origin. It is essential for this posture that a seat should be arranged so that the thighs shall be horizontal while the lower leg is vertical, and the soles of the feet rest steadily upon the floor, or if necessary upon a support. Thus seated, with the spine erect but not stiffly vertical, the feet should be placed side by side as should the knees. The upper arms should hang loosely at the sides and the hands should rest palm downwards upon the thighs. The head should be held so that if open the eyes gaze straight ahead.

B. *The Wand Posture* is a normal and well-balanced standing position. The head is held erect, the shoulders are dropped back so that they are neither drooping nor held rigidly square. The arms hang by the sides with a slight natural curve at the elbow; the feet are placed side by side, the toes being turned neither in nor out.

If this posture is correctly maintained, it should be possible to take a step forward with either foot as required, without shifting the weight.

C. *The Earth Posture* is a position in which the subject lies flat on his back. The legs are straight and the arms lie

3

straight at the sides of the body. It is essential for this posture that tight clothing and unnecessary discomforts should be avoided.

The standard breathing technique used in connection with Aurum Solis practices is referred to as the *Rhythmic Breath*. This particular rhythm of breathing is termed by some people the *Healing Breath*, because one of the good results of its proficient use is the rapid and powerful release of energy: for oneself if need be, or to implement works of healing and magical acts generally.

To practice this Rhythmic Breath, begin by counting your own heartbeats. At first it may be difficult to concentrate upon the heartbeat, so keep away while practicing from sounds such as a ticking clock or strongly rhythmic music. In time you will be able to disregard sounds which do not relate to what you are doing.

When you first begin to concentrate upon your heart-beat, it may slow down to some extent before steadying itself. This is quite normal, and with more practice will cease to occur.

The rhythm of this form of breathing consists in taking the breath in during a count of 6 heartbeats, holding the breath for a count of 3, exhaling during a count of 6, then counting 3 before beginning to inhale again. The critical point is the count of 3 before beginning to inhale: some students may at first find this pause impossible or distressing. In such a case, strain is to be avoided. A count of 2 heartbeats should then be used, but the characteristic rhythm of the practice should be maintained: this will mean inhaling during a count of 4, holding the breath during a count of 2, exhaling during a count of 4, and thus coming to the pause of 2 heartbeats before again inhaling. In time the standard count will become easy.

When Rhythmic Breathing is achieved, whether 4-2-4-2 or the full 6-3-6-3, it may be used whenever opportunity offers, and certainly should be used when any magical or meditative practice is undertaken. The intention in Rhythmic Breathing is *not,* as it may at first seem, to keep attention focused upon counting heartbeats or upon the flow of breath; but to facilitate a total concentration of attention upon other matters in confidence that the Rhythmic Breath, once established, will continue in a smooth and entirely adequate manner for as long as it is needed, without counting, without another conscious thought. A natural, easy flow of rhythmic breathing thus becomes "second nature".

## II

## *THE CALYX*

*(Face East, assume the Wand Posture, develop the Rhythmic Breath.)*

i.    Draw in a deep breath; on the expelled breath, vibrate:– אתה ❙ EI

ii.    Draw in a deep breath, raise the arms gently at the sides so that they are held almost horizontally, but not stiffly so: the palms being upturned. The breath is expelled.

iii.    Draw in the breath; on the expelled breath, vibrate: מלכות ❙ Η ΒΑΣΙΛΕΙΑ

iv.    Lowering the elbow as may be necessary, on the next indrawn breath bring the palm of the left hand across to the right shoulder. On the expelled breath, vibrate:– וגבורה ❙ ΚΑΙ Ή ΔΥΝΑΜΙΣ

v.    On the indrawn breath bring the palm of the right hand across to the left shoulder, across the left arm. On the expelled breath, vibrate:– וגדולה ❙ ΚΑΙ Ή ΔΟΞΑ

vi.    Keeping the arms crossed, incline the head slightly forward on the pause at the end of the breath. Draw in the breath. On the expelled breath vibrate:– לעולם ועד ❙ ΕΙΣ ΤΟΥΣ ΑΙΩΝΑΣ

### (Commentary)

The Calyx is a fundamental technique of Art Magick, which

7

both aligns the practitioner with the forces of the cosmos, and awakens awareness of the counterparts of those forces with the psyche. It can thus be said to encapsule in brief compass the chief method and purpose of all workings of High Magick.

The Calyx is variously employed as a psychic energizer, as a mode of adoration, or as a preparatory formula for the bringing through of power.

It forms, for example, an integral part of the rites of the Setting of the Wards (Papers III, IV, and V following), where its primary function is to imbue the operator with the power necessary to establish a sealed and sanctified environment, a vibrant astral matrix, in which to conduct his work.

Again, at the conclusion of some of the Ritual Formulae of Part VI of this book, the Calyx is employed as a *gratulatio*, a magical thanksgiving. In this context, the function of the Calyx is twofold: in the ambience of an achieved rite it honors the sublime reality of the forces of cosmos and microcosmos, and it affirms and establishes the equilibrium of potencies within the psychic organism of the operator.

Although relatively simple, the Calyx is a complete spiritual "toner" in its own right, and the student should use it frequently: whether to enhance the personal psychic energies in preparation for a further activity (ritual, meditative, or other), or as mode of attunement to the great forces of life, or for the sheer joy of the work or for bliss of being.

In the text of the Calyx, the Words of Power are given in both Hebrew and Greek forms. The transliterations and meanings of these words are as follows:

| (Hebrew) | (Greek) | |
| --- | --- | --- |
| ATOH | EI | *THOU ART* |
| MALKUTH | HE BASILEIA | *THE KINGDOM* |
| V'GEBURAH | KAI HE DUNAMIS | *AND THE POWER* |
| V'GEDULAH | KAI HE DOXA | *AND THE MAJESTY* |
| L'AULOM VO-ED | EIS TOUS AIONAS | *TO ETERNAL AGES* |

After mastering the "mechanics" of the Calyx—the synchronization of breath, intonation and gesture—the student is ready to undertake the Calyx in its complete form, to include the use of visualization and a contemplative awareness of the successive principles involved. This complete form is exemplified below: in this, for convenience, the Words of Power are given in their Hebrew form alone.

i.     When the Rhythmic Breath has been developed, a Tongue of Flame is visualized above the head. This Tongue of Flame represents the Higher Genius, the source of magical power, that Sacred Flame by virtue of which the practice of Magick is possible. Its situation above the head should prevent any confusion of it with the everyday personality or Ego. Holding this visualization steadily in mind, on the expelled breath we vibrate:—

ATOH

ii.     On the indrawn breath the arms are raised. In raising the arms, the vertical line of the body is balanced by a symmetrical, horizontal extension. This horizontal evokes an awareness of Jupiter, Mercy, to the left, with Mars, Strength, to the right, as balanced powers within us. The palms are upturned to signify that this balanced being is ready to receive the power of the Higher Self. The breath is expelled.

iii.     As the breath is drawn in, a brilliant shaft of light is visualized which descends swiftly from the Tongue of Flame, passing through the crown of the head and the center of the body to the ground between the feet.* On the Expelled breath we vibrate:—

---

* As in all magical operations involving the central column energies, whether visualized as the downward-coursing light or as the Centers of Activity themselves, the primary domain of controlled function is the astrosome. Initially, therefore, the effect of such practices is likely to consist solely in the increase and harmonization of energy patterns within the astral body. But this is only the beginning of the process, for through continued and regular use of these practices, higher and more inward faculties of the psyche will become increasingly involved in the work, and a true harmony and interaction of forces will thus be wrought through all levels of the psyche.

## MALKUTH

iv.   On the indrawn breath the palm of the left hand is brought across to rest on the right shoulder. We acknowledge the forces of Mars at the right side. On the expelled breath we vibrate:—

## V'GEBURAH

v.   On the indrawn breath the palm of the right hand is brought across to rest on the left shoulder. We acknowledge the forces of Jupiter at the left side. On the expelled breath we vibrate:—

## V'GEDULAH

vi.   Keeping the arms crossed, on the pause at the end of the breath we lower the head. The breath is drawn in: we feel the shaft of light within, radiating energy into our being. We feel a great concentration of light and power at the heart-center, which lies upon the vertical line under the crossing of the arms. On the expelled breath we vibrate:—

## L'AULOM VO-ED

*III*

## THE SETTING OF THE WARDS OF POWER
### (Hebrew)

*(Stand in the centre of the place of working, or as nearly the centre as the arrangement of the chamber will allow.\*)*

i.   Facing East, assume the Wand Posture. Vibrate אתה

ii.  Raise the arms at the sides, vibrate מלכות

iii. Touch the right shoulder with the left hand, vibrate וגבורה

iv.  Touch the left shoulder with the right hand, vibrate וגדולה

v.   Keeping the arms crossed, bow the head and vibrate לעולם ועד

vi.  Advance to the East. Beginning at that point and returning thereto, move widdershins round the place of working, with hand outstretched tracing the circle.

vii. After completing the circle, return to the centre. Facing East, make the Gesture *Cervus*: at the first point vibrate אהיה, at the second יהוה.

viii. Turn to face North: make the Gesture, vibrating אגלא at the first point, אדני at the second.

ix.  Face West: make the Gesture, vibrating אגלא, then אל.

x.   Turn to face South. Make the Gesture, vibrating אהיה and אלהים.

---

\* If the Bomos is stationed at the centre of the place of working, begin East of Bomos.

11

xi.       Face East. Assume the Wand Posture then raise the
          arms to form a Tau. Vibrate ·—
            TO THE EAST רוחיאל
            TO THE SOUTH אשיאל
            TO THE WEST מיאל
            TO THE NORTH אופיריאל
xii.      Repeat the Calyx, i to v.


(Commentary)


The purpose of the present ritual is to demarcate and
prepare the area in which the magician is to work, with astral
and Briatic defenses. The ritual consists of both banishing and
invocation: the four Elements having been banished from the
Circle in their naturally confused and impure state, the mighty
spiritual forces ruling the Elements are invoked into symbolic
egregores, to become Guardians of the Circle.

In the text of the Setting of the Wards of Power given
above, the Gesture Cervus is indicated. This Gesture is performed as follows:

1.   The Wand Posture is assumed.
2.   Both hands are raised to the brow, so as to frame
     the center of the forehead in the space formed by
     conjoining thumb with thumb, forefinger with fore-
     finger, palms facing forwards. (The two middle
     fingers will also touch.) This constitutes the first
     point of the Gesture; while this position is held,
     the first Word of Power is vibrated.
3.   In one vigorous movement the hands are separated
     and flung forward, slightly apart and upward: the
     elbows should be straightened and the fingers slight-
     ly spread. The palms are still facing forwards. This
     position constitutes the second point of the Gesture.
     The second Word of Power should be forcefully
     uttered while this movement is being made. The
     arms are then lowered.

When the student has mastered the physical performance of the rite (that is, vibration, movement and gesture) as detailed in the text, he should proceed to employ the full form of the Setting, incorporating visualization and reflection, as follows. *From the beginning, however, he should perform the Calyx fully, as set forth in Paper II.*

The Calyx is performed.

The operator advances to the East. He moves widdershins round the place of working, tracing the circle with his out-stretched right hand. As he proceeds, he visualizes a shimmering wall of silver mist which he is thus drawing round the limits of the chamber: when he links the circle in the East this silver wall completely encompasses the place of working.

The operator returns to the center. Facing East, he makes the Gesture Cervus; at the completion of the first point he visualizes a pentagram of brilliant light on his brow, framed by his hands. Holding this in mind he vibrates *EHEIEH*. The pentagram is flung forth with the second point of the Gesture, the operator vibrating YAHWEH: as the pentagram is flung forth it is seen to diffuse as a burst of light into the shimmering mist-wall. The result of this is twofold: the forces of Air are banished from within the circle, and the first Ward is established.\*

Remaining on the same spot, but turning to face the North, the operator repeats the Gesture and visualizations, using the names AGLA and ADONAY.

Still at center, the operator turns to face West. He repeats the Gesture and Visualizations, using the names AGLA and EL.

---

\* The Gesture by its nature causes diffusion, but does not lessen banishing force within a small area. Magical practice has established that Cervus is fully efficacious to a distance of approximately thirty feet from the operator, and thus in a working area sixty feet in diameter. Beyond this range the full astral reality of its power begins to diminish. The fortification of the circle by the method of the Cervus is only possible because the projected force is diffused thereby; a concentrated projection of force would, inevitably, pierce the barrier. The circle alone will contain forces, but will provide no adequate defense.

Turning to face South, he again repeats the Gesture and visualizations, using the names EHEIEH and ELOHIM.

The operator now faces East. He assumes the Wand Posture, then raises his arms to form a Tau, palms downwards. He remains thus, at center and facing East, arms raised in the Tau, throughout the fourfold invocation of the Archangelic powers (section xi of the text).

Before him he visualizes a tall and slender form clad in a voluminous and billowing robe of yellow, heightened with traces of violet. While this figure is contemplated, a cool rushing of wind is to be felt as emanating from the East. This wind should be felt inwardly to awaken the hidden aspirations and wordless hopes which have lain dormant in the toils of sloth and habitude: it sings to the inner ear of the potentialities of a life which reaches forth to the spiritual heights. When this image has been formulated and realized, the operator vibrates TO THE EAST RUACHIEL.

To the South he visualizes a lean muscular figure with an appearance of great strength, clad in a robe of brilliant red with changeful sparks of green, and standing amid flames. This figure holds in his right hand a wand of burnished copper. While this figure is contemplated, a sensation of powerful heat is to be felt as emanating from the South. It should also be perceived inwardly that the fire from which this heat is generated is the fire of inspiration: there is in its power a kernel of inebriation too, as may be understood by recalling that Dionysus took birth from the all-consuming fire of Zeus. When this image has been formulated and realized, the operator vibrates TO THE SOUTH ASHIEL.

To the West he visualizes a tall and powerful figure standing amid foaming turbulent waters, clad in a robe of blue merging into highlights of orange, and holding in his left hand a silver cup. While this figure is contemplated, the mighty surge of the sea tides is imagined, pouring in successive waves from the West. Inwardly it should be felt that these waves are of the cold and shining waters which purify the intellect in their flood, healing it of unreason's fever and tempering it as steel is tempered. When this image has been formulated and realized, the operator vibrates TO THE WEST MIEL.

To the North he visualizes a broad-shouldered, placid figure, robed in indigo which gleams with flashes of pale gold, and standing upon wild grass studded with yellow flowers. In his left hand the figure bears a golden orb, in his right a golden sickle. While this figure is contemplated, a feeling of great peace and stability is to be imagined, for the succession of the seasons wipes out or mitigates past errors: the innocence of the Golden Age ever awaits us in earth's renewal. Elemental Earth itself is the medium of nature's work, and the instinctual faculties of man find their repose therein. When this image has been formulated and realized, the operator vibrates TO THE NORTH AUPHIRIEL.

The fourfold invocation having been accomplished, the operator, still at center and facing East, concludes with the Calyx.

When the integration of gestures, vibrations, visualizations and other parts of the Setting has been achieved, the student should accustom himself to performing the Setting of the Wards, and to working within their protection. To this end, he should carry out the Setting very often, and always before his exercise sequence or any other magical work.

One of the effects of the practice is a personal attunement to the equilibrium of the great forces invoked therein. Long familiarity with this ritual will but render it more rewarding; care must be taken, however, that it is always performed attentively and with unabated heed to all its parts.

The circle traced about the place of working (section vi of the text) should encompass the whole area, all necessary equipment having been duly placed beforehand within its limits. This is of vital importance, as no-one is to cross the bounds of the circle during the working. No relaxation of this rule should be permitted. If the circle is disturbed in this way, there is a real danger that undesirable influences attracted by the magick may enter through the breach and vitiate the working. A more insidious danger, however, is that the operator who is careless concerning the breaking of his defences will find that he has weakened his own belief in their reality; and such doubts carry their own perils. One's work must be sound, and one must know it to be sound.

*IV*

## THE SETTING OF THE WARDS OF POWER
### (Greek)

*(Stand in the centre of the place of working, or as nearly the centre as the arrangement of the chamber will allow.)*

i.      Facing East, assume the Wand Posture. Vibrate EI

ii.     Raise the arms at the sides, vibrate Ἡ ΒΑΣΙΛΕΙΑ

iii.    Touch the right shoulder with the left hand, vibrate ΚΑΙ Ἡ ΔΥΝΑΜΙΣ

iv.    Touch the left shoulder with the right hand, vibrate ΚΑΙ Ἡ ΔΟΞΑ

v.     Keeping the arms crossed, bow the head and vibrate ΕΙΣ ΤΟΥΣ ΑΙΩΝΑΣ

vi.    Advance to the East. Trace the circle, returning to the East.

vii.   Return to the centre. Facing East, vibrate:—
          Ἡ ΠΕΛΕΙΑ ΚΑΙ Ἡ ΥΓΡΑ
          Ὁ ΟΦΙΣ ΚΑΙ ΤΟ ΩΙΟΝ

viii.  Facing East, make the Gesture *Cervus:* at the first point vibrate ΑΘΑΝΑΤΟΣ, at the the second ΣΕΛΑΗ-ΓΕΝΕΤΗΣ.

ix.    Turn to face North: make the Gesture, vibrating ΙΣΧΥΡΟΣ at the first point, and ΚΥΡΙΟΣ at the second point.

x.     Face West: make the Gesture, vibrating ΙΣΧΥΡΟΣ then ΠΑΓΚΡΑΤΗΣ.

xi.    Turn to face South. Make the Gesture, vibrating ΑΘΑΝΑΤΟΣ and ΘΕΟΣ.

17

xii.        Face East. Assume the Wand Posture. Vibrate:—
            ΓΑΙΑ ΚΑΙ ʹΟ ΙΧΩΡ ΤΟΥ ΟΥΡΑΝΟΥ
            Raise the arms to form a Tau, vibrate:—
                TO THE EAST ΣΩΤΗΡ
                TO THE SOUTH ΑΛΑΣΤΩΡ
                TO THE WEST ΑΣΦΑΛΕΙΟΣ
                TO THE NORTH ΑΜΥΝΤΩΡ

xiii.       Repeat the Calyx, i to v.


                        (Commentary)
        The Calyx is performed:
            EI—*Thou Art*
            HE BASILEIA—*The Kingdom*
            KAI HE DYNAMIS—*And the Power.*
            KAI HE DOXA—*And the Glory*
            EIS TOUS AIONAS*—*To the Ages.*

        The operator advances to the East. He moves widdershins
round the place of working, tracing the circle with his out-
stretched right hand. As he proceeds, he visualizes a silver
mist which he is thus drawing round the limits of the chamber:
when he links the circle in the East, the place of working is
completely encompassed by this shimmering wall.

        The operator returns to the centre. Facing East, he
vibrates:—
            HE PELEIA KAI HE HUGRA—*The Dove and the Waters*
            HO OPHIS KAI TO OION—*The Serpent and the Egg*

        He makes the Gesture Cervus: at the completion of the
first point he visualizes a pentagram of brilliant light on his
brow, framed by his hands. Holding this in mind he vibrates
ATHANATOS. The pentagram is flung forth with the second
point of the Gesture, the operator vibrating SELAE-GENETES:
as the pentagram is flung forth it is seen to diffuse as a burst

---

* As a general note on the pronunciation of Greek, it is pointed out that the
transliterations occurring in this volume are in some respects only approximate,
particularly with regard to the letters Η, Υ and Ω. For exactitude the student is
advised to familiarise himself with the sound-values of the Greek letters.

of light into the shimmering mist-wall.

This procedure is repeated with the paired names ISCHYROS and KYRIOS, ISCHYROS and PANKRATES, ATHANATOS and THEOS, for the North, West, and South respectively.

The operator faces East. He assumes the Wand Posture and vibrates:—

### GAIA KAI HO ICHOR TOU OURANOU
*Earth and the Blood of Heaven.*

He raises his arms to form a Tau, remaining thus throughout the fourfold invocation:—

Before him he visualizes a tall and slender form clad in a voluminous and billowing robe of yellow, heightened with traces of violet. While this figure is contemplated, a cool rushing of wind is to be felt as emanating from the East. (It awakens the hidden aspirations and wordless hopes which have lain dormant in the toils of sloth and of habitude. It sings to the inner ear of the potentialities of a life which reaches forth to spiritual heights. When this image has been formulated, the operator vibrates TO THE EAST SOTER.

To the south he visualizes a lean muscular figure with an appearance of great strength, clad in a robe of brilliant red with changeful sparks of green, and standing amid flames. This figure holds in his right hand a wand of burnished copper. While this figure is contemplated, a sensation of powerful heat is to be felt as emanating from the South. (The fire from which this heat is generated is the fire of inspiration: there is in its power a kernel of inebriation too, as may be understood by recalling that Dionysus took birth from the all-consuming fire of Zeus. Nevertheless, although the nature of this Element is to be acknowledged, it is not to receive in this rite our inner submission to its power; but we salute its great Regent with veneration.) When this image has been formulated, the operator vibrates TO THE SOUTH ALASTOR.

To the West he visualizes a tall and powerful figure

standing amid foaming turbulent waters, clad in a robe of blue merging into highlights of orange, and holding in his left hand a silver cup. While this figure is contemplated, the mighty surge of the sea-tides is imagined, pouring in successive waves from the West. (These waves are of the cold and shining waters which purify the intellect in their flood, healing it of unreason's fever and tempering it as steel is tempered.) When this image has been formulated, the operator vibrates **TO THE WEST ASPHALEIOS.**

To his left he visualizes a broad-shouldered placid figure, robed in indigo gleaming with flashes of pale gold, and standing upon wild grass studded with yellow flowers. In one hand the figure bears a golden orb, in the other a golden sickle. While this figure is contemplated, a feeling of great peace and stability is to be imagined. (The succession of the seasons wipes out or mitigates past errors, the innocence of the Golden Age ever awaits us in earth's renewal. Elemental Earth itself is the medium of nature's work: and the instinctual faculties of man find repose therein.) When this image has been formulated, the operator vibrates **TO THE NORTH AMYNTOR.**

The Calyx is repeated.

# V

## SUB ROSA NIGRA
## THE SETTING OF THE WARDS OF ADAMANT

*(Stand in the centre of the place of working, or as nearly the centre as the arrangement of the chamber will allow.)*

### Calyx

i.     Facing East, assume the Wand Posture. Vibrate **TU ES**

ii.     Raise the arms at the sides, vibrate **REGNUM**

iii.     Touch right shoulder with left hand, vibrate **ET·POTENTIA**

iv.     Touch left shoulder with right hand, vibrate **ET GLORIA**

v.     Keeping arms crossed, bow head and vibrate **IN SAECULIS**

### Circulus

vi.     Advance to the East. Beginning at that point and returning thereto, trace the widdershins circle, encompassing the area of working.

### Praesidia

vii.     Return to centre and face East. Make the Gesture *Cervus:* at the first point vibrate $A\Theta ANATO\Sigma$, at the second point vibrate $\Sigma E\Lambda AH-\Gamma ENETH\Sigma$.

viii.     Face North: make the Gesture, vibrating $I\Sigma X\Upsilon PO\Sigma$ at the first point, $K\Upsilon PIO\Sigma$ at the second.

ix.     Face West: make the Gesture, vibrating $I\Sigma X\Upsilon PO\Sigma$ at the first point, $\Pi A\Lambda KPATH\Sigma$ at the second.

x.    Face South: make the Gesture, vibrating
ΑΘΑΝΑΤΟΣ and ΘΕΟΣ.

### Invocatio

xi.    Face East. Assume the Wand Posture then raise the
arms to form a Tau. Vibrate:—
    TO THE EAST ΣΩΤΗΡ
    TO THE SOUTH ΑΛΑΣΤΩΡ
    TO THE WEST ΑΣΦΑΛΕΙΟΣ
    TO THE NORTH ΑΜΥΝΤΩΡ

### Dedicatio Sub Rosa Nigra

xii.    Lower the arms to the sides. After a few moments'
pause, make the Gesture *Ave*, then declaim:—
FROM THE PORTAL OF EARTH
    TO THE PORTAL OF FIRE,
FROM THE PORTAL OF AIR
    TO THE PORTAL OF WATER,
FROM THE CENTRE OF POWER
    TO THE ENCOMPASSING ADAMANT,
LET THIS SANCTUARY BE ESTABLISHED
    WITHIN THE BLACK ROSE:
IN THE NAMES ΛΕΥΚΟΘΕΑ, ΜΕΛΑΝΟΘΕΟΣ,
    ΑΓΑΘΟΔΑΙΜΩΝ.

### Arista

| xiii. | | |
|---|---|---|
| AVE LUX SANCTISSIMA, | 1st point |
| SOL VIVENS, | 2nd point |
| CUSTOS MUNDI, | 3rd point |
| IN CORDE TE FOVEO, | 4th point |
| MEMBRIS CIRCUMAMICTIS GLORIA TUA. | 5th point |

I

The Gesture *Ave* is accomplished as follows:—

The right arm is raised with the elbow flexed, so that the upper arm is held forward in an almost horizontal position, slightly out from the side as necessary, the forearm and hand being raised vertically, the palm forward.*

The Gesture *Arista* is accomplished as follows:—

*1st point.* Commencing from the Wand Posture, raise the arms at the sides, so that the body and the upcurved arms form roughly the shape of the Greek letter Ψ, with the upturned palms held almost horizontally though not stiffly so.

*2nd point.* In one smooth movement the hands are brought over to cross upon the breast, right arm over left, fingertips touching collarbones.

*3rd point.* In one smooth movement the forearms are fully extended downward and slightly forward from the body (the elbows move only slightly in this change of position), the hands horizontal with palms downward and closed fingertips pointing forward. This position is, in its own right, the Gesture *Pronatio.*†

*4th point.* In one smooth movement return to position 2, as above, but with left arm over right.

*5th point.* In one smooth movement the arms are opened to a gentle curve just below horizontal, so that they are outward to the sides of, and slightly forward from, the body:

---

* This Gesture is customarily used by comites ("companions", sing. *comes)* as a general salutation to the East when passing that station. It is used by all comites who have cause to pass the East but are not at that time involved in a specific ritual action. Comites involved in a specific ritual action, having cause to pass the East, do not employ the *Ave* unless it is an ordained part of their action. If a ritual act culminates in the East, at the conclusion thereof the Gesture is employed if convenient. But the Gesture is also to be used as a salutation to the East whenever a reverent acknowledgment of the Place of Light is felt to be appropriate. (When performing Morning or Evening Adoration, the *Ave* may be made towards Sol.)

† The Gesture *Pronatio* is independently used (according to context) in invoking chthonic forces, or to link the magical purpose with an intended offering.

the hands following the same line but slightly incurved, very slightly cupped.

## II

The Calyx is performed in Latin. (Significance is as in Hebrew and Greek.)

The operator advances to the East. He moves widdershins round the place of working, tracing the circle and linking in the East. As he proceeds, he visualizes a shimmering wall of silver mist which he is thus drawing round the chamber.

He now returns to the centre. Facing East, he makes Cervus: at the completion of the first point he visualizes a pentagram of brilliant light on his brow, framed by his hands. Holding this in mind he vibrates **ATHANATOS**.   The pentagram is flung forth with the second point of the Gesture,  the operator vibrating **SELAE GENETES**: as the pentagram is flung forth it is seen to diffuse as a burst of light into the mist-wall.

Cervus is repeated with the paired names **ISCHYROS**  and **KYRIOS, ISCHYROS** and **PANKRATES, ATHANATOS** and **THEOS**, for the North, West, and South repsectively.

The operator faces East and assumes the Wand Posture. He then raises his arms to form a Tau, remaining thus throughout the formulations and utterances of the "fourfold invocation", as in the Greek Setting of the Wards of Power.

He lowers his arms to his sides; after a pause he makes the Gesture Ave. The Gesture having been dismissed, he declaims:—

**FROM THE PORTAL OF EARTH TO THE PORTAL OF FIRE, FROM THE PORTAL OF AIR TO THE PORTAL OF WATER, FROM THE CENTRE OF POWER TO THE ENCOMPASSING ADAMANT, LET THIS SANCTUARY BE ESTABLISHED WITHIN THE BLACK ROSE: IN THE NAMES *LEUKOTHEA, MELANOTHEOS, AGATHODAIMON.***

The above italicized names are from the *Constellation of the Worshipped*. While vibrating these the operator traces in the air before him with his right hand a circled, equal-armed cross, all lines being visualized in white light as traced; the horizontal line with the first name, the descending vertical line with the second name, the circle—beginning at the top and returning deosil with the third name.

The operator concludes with the five points of the Gesture Arista and their Latin words:—

He establishes the first point of the Gesture and intones AVE LUX SANCTISSIMA—*Hail, most holy Light!*

He establishes the second. point of the Gesture and intones SOL VIVENS—*Living Sun.*

At the third point of the Gesture he intones CUSTOS MUNDI— *Guardian of the World.*

At the fourth point he intones IN CORDE TE FOVEO— *In my heart I hold thee.*

At the fifth point, MEMBRIS CIRCUMAMICTIS GLORIA TUA— *My limbs being girt about with thy glory.*

N.B. No visualizations are employed with *Arista.*

## VI

### CLAVIS REI PRIMAE
#### (1st Formula)
#### THE ROUSING OF THE CITADELS

(Face East, assume the Wand Posture, develop the Rhythmic Breath.)

*The Gates:*
  i.    Visualize the Crown Center, the *Corona Flammae,* as a sphere of intense whiteness.
  ii.   *Exhale,* vibrating AHIH (Eheieh).
  iii.  *Inhale,* drawing down a shaft of brilliance from the Corona and formulating the Brow Center, the *Uncia Coeli,* as a sphere of luminous whiteness.
  iv.   *Exhale,* vibrating YHVH ALHIM (Yahweh Elohim).
  v.    *Inhale.* Maintaining awareness of the Corona and the Uncia Coeli, draw down the shaft of brilliance from the Uncia Coeli and formulate the Throat Center, the *Flos Abysmi,* as a sphere of luminous whiteness.
  vi.   *Exhale,* vibrating OLIVN (Elion).
  vii.  *Inhale.* Maintaining awareness of the preceding Centers, draw down the shaft of brilliance from the Flos Abysmi and formulate the Heart Center, the *Orbis Solis,* as a sphere of luminous whiteness.
  viii. *Exhale,* vibrating YHVH ALVH VDOTh (Yahweh Eloah V'Daath).

ix.     *Inhale.*    Maintaining awareness of the Centers
        previously established, draw down the shaft of
        brilliance from the Orbis Solis and formulate the
        *Cornua Lunae,* the Genital Center, as a sphere of
        luminous whiteness.

x.      *Exhale,* vibrating ShDI AL ChI (Shaddai El Chai).

xi.     *Inhale.* Maintaining awareness of the preceding
        Centers, draw down the shaft of brilliance from the
        Cornua Lunae and formulate the *Instita Splendens,*
        the Feet Center, as a sphere of luminous whiteness.

xii.    *Exhale,* vibrating ADNI HARTz (Adonai Ha-Aretz).

*The Caduceus:*

xiii.   *Inhale,* Visualizing a band of white light emanating
        from the Instita Splendens, and at once beginning
        to spiral swiftly upwards in an anticlockwise direc-
        tion about the Centers and the shaft of brilliance
        until it reaches the Flos Abysmi, the Throat Center,
        into which it is entirely assumed and vanishes.

xiv.    *Exhale,* strengthening awareness of Centers and
        connecting shaft.

xv.     *Inhale,* visualizing a band of reddish-white light
        emanating from the Instita Splendens, and at once
        spiraling swiftly upwards in a clockwise direction
        about the Centers and the shaft of brilliance until
        it also reaches the Flos Abysmi, into which it is
        entirely assumed and vanishes.

### (Commentary)

The 1st Formula of the Clavis Rei Primae is to be a regular part of the personal curriculum, being performed daily or on alternate days as may be found most effective: it should be performed within the protection of the Wards.

The Rousing is a technique of very considerable value. Obviously it is not and cannot be taken as the sum and substance of magical training: but it is a powerful and beneficial foundation to magick (see Book III, Chapter VIII). It refreshes and invigorates the psyche and stimulates the Centers themselves: it accustoms them to participation in organized work as distinct from the random needs of ordinary life. In this exercise, which is performed essentially within the astral level of the psyche, the interaction which naturally results from the correspondence of the levels is intensified by the use, in visualization, of appropriate colours.

The Centers should be conceived of as spherical concentrations of light and energy (as is found to be most satisfactory in magical training) approximately five centimeters in diameter. The Corona Flammae is above the crown of the head; the Uncia Coeli projects in a hemisphere from the brow. The Flos Abysmi is completely external to the throat; the Orbis Solis projects from the breast in a hemisphere; the Cornua Lunae, broadly speaking, projects in a hemisphere; the midpoint of the Instita Splendens is between the insteps, hemisphere above and hemisphere below ground. These, the *Positions Potent of the Centers of Activity*, are in no circumstances to be varied.

The student of these volumes who intends to follow the Aurum Solis system in its entirety should, from the outset, employ the following Sub Rosa Nigra Words of Power in connection with the Rousing, in place of the Hebrew Divine Names:—

>*For the Corona Flammae* — EN TO PAN
>*For the Uncia Coeli* — TURANA
>*For the Flos Abysmi* — DESTAPHITON
>*For the Orbis Solis* — ONOPHIS
>*For the Cornua Lunae* — IAO
>*For the Instita Splendens* — BATH-MENIN-
>                                          HEKASTOU

In order to achieve sound proficiency in the 1st Formula, the student should develop the technique methodically and carefully in accordance with the following plan of practice. The student should consider his work critically. In the polish-

ing of the exercise he should prefer, before proceeding to a
further stage of its development, to continue with the stage
in hand if he feels the slightest doubt as to his performance.
*First stage of practice*

The student should use the text of the Rousing as given
above, building the Centers in white light only, and forcefully
vibrating the Words of Power (whether Hebrew or Sub Rosa
Nigra). To achieve smooth performance of the Caduceus the
student may, in this initial stage of practice, repeat the sequence xiii, xiv and xv several times (not exceeding five) to
conclude the Rousing.

After a minimum of three weeks of regular practice, the
student may proceed to the following:
*Second stage of practice*

Instead of visualizing the Centers of Activity in luminous
whiteness as hitherto, the student should now visualize them
in color:

> *Corona Flammae* — Intense brilliance, like burning
> magnesium.
>
> *Uncia Coeli* — glimmering soft dove-grey.
>
> *Flos Abysmi* — billowing intense mid-purple.
>
> *Orbis Solis* — pulsating radiant yellow.
>
> *Cornua Lunae* — pure lavender, radiant and fast-
> swirling.
>
> *Instita Splendens* — seven prismatic colors, swirling
> lazily and shimmering.

The colors for the Crown, Brow and Throat Centers are
drawn from the Atziluthic or *Radical Scale* (see Book III,
Chapter VIII), the color for the Heart Center from the Briatic
or *Prismatic Scale,* the color for the Genital Center from the
Yetziratic or *Contingent Scale,* and the colors for the Feet
Center from the Assiatic or *Iconic Scale;* the whole series of
colors thus betokening the correspondences of the Centers
according to the pattern of the Composite Tree (see Book III,
Chapter III).

In this 1st Formula, the shaft connecting the Centers

remains, at every stage, in white light.

After a minimum of three weeks of regular practice, the student may proceed to the following:

*Third stage of practice*

When the student has opened the doorways of interior power by his continuing work, so that he is aware of the real and potent formulation of the Centers in his practice, he should expand the formula to incorporate a threefold vibration of each Name of Power. In this, the Rhythmic Breath, visualization and vibration are to be correlated in the following manner (the pause at the top and bottom of the breath is taken for granted):

> *Inhale—* formulating the Corona Flammae.
> *Exhale—* vibrating the Name of Power.
> *Inhale—* strengthening the Corona.
> *Exhale—* vibrating the Name of Power.
> *Inhale—* strengthening the Corona.
> *Exhale—* vibrating the Name of Power.
>
> *Inhale—* drawing down the shaft of brilliance rapidly and formulating the Uncia Coeli.
> *Exhale—* vibrating the Word of Power.
> *Inhale—* strengthening formulation of Uncia Coeli.
> *Exhale—*vibrating the Name of Power.
> *Inhale—* strengthening Uncia Coeli.
> *Exhale—* vibrating Name of Power.

This expanded pattern is employed for each successive Center, and the Rousing is concluded with the Caduceus in the normal manner.

After a minimum of eight weeks of practice, the student may proceed to the final necessary development of the Rousing.

*Final stage of practice*

While formulating or strengthening each Center, at each inhalation let the student inweave with his work a reflection upon the essential cosmic principle to which the Center is referred. *But on each exhalation, while the Center is dynamic and radiant, he must charge it with only the stark utterance, the vibration of the Name of Power.*

When this stage has been reached successfully, the Rousing of the Citadels can be considered an efficient instrument for its purpose: continued use can but enhance its benefits.

An example of the full and perfect use of the 1st Formula of the Clavis Rei Primae now follows; in this instance the Sub Rosa Nigra Words of Power have been employed:

*Inhale—* Visualizing the Corona Flammae as a sphere of intense brilliance, like burning magnesium, and reflecting upon the cosmic principle to which the Corona is referred.

*Exhale—* vibrating EN TO PAN.

*Inhale—* strengthening the Corona and reflecting.

*Exhale—* vibrating EN TO PAN.

*Inhale—* strengthening the Corona and reflecting.

*Exhale—* vibrating EN TO PAN.

*Inhale—* drawing down the shaft of brilliance from the Corona, formulating the Uncia Coeli as a sphere of glimmering dove-grey, and reflecting upon the cosmic principle to which the Uncia Coeli is referred.

*Exhale—* vibrating TURANA.

*Inhale—* strengthening the Uncia Coeli and reflecting.

*Exhale—* vibrating TURANA.

*Inhale—* strenthening the Uncia Coeli and reflecting.

*Exhale—* vibrating TURANA.

*Inhale—* maintaining awareness of the Corona and Uncia Coeli, drawing down the shaft of brilliance from the Uncia Coeli, formulating the Flos Abysmi as a sphere of billowing intense mid-purple, and reflecting upon the cosmic principle to which the Flos Abysmi is referred.

*Exhale*—vibrating DESTAPHITON.

*Inhale*— strengthening the Flos Abysmi and reflecting.

*Exhale*— vibrating DESTAPHITON.

*Inhale*— strengthening the Flos Abysmi and reflecting.

*Exhale*— vibrating DESTAPHITON.


The procedure is continued through to the Instita Splendens, with the appropriate color visualizations and reflections, and the Rousing is concluded with the Caduceus in the normal manner.

*VII*

*CLAVIS REI PRIMAE*
*(2nd Formula)*

i.   Assume the Wand Posture.

ii.  Visualize the Corona Flammae as an intense pulsating sphere of *white brilliance* (rather like burning magnesium).

iii. *Inhale.* As the breath is drawn in, a shaft of brilliance desends from the Corona to the breast, where it expands into a sphere of radiant *golden yellow light.*

iv.  *Exhale.* As the breath is released, the shaft of brilliance descends from the Orbis Solis to the feet, where it expands into a sphere of *whiteness*, radiant but less brilliant than the Kether.

v.   *Inhale.* As the breath is drawn in, a reflux charge of intense rose-gold flame rises from the Instita Splendens and passes into the Orbis Solis.

vi.  *Exhale.* The light rests.

vii. The sequence iii through vi is repeated five or six times.

viii. Concentrate on the Orbis Solis. The central solar-nucleus remains quite distinct as a blazing and vibrant inner sun, but emits a powerful radiance which steadily grows until the total sphere of sensation  is charged with golden yellow light. (See note D below).

Notes:

A) Wand Posture and Rhythmic Breath are maintained throughout this work, but a strict correlation of breath to visualization is necessary only for the repeated sequence iii through vi.

B)   The Sequence iii through vi is repeated five or six times without a break; thus iii, iv, v, vi, iii, iv, v, vi, iii, iv, v, vi, and so on. If the student finds it necessary to re-affirm the Corona Flammae for the re-commencement of the sequence, this should be done during the pause at the bottom of the breath in vi.

C)   When proceeding from vii (the repetitions of the sequence) to viii, several full breaths may be interposed after the exhalation in vi; or viii may be begun immediately after the final exhalation in vi. This is entirely a matter for personal preference.

D)   In step viii, the light radiated by the Orbis Solis forms a three-dimensional ovoid, conceived of as being co-extensive with the aura. While the attention is directed to the Orbis Solis and its radiated light, the student should gradually lose awareness of the Kether and Malkuth centres.

E)   *No Words of Power are employed with the 2nd Formula of the Clavis Rei Primae.*

N.B. The 1st and 2nd Formulae of the Clavis Rei Primae are both fundamental techniques for energisation. The 1st Formula is usually employed where the purpose is to emphasize the unity or the communication of the different levels within an individual (or, occasionally, of individuals in a group). The 2nd Formula is a rapid method for the energisation of the operator, and is usually employed in promotion of a magical working. These are broad generalisations, however, and the uses of both formulae will be most clearly gathered from a careful study of their contextual occurrence in the present volume.

It is here taken for granted that the student will, before undertaking the 2nd Formula, have practiced the 1st Formula Clavis Rei Primae so as to have made of it an efficient instrument for his magical use. As such, it should at this stage form a regular part of his personal curriculum. Proficiency in the Rousing is essential for his ability to use with full force this important three-center technique of the 2nd Formula upon the frequent occasions when this is required in workings.

## *THE ORANTE FORMULA*

The Orante Formula is a method for effecting a projection of power upon a person, substance, or object. The Orante Formula is a development of the Second Formula of the Clavis Rei Primae, but its name *orante* derives from the primary Gesture which is associated with it.

*The Orante Gesture:*— the arms are raised forwards, with elbows flexed; the arms come to rest at a position in which the upper arm is approximately horizontal, the forearm raised to about 45° above horizontal; the hands are raised in a natural manner so that the palms are directed forwards and towards the object or person to receive the projection, the fingers are not separated.\* Having taken the Orante Gesture, projection may be undertaken from this position if suitable: or any adaptation of the posture may be made, which will bring the palms into a more effective relationship with the subject of the projection. When a materium which is to receive projection is upon the Bomos, for example, the hands may be lowered and brought closer together so that the palms are just above the materium. There is no hard and fast rule about this, but symmetry is essential: both palms should be focused upon the subject. In any instance the body also may be

---

\* It is to be remarked that the radiation of power will be from the centres of the palms, where secondary Centres of Activity reside, and not from the fingertips; the transmission of power from the finger-tips is a technique for other purposes, and generally by direct contact.

inclined, and either foot advanced, as the student feels to be right: all should be achieved in one graceful change from the Orante Gesture, but the Orante Gesture is invariably taken first no matter what modification may be adopted for projection.

Projection having been effected, any variations notwithstanding, the projection posture is invariably dismissed by crossing the wrists upon the breast, fingertips touching the collarbone. The left wrist passes outside the right, to seal off the outgoing current and to symbolize the end of the action. The head is *not* bowed as in the Calyx. If it is borne in mind that the right hand and arm are regarded as active, the left hand and arm as passive, it will be easy to recall which arm passes outside.

### *The Orante Formula*

i.     Assume the Wand Posture.

ii.    Visualize the Corona as an intense pulsating sphere of *white brilliance.*

iii.   *Inhale.* As the breath is drawn in, a shaft of brilliance descends from Corona to Orbis Solis, where it expands into a sphere of *golden yellow light.*

iv.    *Exhale.* As the breath is released, the shaft of brilliance descends from the breast to the feet, where it expands into a sphere of *whiteness.*

v.     *Inhale.* As the breath is drawn in, a charge of intense rose-gold flame rises from the Instita Splendens and passes into the Orbis Solis.

vi.    *Exhale.* The light rests.

vii.   The sequence iii through vi is repeated five or six times, as in the Second Formula of the Clavis Rei Primae.

viii.  *Retaining awareness of the three Centres,* the arms are raised in the Orante Gesture (if suitable the posture is then modified), and on an outgoing breath the power of the Orbis Solis is felt as being impelled up the arms and out from the centre of the palms towards the subject of the projection; the eyes are likewise focused upon the subject. Beams of clear golden yellow light from the palms of the hands are to be visualized as converging upon the subject.

ix.    The projection posture is dismissed.

x.    The Wand Posture is resumed, and steps ii through vii are consciously and deliberately repeated.

xi.    The Formula is concluded with the radiation of light from the central solar-nucleus, as in step viii of the 2nd Formula of the Clavis Rei Primae.

*Notes:*

A)   The sole use of the Orante Formula is to effect a concentration or projection of power upon a person, object or substance.

B)   The Formula is a catalyst, and after a substance has received projection a period of latency occurs before the result manifests. The duration of this "fermentation" depends both upon the nature of the materium and upon the type of the operation.

C)   Projection by the Orante Formula is extremely powerful, and transmission of energy need only be maintained for the space of one outgoing breath.

D)   Whatever the dedication and purpose of a rite in which this Formula is employed, at the actual moment of projection a materium is to be charged *purely and simply* with an irradiation of golden yellow light. Nothing more. To appreciate this it is necessary to understand that there are two types of projection of power, differing considerably in method, though not in fundamental principle. These are termed by us "alchemical projection" and "magical projection." Alchemical projection employs a powerfully concentrated inner concept, whether of perfect integration or of a specific natural force: and with the act of projection this inner concept is spontaeously impressed upon the materium. This type of projection is not limited to alchemical work proper, but is frequently found in folk-magick and in other of the less formal types of magick, even of High Magick (which can be very informal indeed.) Examples of alchemical projection are given in Book II, Chapter II. Magical projection is achieved in a different way. The act of projection takes place only after the astral substance of the materium has been conditioned by the rite: projection in this case is of dynamic force unconditioned by any concept of the specific effect to be produced. The Orante Formula is of this latter type of projection.

E)   In a rite of transubstantiation the elements must be projected upon seperately. After projecting upon the first element, dismiss the projection posture as taught, and assume the Wand Posture. Repeat step viii of the Orante Formula, projecting upon the second element. Dismiss the projection posture and continue in the normal manner through x and xi.

## IX

### BANISHING & INVOKING

The banishing and the invocation of various types of force are essential functions in magical works generally. Both banishing and invocation can be brought about in a number of ways, but the use of a distinctive sign, itself both potent and harmonious to the working, is frequently desirable not only to give weight to the act of banishing or invoking, but also to signal the moment of operation. Such a sign is chosen according to the type of force to which it is applied: the pentagram for any of the Four Elements and Spirit, the Heptagram for planetary and zodiacal forces.

*The Pentagram*
*(The Solomonic Seal)*

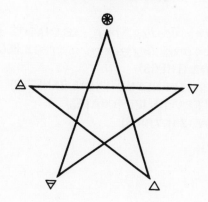

In the A.S. system, when the pentagram is used in invocation, it is traced clockwise commencing from the point attributed to the force to be invoked, the appropriate Divine Name being vibrated meanwhile. When used in banishing, the pentagram is traced anticlockwise from the point attributed to the force to be banished, the appropriate Divine Name again being vibrated. Any pentagram thus traced is referred to as an invoking (or banishing) pentagram of the Element in question. The attributions of the points of the pentagram are shown on the diagram above.*

Because of the great potency of the pentagram, it is a rule to introduce a stabilising factor into banishings and invocations in which this sign is traced: *thus the pentagram of an Element is always preceded by a pentagram, banishing or invoking as the case may be, of Spirit.* The Divine Name to be vibrated while tracing the pentagram of Spirit will depend upon the Element in question, as shown below.

*The Hebrew Divine Names employed with the pentagrams are:—*

⊕ *when preceding* △ *or* △ , אהיה (AHIH)
⊕ *when preceding* ▽ *or* ▽ , אגלא (AGLA)
△ אלהים (ALHIM)
△ יהוה (YHVH)
▽ אל (AL)
▽ אדני (ADNI)

*The Greek Divine Names employed with the pentagrams are:—*

⊕ *when preceding* △ *or* △ , ΑΘΑΝΑΤΟΣ (ATHANATOS)
⊕ *when preceding* ▽ *or* ▽ , ΙΣΧΥΡΟΣ (ISCHYROS)
△ ΘΕΟΣ (THEOS)
△ ΣΕΛΑΗ ΓΕΝΕΤΗΣ (SELAE GENETES)
▽ ΠΑΓΚΡΑΤΗΣ (PANKRATES)
▽ ΚΥΡΙΟΣ (KYRIOS)

*The Enochian Divine Names employed with the penta-grams are:—*

⊛ *when preceding* △, BITOM

⊛ *when preceding* ▲, EXARP

⊛ *when preceding* ▽, HCOMA

⊛ *when preceding* ▿, NANTA

△     OIP TEAA PDOCE

▲     ORO IBAH AOZPI

▽     MPH ARSL GAIOL

▿     MOR DIAL HCTGA

When invoking Elemental Spirits (Elementals, properly so called) by means of the pentagram, the appropriate Kerubic sign is used to represent the power of the Angelic Ruler of the Element. The sign is traced in the centre of the figure, after the second (the elemental) pentagram has been described. ♒ should be used for the Spirits of Air, ♌ for the Spirits of Fire, ♏ for the Spirits of Water, ♉ for those of Earth. The Kerubic sign is not employed in the banishing of Elementals. (See Appendix D.)

When invoking or banishing, it is usual to trace the pentagrams in the air while facing the quarter associated with the Element in question. If however pentagrams are traced over an object with an intention of invoking or banishing which is limited to that object, a circle must first be traced above the object, and then the pentagrams traced within the circle: the Divine Names being vibrated meanwhile, as usual.* For invocation, trace the circle deosil: for banishing, trace it widdershins.†

Theoretically, a pentagram is potent throughout the whole range of its Element of attribution in the Yetziratic World.

---

* Note that in the Rites of the Wards the use of the pentagram is special and distinctive: each pair of Divine Names being linked to one pentagram only, but in connection with the banishing gesture *Cervus.*

† Concerning the widdershins circle, see *Principles of Ceremonial.*

## The Heptagram

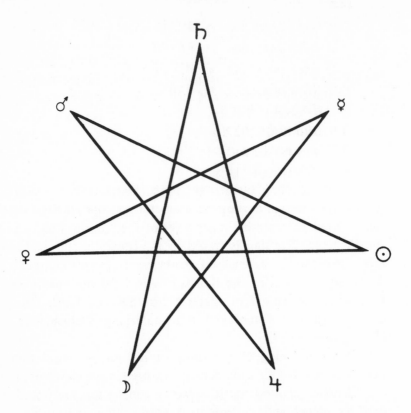

*Planetary or sephirothic forces.* To invoke, first trace the presigillum* of the planet of the working, then, about it, trace the heptagram clockwise from the point attributed to the planet, meanwhile vibrating the appropriate Divine Name. To banish, trace the presigillum of the planet, then, about it, trace the heptagram anti-clockwise from the point attributed to the planet, meanwhile vibrating the appropriate Divine Name. For Malkuth (Earth as planet, not as element), trace the presigillum ♘ , then, about it, the heptagram of Saturn but using the Divine Name appropriate to the Sphere of Malkuth.

* See the paper *Sigils,* where the presigilla are shown.

*Zodiacal forces.* To invoke, trace the presigillum corresponding to the sign of the working, then trace clockwise about it the heptagram of the planet which rules that sign (cf. Vol. III, Ch. V): meanwhile vibrating the applicable Divine Name. To banish, trace the presigillum, then trace the heptagram anti-clockwise, with vibration of the Divine Name.*

To limit planetary or zodiacal invocations or banishings to a specific object, first describe above that object a deosil circle for invocation, or a widdershins circle for banishing: then within that circle, trace presigillum and heptagram, with vibration of the Divine Name.

Theoretically, a heptagram is potent throughout the whole range of its sign of attribution in the Yetziratic World.

---

* The signs ♒, ♌, ♉, ♏, when employed *with pentagrams,* are on no account to be replaced with presigilla.

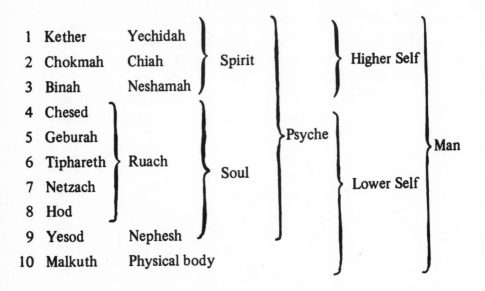

**Part II**

**MAGICK OF THE PSYCHE**

## X

## *IDENTIFYING WITH GOD-FORCES*

In present-day occult working several techniques exist by which identification with God-forces may be achieved. The procedure here given is traditional to the A.S.

This work takes time to complete, but the emphasis throughout is upon the individual character of the chosen deity. If the earlier parts of the work are fulfilled to the highest degree, the final phase will culminate in a profound mystical experience.

N.B. For this work, a deity is not to be chosen from the Voudoun pantheons. The Loa are only to be approached through the cult methods traditionally associated with them.

1

In this, which is one of the nost noble usages of High Magick, the student must as a preliminary make a serious study of the deity which is to be the subject and centre of his operation; of the deity in itself, according to its own nature; of the deity in context of its native pantheon, and in relation to other deities thereof; of the deity furthermore in context of the Qabalah, and in relation to the Sephiroth.

2

This preliminary study accomplished so that he is familiar with every aspect which may have a bearing upon his work, the student must begin the operation itself by undertaking steadfastly the cult of the deity. He will establish his own personal shrine of that deity, equipping the shrine with everything within his power to associate it with both traditional and magical worship of the deity. The student shall devise words and modes of worship for the deity, introducing traditional forms where possible or suitable; these words and modes he may if he desires vary, according to hour or day or season, so that this worship shall be always a living reality to him. For he must in full reality worship, he must meditate, he must adore, he must praise, so as to grow continually in love and in understanding of the divine being about whom this work revolves.

3

When he has grown in his cult, the student will regularly, at the conclusion of his worship, assume the god-form of his deity (that is to say, he will imagine himself to be enveloped in the form characteristic of his deity).* He will learn to feel at ease therein; but he will keep silence while the god-form is maintained. This technique, as his love and understanding of the deity increase, will gather increased meaning and richness for the worshipper.

Whenever he can, the worshipper will visit historic shrines, or sites of shrines, of his deity; there he will worship, always performing at least some act of adoration, spending some time in meditation, and assuming in silence the god-form.

In the use of the forms of worship which he has compiled, the student will give heed continually to their suitability to the deity. Should he find as he advances in understanding and in perceptivity that they fail in that respect, he will amend them. He will make of his cult as it were a mirror of the deific force, so that he may find reflected there all that he has gathered by study and by meditation of the nature of his god; and through the continual interchange,

---

* Assumption of god-form is concluded by re-centring upon the magical personality, while the god-formulation is allowed to fade from the consciousness.

the cult influencing the student and his further work influencing the cult, an increasing affinity with the divine force will be built up.

## 4

As a principal effect of these practices, the student will develop an awareness, which is a completely objective certainty, of the numinous power of his deity. This awareness is a clear sign of the progress of the operation towards success; but still it does not suffice to indicate that the student should proceed to the final phase of the operation. Indeed, the student should postpone the final phase as long as he can, acquiring greater knowledge, giving augmented worship, developing more profound love for the deity, while the power of the god, at once radiant and magnetic, encompasses him and draws him strongly and yet more strongly, onward irresistibly. For it is no light thing, and no small thing, to seek, as the final phase of the operation will do, the uniting of consciousness with a living force of godhead. In developing a relationship with any divine power the operator receives in proportion as he gives; when a deity is approached in the exalted and intensely magical mode which is required by this work, progressively higher levels of the psyche become engaged in reciprocity with the deity.

## 5

*The final phase of the operation will take place when the previous work has been brought to reality and when the bond between god and devotee has become such as to compel the culmination.*

The place may be the personal shrine; equally it may be a traditional shrine of the deity, some historic focal point of that worship; or again in certain circumstances it may be a place which by its natural features and its beauty powerfully brings to the cultist a conviction that his deity is *here*.

To actuate the climax of the work the operator proceeds with the Deific Formula—which combines the Formula of the Triple Vibration with the technique of assumption of god-form —employing therewith the name of his deity.

### The Deific Formula

i.    The operator makes adoration of his deity.

ii.   He states his intention of uniting his consciousness with his deity.

iii.  He assumes the Wand Posture and establishes the Rhythmic Breath.

iv.   He visualizes the Corona Flammae as an intense pulsating sphere of white brilliance.

v.    On an *exhalation* he vibrates the name of the God.

vi.   As he *inhales* he visualizes a shaft of brilliance descending from the Corona to the breast, where it expands into a sphere of radiant golden yellow light.

vii.  He *exhales,* vibrating for the second time the name of the God; while doing so, he visualizes the shaft of brilliance descending from the Orbis Solis to the feet, where it expands into a sphere of whiteness.

viii. As he *inhales* he visualizes a charge of intense rose-gold flame rising from  the Instita Splendens and passing into the Orbis Solis.

ix.   As he *exhales* he vibrates for the third time, and powerfully, the name of the God, simultaneously assuming the god-form.

In using the Deific Formula, the operator opens the door to the fulfillment of the entire work. The successive vibrations of the  name of the deity build up a tremendous and sublime force, which, in combination with the assumption of god-form in the final step of the Formula, precipitates the experience of identification as an exaltation sweeping away and replacing the  personal  selfhood-consciousness  of  the  operator.  He perceives, he knows, he has power as a god: not as himself deified nor as godhead generally, but as the especial and glorious deity of his adoration. It is the presence, the character, and the very nature of that deity which—for a longer or shorter time, as it may be—he experiences from within.

---

When he has returned to normal consciousness, the operator performs the Rousing of the Citadels (1st Formula Clavis Rei Primae.)

## 6

Successful completion of this work will confer the magical power of identification with the god. *On subsequent occasions,* the operator should find it possible to realize the identification by means of the Deific Formula, without recapitulation of the work indicated in the previous sections; but a reverent approach is to be preserved. The Rousing of the Citadels should always be performed after the return to normal consciousness.

## XI

## *RISING ON THE PLANES*

Two operations come under the heading of *Rising on the Planes*:—

### I

The first is the traditionally known operation, which is referred to in Book III, Chapter III. In its pristine conception it is a technique of meditation for Adepti Pleni (full Adepti Minores), involving at its culmination the use of the Briatic consciousness. The usually accepted apogee of this experiment is the mystical experience of Tiphareth in Briah. Some occult writers have referred to an extension of the practice, involving culmination higher upon the central column of the Tree.

The operation has come into use for those below the status of full Adept, that is to say, those in whom the Briatic consciousness is not yet awakened: but it is emphasized here that by its very nature it is specifically for full Adepti.

In all cases the operation is conducted by means of simple key-symbols; those traditionally used by the A.S. are as follows:—

The first symbol: a black and white chequered pavement, in which the forces of light and of darkness are perfectly equilibriated. This is not only the initial symbol but is also the "homing" symbol, *Malkuth*.

The second symbol: a Tau cross of heavy form with

slightly incurved sides and top. The cross is black; upon it at
the junction of the arms is a single drop of blood. *Thirty-
second Path*.

The third symbol: an upward-pointing equilateral
triangle, mist-blue with silver sparkles, supporting a silver
crescent with horns uppermost. *Yesod*.

The fourth symbol: an arrow, barbed and flighted,
speeding vertically upward. Clear brilliant blue with flashing
white detail. *Twenty-fifth Path*.

The fifth symbol: interlacing squares of red and white,
as upon the Tessera (see Note A to *The High Consecration
of the Tessera)*, concentric with a golden circle which passes
through the corner of each square. *Tiphareth*.

After any desired preliminaries, the God-form Posture
is assumed, the eyes are closed, and the Breath is established.
The symbols are reviewed in sequence without consideration
of their meaning; for the first, third and fifth symbol respectively, the appropriate Divine Name is vibrated aloud. The
black and white pavement is then established below. The
operator formulates clearly the intention of rising through the
Gates of the central column into Tiphareth. The work itself
is carried out without advertence to this specific intention,
the volition to rise being all that is required. The second
symbol is established in the higher area of mental vision,
and the spiritual ascent begins.

Imminent entry into a Sephirah produces a feeling of
stress. This is followed by a spontaneous change of symbol,
signalling actual entrance, with sensations relating to the
Sephirah in question: one may be "born into" Yesod, "raised
up" into Tiphareth.

The second and fourth symbols will need to be deliberately established, the third and fifth symbols will appear
spontaneously. Thus is fulfilled the Passing of the Tau and
the Following of the Arrow.

When Tiphareth is entered, a state of ecstasy may

supervene. It is not unknown for physical levitation to occur at such a time, but it is a grave defect. Rising on the Planes can indeed be used as a basis for physical levitation, but then the experiment is somewhat differently undertaken.

The inwardness of Rising on the Planes should not be taken to imply that it is necessarily experienced in complete spiritual isolation throughout, neither is it to be thought that the Adept is bound to passivity in Tiphareth. The Adept is master in this work, not servant.

For the willed return to normal consciousness the first symbol is again employed: however, the mode in which the symbol is to be used is personal to each operator.

## II

The second operation which is known as Rising on the Planes does not consist in any progression from one Sephirah to another, nor in traversing any of the Paths: it is concerned entirely with the experience of one or another planetary Sephirah (one only of the planetary Sephiroth being selected for the work on any given occasion.)

This practice is open to all insofar as each is able to achieve it. For further on this second operation, see *Works Undertaken Through Astral Projection* where it is detailed.

## XII

## "ASTRAL PROJECTION"
## PRIMARY TECHNIQUES OF
## NEPHESH AND RUACH PROJECTION

Projection of Nephesh-material alone, whether as an involuntary occurrence, or under the direction of the conscious mind, is classified by the Aurum Solis under the general head of "Hecatean out-of-the-body experience." In neither the voluntary nor the involuntary type of Hecatean projection does the Ruach-consciousness accompany the exteriorised Nephesh-material.

Involuntary projection of Nephesh-material is not uncommon, and examples are frequently mingled with dreams which are remembered as strangely vivid and objective. Voluntary projection of Nephesh-material takes place in certain magical procedures, as for example in *The Formula of the Watcher*.

———————

Projection of both Nephesh-material and Ruach-consciousness is classified by the Aurum Solis under the head of "Helionic out-of-the-body experience." Here the Ruach-consciousness functions through, and travels with, the vehicle of exteriorised astral substance.

The Ruach is not native to the Astral Light, and generally has awareness of the astral planes only through the Nephesh-substance: this is analagous to the manner in which the Ruach, acting through the Nephesh, normally draws upon sensory brain-consciousness (which is computer, not intelligence) to

61

build up its rational awareness of the physical plane. However, the subject may have the impression that something less than his normal Ruach-consciousness is involved. A person who projects in this manner may be capable of experiencing travels, encounters, etc., with quite high spiritual implications, which he will understand according to the stage of personal development he has reached at the time: but he may while in the state of projection find himself unable to recall technical data or ordinary knowledge of one sort or another, simply because this state has temporarily separated him from the computer-bank of the physical brain which he is accustomed to using all the time.

This difficulty may never arise for some students, and when it does, it belongs altogether to the earlier stages of training; later on, when magical practice, meditation and extraphysical states have become an integral part of the student's own life-experience, the difficulty will disappear, more and more material being passed to the deeper levels of the psyche. Knowledge which is by nature ephemeral, however, is not likely to be retained unless it has especial emotional connotations.

Another problem that may arise is the refusal of the instinctual level of the Nephesh, together with the physical brain, to accept the reality of the experience when the Ruach-consciousness has "returned with knowledge." This happens less often with Order members under training than with people to whom projection of consciousness happens involuntarily: the magical student has usually had experience of other non-material happenings, and generally speaking wishes to succeed in his exercises, but even so it does sometimes occur that there is a hidden resistance. There are two possible reasons for this. The instinctual nature may rebel because to the instinct of self-preservation this type of experience appears as a threat; or the brain itself may react negatively to a remembered event which was not initially recorded in its cells, and an almost obsessive recapitulation of the experience may result. In both these cases the solution is relatively simple: the key-word is *Acceptance,* willingness to progress, acceptance of change, assent to the heightening of one's consciousness and the broadening of one's horizons.

The Rousing of the Citadels (Clavis Rei Primae 1st Formula) will be of great assistance in dealing with these two problems, for it establishes a harmony and balanced interaction between the various levels of the psyche. For this reason, and also to guard against astral bleeding* and to expedite the normal re-linking of the levels after projection, the Rousing is used both before and after the experiment.

The practice of Helionic projection is optional for students of the A.S. (however, see Note B below), but if undertaken is not for spasmodic work: once begun it is essential that it be persevered in, and it should only be dropped if a grave reason compels. However, the student should not essay Helionic projection after the moon begins to wane, until the new moon: in no circumstances should the novice essay Helionic projection during the Tempus eversionis.

*A usual warning must be given.here:— persons afflicted with heart-disease, high blood pressure, or any serious affliction of the nervous, circulatory or respiratory systems, should not attempt Helionic projection.*

Immediate or early success in Helionic projection is not necessarily a hallmark of superior magical aptitude, neither do months or even a number of years of perseverance before succeeding reflect discredit upon the aspirant.

---

* "Astral bleeding" is excessive projection, or leakage, of Nephesh-substance. This can lead to physical weakness and in serious cases to cell damage; it is also a cause of poltergeist-type activity. When its occurrence is not associated with occult work, it indicates a need for self-control of the emotions and, frequently, a compensating creative outlet:— through the arts, or through a suitable athletic activity.

To aid the student who desires to make a special study and practice of Astral Projection, the formula given below is expanded into a detailed and explanatory program, in *The Llewellyn Practical Guide to Astral Projection,* by Denning and Phillips (Llewellyn, St. Paul). That book contains a consideration of many more aspects of the practice of Astral Projection than could find place here, and is commended as a supplement to the present text for all who wish to develop or simply to understand this magical art.

*The Going Forth of the Star and the Chariot thereof*
*(Method of Helionic Projection)*

1.  *Preliminaries:—*
    i. Earth posture
    ii. The Rousing of the Citadels (Clavis Rei Primae 1st Formula.)

2.  *Exteriorisation of Nephesh-substance:—*
    In his visual imagination the operator should send forth to a convenient distance above him a jet of silver-grey mist, which should form at that distance into a small cloud, and which, under pressure of sustained ejection, should grow rapidly, becoming more defined, until it takes on the shape and stature of a human being. He should create this figure as being in the same posture as himself, but facing him. This completes the ejection: the figure and the connecting line of mist should be held in formulation. (The student may image this key-figure as he wishes, but it should be predominantly silver-grey, of dignified appearance, unelaborate and functional.)

3.  *Transference of Consciousness:—*
    Holding clearly in mind the projected "vehicle" and its "cord", he should now centre his consciousness at the level of his eyes, or at his forehead, or at his throat, as seems right, not proceeding further until he experiences a warm and vital sense of selfhood at the chosen point.
    When this is achieved, he is mentally to make this

deliberate resolution:– I, STAR OF BEING, WILL ENTER
THE CHARIOT OF LIGHT. (At no time during the work
which follows shall this resolution be reaffirmed.) Directly he
has made this resolution, he is to imagine himself (that is,
his consciousness) gliding swiftly upward to the figure, and
entering it at the level of eyes, forehead or throat according
as he has centred his consciousness in the physical body.
Then deliberately, in his mind, he is to "turn about" so as to
co-ordinate with the viewpoint of the figure, consequently
perceiving in imagination his surroundings and his recumbent
physical body from that viewpoint.

It is this mental change of perspective which will effect
a veritable transference of consciousness to the exteriorised
vehicle. Success in achieving this transference may occur
suddenly and may be accompanied by the distinct "metallic
click" which is traditional in this context; or the student may
sustain his effort for some while before succeeding. On no
occasion should he continue to seek transference when he
has begun to be fatigued by the necessary concentration.
Perseverance consists in proceeding on the next occasion with
equal care and with increased experience.

(Should he not succeed, he need only re-orientate himself
to normal awareness in his physical body, and then proceed
to re-absorption of the vehicle as detailed in 5 below.)

When transference to the astral vehicle is achieved by the
method described above, the student must, as it were, "feel
himself into" the totality of the vehicle: this is not an easy
thing to describe, but in practice it is quite simple. He will
feel very much as though he is in a physical body, and he
will be able truly to orientate himself to his surroundings
from his new viewpoint.

4.   *The Return:–*
In order to return after having successfully "gone
forth", the operator need only draw near to his physical

body and he will be spontaneously reunited with it. However, it is desirable that he should achieve this approach in the manner following.

He should assume the Earth posture about eight feet above his physical body, and facing in the same direction. In this posture, he should reaffirm his awareness of his astral vehicle and should then descend slowly towards his physical body. At last he sinks gently into it, and after a short time should be able to re-establish his sensory unity with his physical being.*

To conclude the operation he is to perform the Rousing of the Citadels.

*On returning to the body after successful Helionic projection, re-absorption as given under 5 below is not required.*

5.   *Re-absorption:—*

When an astral vehicle has been formulated, but transference of consciousness to it has not occurred, the operator is to conclude the work by deliberately re-absorbing that vehicle: in his visual imagination he should withdraw astral substance so that the figure diminishes to a small cloud of sivler-grey mist, which in turn diminishes, and finally he is to re-absorb the cord.

To conclude the operation he is to perform the Rousing of the Citadels.

*Notes:*

A) The standard conditions for this work are that the student should perform it in the Chamber of Art; that he should assume the Earth posture with his head to the North, his feet to the South; and that he should be free from any

---

* When the consciousness and its astral vehicle return, the body—which has been animated and maintained in a trance state by the lower level of the Nephesh— "awakens" as if from a deep sleep when the levels naturally re-link.

restricting clothing, a single garment or nudity being recommended.

B)    The region of the upper abdomen may be described as "astro-sensitive", and it is from this area that Nephesh-substance is sent forth.

In the early stages, the novice's exteriorisation of substance is likely to be purely imaginative; however, with conscientious practice the "astro-sensitive" region will soon respond to the student's command, and it will not be long before he is able, through this use of his imagination, to send forth astral substance in truth. Preliminary work on the exteriorisation technique (without any attempt at transference of consciousness) is thus urged: and to this end sections 1, 2 and 5 above should from time to time be incorporated into the exercise routine. In this case, however, the student should assume the *Wand Posture* for the work, thus to formulate the key-figure before, rather than above, himself.

*If Helionic projection is not intended to be undertaken, this preliminary work (sections 1, 2 and 5) should still be incorporated,* in Wand posture, *into the exercise routine: developments of this procedure being employed in other operations.*

C)    If incense is burned, a compound of Mastic, Oil of Jasmine, and powdered Orris root will be found suitable. Alternatively, Oil of Jasmine may be lightly applied to the forehead: some find this very helpful. Neither of these things is essential however.

D)    It is to be observed that the Rousing of the Citadels will be performed in the Earth posture, both at the beginning and at the end of the work, if Helionic projection is undertaken; but in the Wand posture if the preliminary work only (1, 2 and 5) is intended.

*XIII*

## *WORKS UNDERTAKEN*
## *THROUGH ASTRAL PROJECTION*

In the course of his magical experience, the student will almost certainly encounter individual situations in which he can operate more effectively through astral projection than in any other manner. We do not enumerate such possible situations: many of them involve some form of intervention in the lives of others, the rightness or desirability of which must be left entirely to the judgment of the operator at the time. Other than such works, there are also vast fields of research, in which the student can increase his own knowledge and ability without the need for such weighty decisions: and two approaches to this research are here considered.

*Rising on the Planes.*
          The commencement of this operation takes place on the physical plane. The place of working is prepared as the operator may be able to devise, in accordance with the symbolism of the planetary Sephirah intended as the sphere of operation: with the appropriate colours, the number and pattern of arrangement of lights, suitable incense, and perhaps music. If desired, the lineal figure attributed to the sphere of operation may be marked out upon the floor, of such size that the operator may lie down within it: a floor cloth with that figure could be utilised, or the figure could be outlined in chalk or tapes as convenient. It is not intended to serve as an astral defence. If a lineal figure is employed, the lights should be positioned at

69

its points. This gives a good example for the placing of lights, even when a lineal figure is not used.

The operator, established within his place of working, now meditates upon the sphere and its significance, while he drinks in the essential qualities of the symbolism which surrounds him.

He traces the invoking heptagram of the sphere after due meditation, vibrating the Divine Name or Magical Formula appropriate thereto. He states his intention clearly, of rising in the particular sphere.

Having assumed the Earth posture and performed the Rousing, he proceeds with Helionic projection. Once out of the physical body he begins to rise without delay, and continues the ascent as far as he is able. This is not such an ascent as can be pictured as the astral equivalent of going up into the sky of the material world. The exercise is actually a device, of a kind frequently found in mysticism, to enable the operator to reach levels of being which are *higher* in the sense of finer or more inward, levels of the Astral Light which manifest themselves to more inward planes of the psyche of the operator.

As he rises, landscapes or parts of landscapes may appear. peopled or not: sometimes as coming to sight out of an intermittent mist, or as isles in the sea; sometimes abruptly terminating as precipitous cliffs or unfinished buildings. Often, on the lower levels especially, he will encounter scenes so material-seeming and realistic that he will find it difficult to recall that he is not travelling in the physical world. This is not strange, for just as his physical body experiences the outer world as "real," because of similar density, so his astral body finds a corresponding reality in some of the astral regions. Always, however, in this work, he will perceive that the scenes and entities partake essentially in the nature of the sphere of operation, though this will be manifested by them in varying modes. Thus he should be able from these visions to learn something of the sphere in which he is rising: but always he should continue the ascent, and should not for anything he sees or hears leave it. The higher he goes, however, the more difficult it will be for him to maintain his upward progress. At last there will come a time when the Light itself will seem to thrust him downwards. At this stage he should will more of his astral substance to return to his physical body:* this voluntary refining of the astral vehicle may permit him to rise still higher, but if it does not, he should cease struggling to ascend further. Sooner or later, he reaches a "high point" consistent with his stage of development. Cessation of the attempt to ascend will at once mitigate the contrary impulse of the Light. He should maintain himself in equilibrium at that level, experiencing the ambience passively. When sated or simply tired, he should not set off on other lines of exploration, but should return directly to his body. The return accomplished, he should as usual perform the Rousing in the Earth posture; then, standing, he should trace the banishing heptagram of the sphere of operation, vibrating therewith the appropriate Divine Name.

The experience of the full Adept is not considered in these notes. The Adeptus Minor who is not a full Adept should be able by virtue of his initiations to penetrate to that highest Yetziratic region of the sphere where the influences of the Briatic level are strongly discernable: if he were not aware that he lacks as yet the Briatic consciousness, he would imagine himself to have penetrated to the World of Briah itself. Those of lesser status will be able to rise through the Yetziratic planes and sub-planes in the sphere as far as their personal development permits. These planes and sub-planes are comprised in two main regions, the Higher and Lower Astral: but although these main regions are distinct in character, there is no sharp change or boundary in the transitional

---

* Although it is common practice when any considerable astral journey is to be undertaken, to send back some Nephesh-substance to the physical body by an initial swift act of will, more can, and in certain circumstances should, be sent back at a later stage. Hence the instructions in the text.

phase between them, and some of the Higher Astral regions of the sphere should be accessible to many who are not yet Adepti Minores.

If the ascent were carried out as a purely imaginative exercise (as is sometimes advocated), the operator might of course conceive of himself as rising to any *nominal* level of a Sephirah, regardless of his state of advancement; but Helionic rising is quite another matter. The actuality of the experience must be viewed soberly. Some will rise to the Higher Astral level of a sphere, others will attain less but cannot do other than benefit by the effort. Neither the labour required nor the reward to be gained should be underestimated however. The beauty and sublimity of the World of Yetzirah are frequently misprized by occultists. In terms of exoteric spirituality the Higher Astral in general is experienced as that which the greater part of the human race would interpret as the "happiness of Heaven"; in other words, it represents the highest bliss and beauty which human nature is capable of experiencing as long as it is wholly dependent for that experience upon a cause conceived of as external to itself.

*Free exploration.*
       A certain robustness of mentality is desirable in the magical student. He should undertake explorations of the various levels and sub-planes of the Astral Light as they exist in themselves:— the Light comprises an indefinitely large number of regions and sub-regions, and the student should not invariably pre-select or "invoke" the area of his exploration. Certainly, however, the operator should go forth armed against any eventuality. He should be thoroughly familiar with the banishing and invoking pentagrams and heptagrams, and the appropriate Divine Names. It is also highly desirable that the student should, with a view to these "free" explorations, familiarise himself with the correspondences, and also with the fundamental principles of magical philosophy.

He will thus be enabled, where needful, to recognise by symbol or analyse by function the Astral regions in which he finds himself, even though he may still encounter particular matters which need his deeper investigation before he can interpret them.

*XIV*

## THE FORMULA OF THE WATCHER

*The formula of the Watcher should not be essayed after the moon begins to wane, until the new moon; nor during the Tempus eversionis.*

The Wand posture is assumed and the Rousing of the Citadels is performed. In the visual imagination Nephesh-substance is ejected from the region of the upper abdomen and the astral key-figure, or whatever shape is to act as Watcher, is formulated. By an act of will this is sent to whatever locality or person the operator desires knowledge of, this technique being normally limited in scope to what may be called "the realm of terrestrial experience." When once the Watcher has been satisfactorily despatched to its destination, the operator must detach his attention from the matter. He can very well go about his ordinary occupations, until the time comes at which he has determined to recall the Watcher.*

For the recall, the operator should take the Wand posture, facing in that direction to which the Watcher was despatched. The Rhythmic Breath is established, and the Watcher mentally summoned. Then, in the visual imagination, the figure is to be made to reappear, and is to be brought to rest about eight to ten feet from the operator; it is then to be re-absorbed by the usual method. Remaining in the

---

* The Setting of the Wards is not employed in connection with this formula.

Wand posture, the operator repeats the Rousing of the Citadels.

Now follows the reviewing of whatever impressions the Watcher has gained. The God-form posture is most suitable for this purpose. Sitting quietly, and re-establishing the Rhythmic Breath, he simply allows impressions to rise into his conscious mind. Until he is experienced in this method of gaining knowledge, the operator is likely to be disturbed by the fact that the impressions coming to consciousness have no sure mark of their origin: they might come from his imagination, they are fairly certain at first to stimulate and to be coloured by his imagination, and he is unsure what value to set upon them. The only remedy for this state of uncertainty is the usual procedure of the magical student: to record faithfully and at once, then later if and when opportunity offers to make comparison with objective fact. Where discrepancies occur, judgment should be reserved. The difference may be due to a simple error, or some other factor may have caused it. Here the intention of limiting perceptions to the terrestrial level should be of help, but it is to be recognised that until the operator has full control of the method, other levels may intrude, whether at the Watcher's end of the experiment or at the operator's. None the less it is of great value to overcome these early difficulties by practice. If persevered with, this Formula can be brought to a stage where much can be learned by means of it.

If the operator prefers not to use the key-figure, the Watcher may be formulated as a simple sphere. The use of animal shapes for the Watcher is to be avoided by any below Adept status:— the less advanced would most likely choose the form of a creature for which his own instinctual nature had an affinity, whether known or not to his conscious mind: this affinity might cause unintended powers to be transmitted to the Watcher from dark and primitive recesses of the lower Nephesh, so that the Watcher would then act with some degree of volition and would continue to grow in strength as it drew in more Nephesh-substance. Experience shows that such invariably become malicious. (These comments have no reference to the adoption of animal forms as transformations of the astral vehicle during Helionic projection, when the conscious mind is present with the astral vehicle and is in full control of it.)

---

When the student has become thoroughly habituated to the use of the Formula of the Watcher already given, another and considerably more advanced practice may be undertaken. For this to be successful, the student must be quite accustomed to the procedures, not only of sending forth and recalling the Watcher, but also of passively bringing into consciousness the impressions gained therefrom.

In this second practice, the gathering of impressions takes place very much as we have described it, *but before the recall of the Watcher,* so that the operator can in fact keep pace with impressions as the Watcher receives them. The one necessary caution here, is that these impressions should continue to be passively received as they arise within the mind, avoiding any direction of the attention towards the Watcher until it is to be recalled.

*XV*

## *ELEMENTARY TECHNIQUES OF SCRYING*

### 1

The art of scrying is profound and of great beauty, ranging from simple operations to elaborate works of ceremonial magick. It is the purpose of the present paper, however, to give only the basic procedures for the opening of the faculty, and the first steps in directing its employment.*

The technique of scrying consists in clearing the mind of external images by fixing the attention visually upon a neutral and featureless surface (which generally is protected from receiving random influences) so that the inner faculties may cause images to be perceived and impressions concerning those images to arise in the consciousness. Scrying is thus allied to several other occult arts, although differing from these in important respects. Furthermore, perceptions akin to those gained by scrying may be experienced by the magician or, indeed, by anyone sufficiently intent upon any material object to gaze long and questioningly upon it;† such examples

---

* These are the first two stages of basic training in scrying. The third stage of basic training is that of *specialized vision,* in which the student pre-determines the area of his investigation.

† In accordance with a magical principle on which we have enlarged elsewhere, the "answer" to the "question" may not be produced at once, but may come after a greater or less period of relaxed attention. The competent operator acquires the knack of turning from the questioning to the receptive state at will; the untrained subject has to let the process take its own course. A well-known anecdote tells of

show by their wide and varied occurrence that the faculty of
scrying is a customary function of the human psyche. If
it seems rare, it is only because the necessary time, attention,
and motivation are not often present for its development.
From these same causes, children have often been considered
more able scryers than adults; but the magical student who
is drawn to cultivate this faculty, and who can create the
necessary conditions for himself, should not doubt of success.

It must be accepted that the seeming materiality of a
visual image differs widely from one seer to another. One
individual perceives images which seem to be solidly within
the scrying instrument, another may see them as if projected
upon a screen; but there is a third, for whom the imagery
remains always within the mind although a strong conviction
of "seeing" in some mode is present. These three states may
indicate different stages of development, *but not necessarily
so;* any of the three is valid in fully developed seership.

## 2

The surface used for scrying may be chosen from several
types. In the East it is traditionally black, as for instance a
small bowl of ink. In the West, grey has been successfully
used, as in the case of Dr. Dee's small sphere of smoke-grey
crystal, or in modern times the discovery made by some
people of their scrying ability by perceiving images and
scenes in an inoperative television screen. The popular
modern instrument for scrying is a colourless and transparent
glass ball, usually three or four inches in diameter.

a certain pioneer of the early days of palaeontology, who spent an evening in
perplexity before a piece of rock which encased a fossil fish. Just enough of the
fish was visible to show that it was of a species not previously discovered; the
researcher had no means of knowing its exact shape or size. To gain that knowledge, it seemed, he must chip; but if he chipped without that knowledge he might
ruin a unique specimen. In this dilemma he ultimately went to bed. That night he
dreamed that he completed his task and saw the unkown fossil within the rock.
Next day he went about his work on the assumption that the shape and size of
the fish would be just as he had seen in his dream; and he was right. The task of
the student is to bring himself by practice from this haphazard state to one of
full control and direction.

The instrument traditional to A.S. working, which is easier for the student to employ and to master, is the black concave "mirror." In one sense this is a misnomer since the instrument is so constructed as to absorb rather than to reflect light which enters it; however, for this very reason it forms an excellent background for that image-forming faculty which, as De Quincey says, "paints upon darkness." This mirror is a concave disc, about eight inches across, of any convenient material. It has a completely smooth inner surface, and is provided with a plain border and means of standing almost vertically. The interior is finished evenly with black *gloss;* the border and the outside are coloured bluish-grey. It is usual for the Signs of the Zodiac to be painted in gold upon the border.

### 3

For the early stages of practice in the art of scrying, a simple arrangement of the Chamber of Art is desirable, and we recommend the following:—

*A black drape covers the Bomos, which is set up for the operator to face East across it. The Magick Mirror is set thereon, somewhat forward (westward) from centre. Two candles are placed, one at each of the corners behind the Mirror, so that no light falls directly into it. Also upon the Bomos are placed, as preferred, Thymiaterion and incense casket. A chair is placed to the West of, and facing, the Bomos.*

Early morning is the best time of day for scrying, evening is the next best. The student may practice at both these hours if he wishes, for not less than forty minutes and not more than two hours at a time. He may perceive no images at all during a number of his early sessions; he should not be discouraged, but should continue patiently to sit before the scrying surface for the appointed time. Great perseverance may be needed to open the faculty.

4

The operator performs the Setting of the Wards of Power,
then standing before the Bomos, he places incense* in the
thymiaterion. He then utters an earnest aspiration to find
and to control the powers of knowledge and vision which are
in his psyche, letting this take what form he feels proper.
Whatever words are employed, he should dwell upon them
meanwhile so that a true attunement is brought about.
Seating himself before the Bomos, he assumes the God-form
posture, and proceeds according to one or other of the methods
given below, or a combination:—

(a) The operator keeps the gaze fixed upon a point about
the centre of the scrying surface. Rhythmic Breath is established. The mind is cleared from any intense cogitations, but
no effort is made to "switch off" the reflective processes: the
mind can wander over any range of subjects, so long as these
cause no intellectual or emotional tension. The eyes may at
first play tricks, but should always be brought back as soon
as possible to their steady gaze at the central point. There
should in this method be no toying with optical illusions, nor
should the student hope to gain true vision by pursuit of
what he knows to be only a physical reaction. When images
genuinely begin to appear, these will be of a nature quite
different from such optical devices, but will probably be
somewhat away from the actual point of gaze. The operator
should try whether he can transfer his direct gaze to them
without their vanishing or shifting. If not, more time is
needed for the images to develop on the periphery of vision
before they are looked at directly.

(b) Rhythmic Breath is established. The eyes are half-
closed, so that the featureless scrying surface is quite indistinct.
Maintaining the eyes thus, not one point but the whole scrying

---

* Crushed coriander seeds and pure frankincense. This incense is one of those
traditional to the Moorish scrying rites, *Darb-el-Mendel,* and is of great avail in
general and simple operations of scrying.

surface is taken as the object of gaze. Again, the mind is allowed to move placidly meanwhile. When images begin to appear, they should continue to be watched with half-closed eyes.

(c) In this method, the eyes are kept directed upon the scrying surface, but the action of the mind is governed by use of a "mantram." It must be realised that there is no question here of evoking any objective being or power; the mantram is directed entirely to the student's own faculties. Such a phrase as VIDEO-COGNOSCO-SCIO (I see, I understand, I know) is useful, this to be continually and rythmically repeated in a low tone, the consciousness being lulled from its discursive activity by the repetitions. When images begin to appear, the repetitions should gently be stopped. If this method is used, the faculty of scrying may to a slight extent become dependent upon the mantram employed, but, even so, with adequate practice two or three repetitions of the chosen word(s) should then suffice to open the vision.

(At the close of the scrying session, the operator gives the usual battery, preceding this with any other action or utterance he may deem fitting.)

5

Having begun to experience the appearance of images, the student should continue regular practice to maintain and to strengthen his ability. All should be carefully recorded in the Magical Diary, and even the most pointless-seeming perceptions should be given in detail. Many of them may for ever remain pointless, but it may chance that some will be judged otherwise in the light of later understanding or of later experience. In the development of the faculty of scrying, however, the prime requirement for the student at this stage is that the images and scenes, whether stills or moving pictures, should be distinctly perceived.

6

The student who has achieved this clear perception should next in his scrying sessions seek comprehension and amplification of that which he sees. An effective way of doing this, when something has become visible in the scrying surface, is to ask himself questions about it. To ensure precision, the questions should be uttered aloud. The student should not ask more than one simple question at a time, and should not easily give up seeking an answer to it; thus he will by practice gain control of his means of exploration.

One type of response which he is likely to experience is in the form of a series of impressions or quasi-memories arising to his consciousness. After he has uttered a question, he should still his mind so as to enable the answer to be formulated in this way; at first there may be delay, but in this inner work a swift conviction is to be desired rather than an outcome of long meditation. Another type of response consists in a relevant change (complete or otherwise) in that which is seen. The two types of response may occur in conjunction, and in scrying generally this is a most effective manner of proceeding; but the student can, if he wishes, so frame his question as to require the one or the other type of response. "I see a man looking over a bridge: what are his thoughts?" he may ask; or, the image of a summer forest having presented itself, "How will this look during a winter storm?" Visually, he can seek change after change; for example, he can proceed to questions concerning human figures which he sees, so as to involve their appearance in scene after scene. Should the result of any question prove unsatisfactory—as for example an inconsequent change in the vision—he should repeat the question in new and exact terms. With increasing experience and skill, he should be able to build up this stage of his work into a strong but delicate method of exploration, of finding and feeling a way into the worlds of past, present and future.

# PART III

# FORMATIVE PRINCIPLES & METHODS

## XVI

## *SUB ROSA NIGRA*
## *THE AURUM SOLIS*
## *CONSTELLATION OF THE WORSHIPPED*

The three principles of the Constellation are the male, the female, and that which is in one aspect the result of their union and in another aspect is their origin. These principles are named as LEUKOTHEA (the *White Goddess*, the female principle); MELANOTHEOS (the *Dark God*, the male principle); and AGATHODAIMON (the *Benign Spirit*, the androgynous principle).

Before proceeding, it should be understood that the deities composing the Constellation of the Worshipped are a means of representing to the imagination fundamental spiritual realities in magically intelligible form, and are formulated in accordance with the age-old tradition of mythological and magical image-making. Entirely harmonious to the forces they represent, they provide powerful vehicles for the operation of the Illimitable Fire of the Godhead.

### *(The Circled Cross)*

The relationship of the three principles can, if we wish, be considered in a most abstract manner. Eternity—a metaphysical aspect of LEUKOTHEA—is the horizontal beam of an equal-armed cross; Energic-Being—a metaphysical aspect of MELANOTHEOS—the vertical beam thereof. The point of intersection is Time, a metaphysical aspect of AGATHODAIMON. In considering this point of intersection it should be brought to mind that eternity, Energic-Being and Time are qualities in themselves and have nothing to do with duration. An instant of Eternity is of the nature of Eternity, and thus is eternal: An instant of Energic-Being is Energic-Being entirely and completely. An instant of Time is nothing more nor less than Time. AGATHODAIMON, simultaneously with his generation, is no longer contained in, but encompasses, that moment of Eternity and that moment of Energic-Being whose synchronicity begat him: he is thus a circle containing that equal-armed cross which defines his point of generation. Yet that circle which represents All Time is omnipresent, even as Eternity is omnipresent and Energic-Being is omnipresent; thus where the circumference is, the centre is: and where AGATHODAIMON is, there neither LEUKOTHEA nor MELANOTHEOS is absent.

### Leukothea

LEUKOTHEA, the White Goddess, is in her primal aspect Goddess of the Vast Ocean: Ocean of Space or Ocean of Light in some connotations, but pre-eminently Ocean of Water. Among the ancient Greeks, this Shining One was held in high honor, not only as a marine diety but as the nurse of Dionysus.

LEUKOTHEA is the Great Mother, the MAGNA MATER, the PAMMETEIRA, the mother of divine as well as of lower "all things." Beneficent and terrible, she is called "white rose with a centre of darkness;" neither aspect can be disregarded, for mankind has always been aware that besides her lifegiving and luminous character she has also another, no less brilliant but fatally magnetic. In the one aspect the Great Mother is giver of mystical enlightenment, divine patroness of many arts, and bestower of all bounties; in the other she presents the allurement of the deeps, she is the fulfiller of the death-wish, the enchantress who seals her victims beneath the dominion of the unconscious. These two, the bright lifegiving aspect and the dark binding aspect, are represented by AGLAIA and AIANA respectively, and each of them can equally be interpreted as Virgin or as Mother.

The dark aspect of LEUKOTHEA is not always perceptibly related to the sea, but lines of association are never hard to find:— AIANA is also Dictynna, "she-of-the-net," often a hunting net (as of Diana) but in some contexts a fishing net: also it is the web of the Spider-aspect of the Mother, but in the background of that dark shape is the great maternal Water-sign Cancer.

### (God-forms)

LEUKOTHEA. The Great Goddess is robed in a shimmering white peplos, the upper back portion of which is draped to form a covering for her hair. Over this veil she wears a circlet of silver, bearing a single beryl cabochon. Her face is almond-shaped with high forehead and cheekbones; her customary expression is of great dignity and gentleness. Her right hand grasps in a pacific manner, near the blades, which thus are not raised above the level of her shoulders, the shaft of the most sacred Double Axe. The blades of the axe are of silver, the shaft of dark wood; the extremity of the shaft is bound with a bright scarlet thong. Upon her right wrist is worn a bracelet of special form:— it shows on each edge a border of heavy gold, the area between the borders being filled with slender transverse bars of various stones, red, dark green, black, white, yellow and deep blue. Her left arm is raised, and upon the palm is poised a seamew with outspread wings.

AIANA is seen through a net which hangs before her, supported by two hovering doves. She is nude, her white-blond hair falling over her shoulders. Black flowers are entwined in her circlet of silver and beryl. The bracelet is upon her right wrist; her arms are held out in an expansive and welcoming gesture.

AGLAIA wears a dark blue peplos, unfastened at the left shoulder so as to reveal her breast on that side. Her hair, veilless, is dark and flowing. Upon her head is the circlet, and upon her right wrist is the bracelet. Her right hand is extended, palm uppermost, as offering a tongue of flame which seems to spring from the centre of the palm. The other hand supports her left breast, this also as in offering.

### Melanotheos

In his primal aspect MELANOTHEOS, the Dark God, is the celestial (ouranian) Primogenitor, the all-potent mover. His influence is seen in all that may be termed fatherhood, whether actual parenthood (human or not) or creative evocation of any kind. As spouse of the Goddess in their primordial union specifically, MELANOTHEOS is symbolized as the high serpent of the Zodiac held in the night's embrace: for he is archetypally one with that mighty spirit Ophion of pre-Hellenic Greece.

Under the dominion of MELANOTHEOS are fertility and magick power: he is wielder of the heavens and giver of seed to the worlds; he is far-hurler of the javelins of will and of purpose, and lord of the hidden forces of the universe. He is also the Divine Fool or Jester, the Harlequin, the Pied Piper, "the Divine Madness of God," and his is that unreason with which a person seizes upon his destiny, regardless of pain or pleasure, good or ill.

As lover of the Goddess, MELANOTHEOS is drawn to her in her every aspect: it is her essential identity which attracts him, whatever guise or function may veil her.

MELANOTHEOS is also, in high mystical thought, the Many, the *Daimones Poliastres*, the Star-Lords. In their origin these are the totally unmanifest and humanly unthinkable *logoi spermatikoi* of his primal aspect,* the seminal archetypes of the universe.

---

* The term *logoi spermatikoi* is here used in context of the writings of Plotinus, who partly borrows it from certain Stoic writers, although he uses it with wider

*(God-forms)*

**MELANOTHEOS.** The form is of a huge and powerful serpent with many great coils, writhing and threshing in darkness. The scales of the serpent are indigo with purple highlights. The eyes are large and brilliant red with black pupils, the long ivory fangs are python-like. The head and forepart of the body has a dorsal crest of dark red.

**MELANOTHEOS.** Male human figure, of muscular but slender form, youthful and powerful, dancing and wildly ecstatic. His skin is pale indigo; his hair is long and dark, and entwined in it are flowers of many colours. The figure is nude but for a long silver pallium draped from his left upper arm; this garment moves with the movement of the God, sometimes falling across his body, sometimes flowing behind him, sometimes twining loosely about him. Upon his hair rests a crescent of silver light, appearing either as horns of power or as the moon.

*Agathodaimon*

**AGATHODAIMON**, the vital equilibrium of opposites, is the power which is generated by and which encompasses the male and the female principles.

In its primal aspect, as origin of god and goddess, this principle is named **HA**, representing the Undifferentiated Divine Essence, transcendent and formless, the root of all manifested principles.

**AGATHODAIMON** is a central and timeless presence in deep human experience. Perpetuated in Gnostic tradition from an earlier Egyptian formulation, **AGATHODAIMON** is identified with the beneficent and life sustaining aspects of the solar force descending to earth, and likewise with the

---

variation of meaning. With Plotinus, a *logos* is always an emanation: generally, as here, the term is used as the Stoics themselves used it, to mean an Archetype or "Idea" in the Divine MInd. The *logoi spermatikoi* as generally identical with the Ideas emphasise an aspect which is further elaborated by Ficino, "These great Ideas are not at all sterile, they multiply their likenesses throughout the Universe." Augustine's "Archetypes" in the Divine Mind (with regard to which he follows Nicomachus of Gerasa) continue the succession of terms having reference to the Ideas.

spiritual response which leads the psyche upwards. He is thus the prototypic solar hero, the *Shemesh Aulom* or sempiternal spiritual sun, whose rising is the ensign of attainment. He is the Eternal High Priest, whose intelligible Tipharic manifestation mediates between man and the vastness of HA. He is *Dumu-zi-da*, the Faithful Shepherd, and he is the healing serpent *Nachash* which Moses lifted up in the wilderness.

AGATHODAIMON is the transforming vision of the Light Divine which arises within the soul; and he is the Holy Guardian of the Kosmos, the spiritual consciousness of the Logos immanent in the manifested worlds.

AGATHODAIMON is both anthropomorphic and ophiomorphic; he is the Winged Solar Serpent (to whom the title KNOUPHIS belongs) and he is the Priest of the Sun. His number is 989, 9 + 8 + 9 = 26 = 8, signifying the force of Regeneration.

### (God-forms)

AGATHODAIMON. Completely human figure, tall and commanding. He has a youthful and spiritual face with lofty resolute expression and compassionate eyes; his hair is yellow-blond and of medium length, falling in curling locks, and upon his head is the golden crown of twelve rays. He wears a white robe, ample and wide-sleeved, which sparkles with light of every colour. He wears also a long and wide stole of rich green, embroidered with interlacings of gold; this rests upon his shoulders somewhat away from his neck, the ends falling before him. His feet are bare.

AGATHODAIMON (In his name *Knouphis*). Serpent form with nacreous white scales. Eyes yellow, with black pupils. Wings as of an eagle, plumage of rich green, feathertips bordered with gold. From the serpent's head dart rays of brilliant golden light.*

---

*But in secret silence doth the Snake slough its skin; and then is the Scourging and the Hidden Splendor, the adoration of the midnight sun and the forthshowing of Abrasax, Living Caduceus and Act of Abraxas.

Whoso perceives truth shall never pierce the Veil! Whoso understands wisdom shall never unlock the Vault of the Adepti!

0 + 1 = 5. Be it accomplished and concealed beneath the Black Rose!

## (Concerning HA)

To the holy name HA no image is applied, and no attributes are ascribed which would imply limitation of the divine essence represented by this name. HA transcends, sustains and is the absolute reality of, all things. All that would be stated of the deific force of Kether can, however, be applied to HA. Thus HA is:

> Eternal Fount of Life,
> Illimitable Light and Splendour,
> Infinite Power underlying all,
> Changeless and Pure Being,
> Light beyond Sight,
> Existence of all Existences,
> The All-Holy, Eternal,
> The Incomprehensible giving the Light of
>     Comprehension,
> Mystic Glory beyond compare.

The name HA is uttered on a non-vocalized aspirate, that is, on a harsh breathing. Then may follow silent or spoken aspiration to, or invocation of, the divine Light and Life of Godhead, as suitable to the occasion.

Invocation of HA may be as rich in imagery as may be proper to the circumstances, provided only that no limitation is stated or implied in the essence of HA. In whatever context, HA is always the infinite containing the finite.

It is always permissible, when circumstances allow, to trace in the air before one with the right hand the Greek letter Ψ *(psi)* when the holy name HA is uttered. The method of so doing is as follows:

To trace, first, the "bowl" from left to right, *in silence:*

(This signifying the universe, all images and vehicles.)
Then, *while breathing* HA, to trace the vertical:

(This signifying the Inflowing Life, the Inspiring Breath.)
The letter *Psi* is traditionally used in the Western Mysteries to symbolize the action of the *Ruach Elohim* upon, and through, the contingent universe.

The principles of the Constellation are related in general character to certain deific concepts of Hebrew Qabalah, and these correspondences can properly be indicated, to illustrate with greater richness and depth the interrelationship of the principles. Thus LEUKOTHEA is AIMA ELOHIM and SHEKINAH. In her name AIANA she is AMA, the "dark sterile Mother"; in her name AGLAIA she is AIMA, the "bright fertile Mother". MELANOTHEOS is ABBA, "Father of Lights". AGATHODAIMON, as has been indicated, is NACHASH: thus also YEHESHUA of later Judaeo-Christian Qabalah.

While the principles of the Constellation may validly be seen to have a primary association with certain of the Sephiroth, they should not, in fact, be conceived of as limited to those aspects. LEUKOTHEA is the godforce of Binah, but she is also the Column of Severity and has aspects which relate to the Sephiroth Netzach, Yesod and Malkuth. MELANOTHEOS is the godforce of Chokmah, but he is also the Column of Mercy and has aspects which relate to the Sephiroth Geburah, Tiphareth, Hod and Yesod. AGATHODAIMON is the godforce of Tiphareth, but he is also the Column of Equilibrium and has aspects which relate to the Sephiroth Chesed, Geburah, Netzach and Hod. The primal aspect of AGATHODAIMON, named as HA, is the godforce of Kether, but also the total reality of the Divine Essence in Atziluth.

It is essential, therefore, that the principles of the Constellation, which represent as it were the intrinsic aspects of the Divine Life, should not be confused with—or considered as alternatives to—the Magical Formulae, the Divine Names of the Sub Rosa Nigra system which are specific to each of the Sephiroth and of the Paths. These latter can be regarded as powers of HA—that is, as modalities of the Divine Life as it extends through the World of Atziluth—or as powers of the other principles of the Constellation, as context and the thought of the individual magician may require.

The Magical Formulae are tabulated below: they are followed by the "Archontic sequence", the tables of related hierarchical names for the Worlds of Briah and Yetzirah.

## MAGICAL FORMULAE
### Divine Names in Atziluth

| | | | |
|---|---|---|---|
| 1 | ♅ | ΕΝ·ΤΟ·ΠΑΝ | EN-TO-PAN |
| 2 | ♆ | ΙΕΗΩΟΤΑ | IEEOOUA |
| 3 | ♄ | ΤΥΡΑΝΑ, ΙΑΛΔΑΒΑΩΘ | TURANA, IALDABAOTh* |
| 4 | ♃ | ΖΑΡΑΙΗΤΟΣ | ZARAIETOS |
| 5 | ♂ | ΣΑΒΑΩ | SABAO |
| 6 | ☉ | ΟΝΟΦΙΣ | ONOPhIS |
| 7 | ♀ | ΑΛΒΑΦΑΛΑΝΑ | ALBAPhALANA |
| 8 | ☿ | ΑΖΩΘ | AZOTh |
| 9 | ☽ | ΙΑΩ | IAO |
| 10 | ⊕ | ΒΑΘ·ΜΕΝΙΝ·ῙΕΚΑΣΤΟΥ | BATh-MENIN-HEKASTOU |
| 11 | △ | ΣΕΛΑΗ·ΓΕΝΕΤΗΣ | SELAE-GENETES |
| 12 | ☿ | ΑΖΩΘ | AZOTh |
| 13 | ☽ | ΙΑΩ | IAO |
| 14 | ♀ | ΑΛΒΑΦΑΛΑΝΑ | ALBAPhALANA |
| 15 | ♈ | ΣΑΒΑΩ | SABAO |
| 16 | ♉ | ΑΛΒΑΦΑΛΑΝΑ | ALBAPhALANA |
| 17 | ♊ | ΑΖΩΘ | AZOTh |
| 18 | ♋ | ΙΑΩ | IAO |
| 19 | ♌ | ΟΝΟΦΙΣ | ONOPhIS |
| 20 | ♍ | ΑΖΩΘ | AZOTh |
| 21 | ♃ | ΖΑΡΑΙΗΤΟΣ | ZARAIETOS |
| 22 | ♎ | ΑΛΒΑΦΑΛΑΝΑ | ALBAPhALANA |
| 23 | ▽ | ΠΑΓΚΡΑΤΗΣ | PANKRATES |
| 24 | ♏ | ΣΑΒΑΩ | SABAO |
| 25 | ♐ | ΖΑΡΑΙΗΤΟΣ | ZARAIETOS |
| 26 | ♑ | ΙΑΛΔΑΒΑΩΘ | IALDABAOTh |
| 27 | ♂ | ΣΑΒΑΩ | SABAO |
| 28 | ♒ | ΙΑΛΔΑΒΑΩΘ | IALDABAOTh |
| 29 | ♓ | ΖΑΡΑΙΗΤΟΣ | ZARAIETOS |
| 30 | ☉ | ΟΝΟΦΙΣ | ONOPhIS |
| 31 | △ | ΘΕΟΣ | ThEOS |
| 32 | ♄ | ΤΥΡΑΝΑ | TURANA |
| 32 | ▽ | ΚΥΡΙΟΣ | KYRIOS |
| 31 | ⊕ | ΑΘΑΝΑΤΟΣ, ΙΣΧΥΡΟΣ | AThANATOS, ISChYROS |
| Daath | | ΔΕΣΤΑΦΙΤΟΝ | DESTAPhITON |

*Binah, depending on whether it is considered in its supernal or its planetary aspect, is represented by *Turana* and *Ialdabaoth* respectively.

ΑΡΧΟΝΤΕΣ
*Archons in Briah*

| 1 | ✹ | ΠΡΩΤΙΣΤΟΣ | PROTISTOS |
|---|---|---|---|
| 2 | ↑ | ΚΛΕΟΦΟΡΟΣ | KLEOPhOROS |
| 3 | ♄ | ΜΕΝΕΣΘΕΥΣ | MENESThEUS |
| 4 | ♃ | ΟΡΘΩΤΗΡ | ORThOTER |
| 5 | ♂ | ΔΟΡΥΞΕΝΟΣ | DORYXENOS |
| 6 | ☉ | ΠΥΛΩΡΟΣ | PYLOROS |
| 7 | ♀ | ΖΩΘΑΛΜΙΟΣ | ZOThALMIOS |
| 8 | ☿ | ΑΝΑΞΕΦΥΔΡΙΑΣ | ANAXEPhYDRIAS |
| 9 | ☽ | ΘΕΟΝΟΗΜΗΝΟΣ | ThEONOEMENOS |
| 10 | ⊕ | ἙΣΤΙΑΤΩΡ | HESTIATOR |
| 11 | △ | ΣΩΤΗΡ | SOTER |
| 12 | ☿ | ΣΘΕΝΟΣ | SThENOS |
| 13 | ☽ | ΑΝΑΚΤΩΡ | ANAKTOR |
| 14 | ♀ | ΑΛΑΛΗ | ALALE |
| 15 | ♈ | ΦΙΛΑΜΜΟΝ | PhILAMMON |
| 16 | ♉ | ΚΟΡΗΣΥΣ | KORESUS |
| 17 | ♊ | ἈΡΜΑΚΟΝ | HARMAKON |
| 18 | ⊗ | ΤΕΛΕΦΑΣΣΑ | TELEPhASSA |
| 19 | ♌ | ΠΕΡΦΡΟΜΕΔΑ | PERPhROMEDA |
| 20 | ♍ | ΔΗΛΙΟΝ | DELION |
| 21 | ♃ | ΒΑΛΗΝ | BALEN |
| 22 | ♎ | ΚΥΠΡΟΦΟΝ | KYPROPhON |
| 23 | ▽ | ΑΣΦΑΛΕΙΟΣ | ASPhALEIOS |
| 24 | ♏ | ΒΑΘΟΝΑΟΣ | BAThONAOS |
| 25 | ♐ | ΤΑΘΕΝΗΛΗ | TAThENELE |
| 26 | ♑ | ΚΑΛΟΦΑΡΙΣ | KALOPhARIS |
| 27 | ♂ | ΡΥΤΩΡ | RUTOR |
| 28 | ♒ | ΑΜΑΛΔΙΣ | AMALDIS |
| 29 | ♓ | ΖΑΝΘΗΜΟΣ | ZANThEMOS |
| 30 | ☉ | ΑΣΠΙΣ | ASPIS |
| 31 | △ | ΑΛΑΣΤΩΡ | ALASTOR |
| 32 | ♄ | ΞΑΙΣ | XAIS |
| 32 | ▽ | ΑΜΥΝΤΩΡ | AMYNTOR |

## ΚΟΥΡΟΙ
*Powers in Yetzirah (Ruling)*

| | | | |
|---|---|---|---|
| 3 | ♄ | ΑΣΧΕΡΙΑΣ | ASChERIAS |
| 4 | ♃ | ΚΑΠΑΙΟΣ | KAPAIOS |
| 5 | ♂ | ΚΑΣΑΡΤΗΣ | KASARTES |
| 6 | ☉ | ΑΓΑΜΑΝΟΣ | AGAMANOS |
| 7 | ♀ | ΑΜΕΡΟΦΗΣ | AMEROPhES |
| 8 | ☿ | ΆΒΕΡΟΦΗΣ | HABEROPhES |
| 9 | ☽ | ΑΡΜΑΤΕΟΝ | ARMATEON |
| 10 | ⊕ | ΟΖΗΡΙΤΗΣ | OZERITES |
| 11 | △ | ΑΣΤΗΡΙΟΝ | ASTERION |
| 12 | ☿ | ΆΒΕΡΟΦΗΣ | HABEROPhES |
| 13 | ☽ | ΑΡΜΑΤΕΟΝ | ARMATEON |
| 14 | ♀ | ΑΜΕΡΟΦΗΣ | AMEROPhES |
| 15 | ♈ | ΕΡΙΘΕΙΟΝ | ERIThEION |
| 16 | ♉ | ΑΡΙΣΤΕΥΣ | ARISTEUS |
| 17 | ♊ | ΝΗΤΗ | NETE |
| 18 | ⊗ | ΑΡΓΥΡΩΠΙΣ | ARGYROPIS |
| 19 | ♌ | ΎΠΑΤΙΟΣ | HYPATIOS |
| 20 | ♍ | ΜΝΕΜΕΟΣ | MNEMEOS |
| 21 | ♃ | ΚΑΠΑΙΟΣ | KAPAIOS |
| 22 | ♎ | ΜΕΛΕΤΩΡΟΣ | MELETOROS |
| 23 | ▽ | ΤΕΘΙΑΣ | TEThIAS |
| 24 | ♏ | ΜΕΣΗΡΟΝ | MESERON |
| 25 | ♐ | ΚΑΣΤΑΛΙΟΣ | KASTALIOS |
| 26 | ♑ | ΑΕΓΑΝΙΟΣ | AEGANIOS |
| 27 | ♂ | ΚΑΣΑΡΤΗΣ | KASARTES |
| 28 | ♒ | ΘΑΛΕΙΟΝ | ThALEION |
| 29 | ♓ | ΑΙΟΔΑΞ | AIODAX |
| 30 | ☉ | ΑΓΑΜΑΝΟΣ | AGAMANOS |
| 31 | △ | ΈΦΑΣΙΟΣ | HEPhASIOS |
| 32 | ♄ | ΑΣΧΕΡΙΑΣ | ASChERIAS |
| 32 | ▽ | ΚΙΑΝΗΣ | KIANES |

## ΚΟΥΡΑΙ
*Intelligences in Yetzirah (Intermediate)*

| | | | |
|---|---|---|---|
| 3 | ♄ | ΑΣΧΙΑ | ASChIA |
| 4 | ♃ | ΖΑΘΑΝΑΤ | ZAThANAT |
| 5 | ♂ | ΖΟΣΘΗΜΗ | ZOSThEME |
| 6 | ☉ | ΒΑΛΘΑ | BALThA |
| 7 | ♀ | ΑΝΑΙΤΟΣ | ANAITOS |
| 8 | ☿ | ΑΣΤΑΦΙΑ | ASTAPhIA |
| 9 | ☽ | ΚΑΜΑΙΡΑ | KAMAIRA |
| 10 | ⊕ | ΜΕΡΟΦΙΑ | MEROPhIA |
| 11 | △ | ΦΩΣΤΡΕΙΑ | PhOSTREIA |
| 12 | ☿ | ΑΣΤΑΦΙΑ | ASTAPhIA |
| 13 | ☽ | ΚΑΜΑΙΡΑ | KAMAIRA |
| 14 | ♀ | ΑΝΑΙΤΟΣ | ANAITOS |
| 15 | ♈ | ΥΕΛΚΕΘ | VELKETh |
| 16 | ♉ | ΚΑΒΥΡΑΣ | KABURAS |
| 17 | ♊ | ΑΜΝΕΦΙΛΗΣ | AMNEPhILES |
| 18 | ⊗ | ΣΕΘΑΚΛΗ | SEThAKLE |
| 19 | ♌ | ΚΑΘΑΝΕΥΣ | KAThANEUS |
| 20 | ♍ | ΣΕΡΙΦΥΣ | SERIPhUS |
| 21 | ♃ | ΖΑΘΑΝΑΤ | ZAThANAT |
| 22 | ♎ | ΚΙΛΑΝΣ | KILANS |
| 23 | ▽ | ΝΑΣΑΜΑΛΗ | NASAMALE |
| 24 | ♏ | ΞΩΣΤΕΘ | XOSTETh |
| 25 | ♐ | ΦΩΛΩΤΟΣ | PhOLOTOS |
| 26 | ♑ | ΥΕΘΥΝΙΣ | VEThUNIS |
| 27 | ♂ | ΖΟΣΘΗΜΗ | ZOSThEME |
| 28 | ♒ | ΣΑΤΡΑΝΙΣ | SATRANIS |
| 29 | ♓ | ΚΥΛΑΘΙΟΣ | KULAThIOS |
| 30 | ☉ | ΒΑΛΘΑ | BALThA |
| 31 | △ | ΤΙΒΥΛΚΑΝ | TIBULKAN |
| 32 | ♄ | ΑΣΧΙΑ | ASChIA |
| 32 | ▽ | ΕΘΑΧΩΝ | EThAChON |

## ΕΥΔΑΙΜΩΝΕΣ
*Spirits in Yetzirah (Servient)*

| | | | |
|---|---|---|---|
| 3 | ♄ | ΑΒΗΘΗΣ | ABEThES |
| 4 | ♃ | ΔΕΜΩΡΟΣ | DEMOROS |
| 5 | ♂ | ΝΑΖΙΡΙΑΣ | NAZIRIAS |
| 6 | ☉ | ΣΟΒΙΑΣ | SOBIAS |
| 7 | ♀ | ΙΖΗΘΟΣ | IZEThOS |
| 8 | ☿ | ΨΑΡΧΙΑΣ | PsARChIAS |
| 9 | ☽ | ΙΗΡΟΧΟΣ | IEROChOS |
| 10 | ⊕ | ΜΕΖΑΘΙΟΝ | MEZAThION |
| 11 | △ | ΦΑΛΔΑΡΟΣ | PhALDAROS |
| 12 | ☿ | ΨΑΡΧΙΑΣ | PsARChIAS |
| 13 | ☽ | ΙΗΡΟΧΟΣ | IEROChOS |
| 14 | ♀ | ΙΖΗΘΟΣ | IZEThOS |
| 15 | ♈ | ΖΑΡΚΥΝΩ | ZARKUNO |
| 16 | ♉ | ΝΕΤΑΦΙΟΣ | NETAPhIOS |
| 17 | ♊ | ΤΑΜΑΣΘΗΣ | TAMASThES |
| 18 | ⊗ | ΦΑΡΖΩΝΙΟΣ | PhARZONIOS |
| 19 | ♌ | ΡΕΦΑΝΙΑΣ | REPhANIAS |
| 20 | ♍ | ΙΣΑΖΩΝ | ISAZON |
| 21 | ♃ | ΔΕΜΩΡΟΣ | DEMOROS |
| 22 | ♎ | ΖΟΙΘΗΝΗΣ | ZOIThENES |
| 23 | ▽ | ΛΑΒΕΝΘΙΟΣ | LABENThIOS |
| 24 | ♏ | ΑΡΙΦΑΝΙΣ | ARIPhANIS |
| 25 | ♐ | ΚΑΜΑΘΩΡΟΣ | KAMAThOROS |
| 26 | ♑ | ΘΑΛΟΝΦΗΣ | ThALONPhES |
| 27 | ♂ | ΝΑΖΙΡΙΑΣ | NAZIRIAS |
| 28 | ♒ | ΡΑΒΑΣΘΗΣ | RABASThES |
| 29 | ♓ | ΣΕΜΙΡΙΑΣ | SEMIRIAS |
| 30 | ☉ | ΣΟΒΙΑΣ | SOBIAS |
| 31 | △ | ΑΓΑΖΥΦΙΑ | AGAZUPhIA |
| 32 | ♄ | ΑΒΗΘΗΣ | ABEThES |
| 32 | ▽ | ΖΥΘΩΡΟΝ | ZUThORON |

## XVII

## *PRINCIPLES OF CEREMONIAL*

**Magical** ceremonial can be built up and elaborated to forms of great subtlety and complexity, but the initial principles which cause its creation are simple in the extreme. In the first place, ceremonial is a different thing from meditation, and it is a different thing from merely wishing or praying that a certain result should come about: the magician sets himself to move the Astral Light in an especial way, and for that purpose certain acts, certain movements and gestures, sometimes an entire dramatic presentation, have to be co-ordinated appropriately. If they are not only chosen for their correspondence to this or that aspect of the Light but also to evoke an inner response in the psyche of the operator, they will have twice the potency which they might otherwise have had.

Magical principle is in this sense "artificial," and owes its effectiveness to that artifice. Once again it can be pointed out that it is not the operator's natural emotion or aspiration, fraught with fears of failure or involvement with other considerations, which carries him to success. This is replaced, for the nonce, with the play of the ritual. The purpose of the magician is not sealed within him, to be subjected to all the forces of negation, but, directed into the performance and the experience of the rite, it moves the currents of the Astral which in turn place him in contact with the cosmic forces of his seeking.

Before considering any assemblage of ritual acts in detail,

we find that such acts in general can be grouped under the
following heads:—

I    a)    *Acts directly imitative of an intended project,
           including the desired outcome.*

I    b)    *Acts imitative of cosmic and meteorological
           processes.*

II   a)    *Acts meant indirectly to induce or to avert
           influences by allusive or symbolic association.*

II   b)    *Mythic presentments and acts of propitiation or
           of worship, intended to link the rite with a specific
           divine force.*

Any or all of these types of action may be present in a
particular ritual, depending upon its complexity and upon the
magician's assessment of the situation. The classification of
magical works according to method, which is more usually
given by various authorities, will be found to furnish sub-
groupings within the above tabulation. Thus I a) contains the
simpler aspects of substitution-rites such as those found
(apparently) in Neolithic hunting-magick, and in the Egyptian
use of images representing enemies for the purpose of their
subjugation: in doll-sorcery generally, and in Mesopotamian
rites utilising not only images, but animals or human beings
(slaves, prisoners) to represent the person who will benefit or
otherwise from the rite. Also included in this category,
fundamentally, is the method prescribed by Sir Kenelm Digby
for the use of his curative "Powder of Sympathy."

I b) comprises not only some very primitive works—the
type of rain-magick which directly imitates thunder or involves
libation as a main feature—but also some imagery of refined
mysticism. Of the many examples which can be given of turning
about in imitation of celestial revolution, at present it will
suffice to refer to the literature of the Dervishes, which seems
in places to imply that thus to revolve fulfills the obligation
of the microcosm to continue the work of the macrocosm:
The right hand of the Dervish dancer having the palm upward

to receive the celestial influences, the left hand having the palm downward to transmit those influences to lower planes of being. A number of writers give other and more elaborate traditions as to the significance of the mystical whirling dance: the one just given is probably the best-known, and shows something of the Pythagorean heritage which has in various particulars been as faithfully handed down by the Arabic tongue as by the Hellenic.

However, it is not only in such notable developments that we find actions which directly imitate phenomena in order to participate in their movement or to induce it. To this category also relates the spontaneous feeling that rites of Fire for instance should be performed with swift quiet movements and aspiring gestures, rites of Water in a slow and undulating mode, rites of Earth with periods of complete stillness and silence, rites of Air with vigour, expansive gestures and musical sound. These characteristics can be varied according to particular circumstances and individual requirements—the clash of cymbals can evoke Fire, while taurine bellowings and stampings belong to some aspects of Earth—the important consideration is not that a particular Element or Power should be represented according to any fixed rule, but that the participants in the rite should feel their actions to be in harmony with the force to be evoked, and above all with the aspects thereof which are related to the working. Real charact-erization can be drawn from the attributes of any power within the range of magical working. Besides personal experience and meditation, the student should encourage imagination by searching in his literary heritage. If a study were being made of the cardinal points or of their Winds (as an example), such a passage as this on the North Wind, from the Sixth Book of Ovid's *Metamorphoses,* would merit attention:—

"Force is my nature: with force I urge the dark clouds, with force I stir the seas and uproot knotty oaks: I harden the snow and scourge with hail the lands. Thus too when I

meet my brothers in open sky (that sky my plain) so mightily
do I contend with them that the mid-air rings, and from hollow
clouds there leap broken fires. Or when tameless I have
descended into vaulted pits of the earth, and have put my
shoulders beneath the deepest caverns, with quakings I affright
the shades of the dead, and all the world."

This passage can be compared with the vivid description
of the North Wind, "the fierce Kabibonokka," in Longfellow's
Hiawatha: the second canto, The Four Winds, has passages
of considerable interest and beauty regarding each quarter.
Essential to a study of the West Wind, again, would be Keats'
superb Ode; considerable work might be put in on the
characters of the Four Winds, and it is one of the subjects
which has always fascinated mankind. Of great antiquity
in Egypt, the "Song of the Four Winds" appears by the time
of the Twelfth Dynasty to have developed a dramatised form,
a dance-game apparently in which four performers at the
quarters of a circle presented each the character of a wind,
and another whose base was at the centre tried in some
manner to "steal the treasure" of the Winds. It may have
been an entertainment simply: or its performance may have
been a "wind-stealing" rite, having the purpose of raising a
wind by means of an allusive drama.

This latter possibility would impinge upon the subject-
matter of our next classification, II a), the attraction of forces
by indirect, sometimes symbolic means. To the subject of
characterisation we shall return presently. Symbolism, as the
language of the Unconscious, becomes hallowed as a means
of communicating with the spiritual world: but an element of
personal insecurity can also in some instances be suspected,
a degree of caution against making too plain a declaration
of one's desire: perhaps also too simple a sequence of cause
and effect is avoided, in order to strengthen both the power of
the operation and the resolve of the operator by introducing
mystifications. The transition from direct enactment to

symbolism is sometimes so slight and so natural as to need no especial reason. Thus in the *Fasti* with regard to the Roman celebrations of New Year's Day, we are told that this day was not made a public holiday for fear such an omen might lead to a workless year: and then that dates and figs, honey and gold were offered to Janus, that their sweetness might bring a year of joy and abundance. A similarly simple transference of ideas is indicated by the shrine and emblems of the fertility cult which were found in a pit of the flint-mines at Grime's Graves, Norfolk: since the nature of the site precludes for the shrine's purpose any ordinary connotations of fertility, it is deduced that the intent here was to render the earth prolific in flints.

In other instances, however, the indirectness of the ritual approach is more developed and conspicuous. A notable example is the Hopi Snake-dance, of which the final purpose is to bring not serpents but rain. The serpentine movements of the dance are intended to attract the fiery Lightning-snakes, who in similar manner will begin to play in the heavens: and it is their play which causes the rain. At a more sophisticated level, to the same category belong rites intended to induce a planetary influence, so as to correct an astrological imbalance and thus avert misfortune, for instance.

II b). With a union of mythic themes and magical concepts, both the possible formulae and the actual power of workings are tremendously enriched. This other dimension, the link with a specific spiritual force, not only brings its own formulae into being, but adds significance and power to rites of the foregoing types. It was early realised that to enact a desired project with its successful outcome, or to represent either directly or symbolically a cosmic occurrence over which the performer has ordinarily no control, became transformed from a primitive attempt to a truly magical work when a myth of similar connotations was enacted, declaring or implying such a Magical Link as, "As the Son of Isis thus triumphed over his enemies, so shall my cause be victorious!"

Myth from one source or another has everywhere provided the major dramatic bases for rites of many kinds, and magical ritual has thereby taken on a special dignity. Predominant in showing forth this influence are the great rites both initiatory and sacrificial of the various solar cults. There are also, however, rites of sheer adoration or of the celebration of some cosmic or mythic fact, rites which from an exoteric viewpoint belong, not to magick, but to religon: these, when considered with occult understanding, are truly magical in their operation of building up an egregore, and of maintaining a channel thereto from the Divine Mind.

From the least to the greatest of magical rites, then, a high degree of dramatic presentation can be recognised throughout. It is dramatic presentation of a particular kind, intended both to stir the Light and to attune the operator to whatever powers are to be associated with the working.

The degree of preparation for a rite will largely depend upon the importance of the occasion. To utilise the more convenient correspondences to which reference is made in these volumes, is a normal standard of working: the magician will on occasion do well with less, according to need or judgment, but it is sometimes desirable to do considerably more. He, and also the other participants if great and specialised force is required, should in such cases devote pre-arranged periods to meditation or reading which centres upon aspects of the sphere in question: for these periods they need not meet, but the times arranged should be as harmonious to the sphere as is possible. Some authorities, particularly in older writings, would have those concerned, and particularly the leader of the working, to keep during the preparatory phase to a diet specially devised to be in harmony with the intended sphere of working, and it evidently is their intention in prescribing solitude also that the magician should be able at that time, and not merely during the working itself, to attune his psychic and physical organization to the sphere. A remarkable example of this counsel is to be found in the *Picatrix*, a medieval Latin translation of an eleventh-century Arabic text attributed to Maslama b. Ahmad al-Majriti, which makes reference to much Greek as well as Arabian lore: a general life of retirement in desert places, and fasting, is recommended to the magician, but then for evocation of the Planetary Spirits he is bidden to choose his food according to the correspondences of the planet whose Spirit he will after due preparation evoke. The rite itself is eventually performed with conformably coloured raiment, appropriate perfume and incense, and images suited to the reason for the work. A modern example, no less thorough in operation, is presented in Crowley's "Moonchild." In all counsel concerning the correspondences, however, no matter how simple or how elaborate the means employed, it is a main objective that when the working itself takes place, the principal person in the group, preferably with any other participants, should be able without difficulty to enter into the temper of the sphere.

In the type of magical rite which we are chiefly considering, the need for long and elaborate preparation is almost completely replaced by development of the mythic element, which means that in the psyche an affinity with the character of the working does not need to be created, so much as contacted where it already exists. This brings out a further important aspect of the relationship of myth to magick. The problem which it helps to resolve is one which has been considered from different viewpoints elsewhere in these volumes: the need for involvement, in the sense of conviction of the necessity for one's work, and at the same time for non-involvement, in the sense of freedom from anxiety as to the outcome of the work. While anything approaching psychodrama (that is to say, in context, an exact presentation of an individual's inner personal situation requiring a specific

outcome) must be banished from enactment in any rite of
High Magick and could only ruin the work, it can cogently
be pointed out here that the great myths of mankind are
such as to awaken a response, conscious or otherwise, in any
human psyche to which they are adequately presented, so that
each participant can have a true sense of "belonging" in the
work at a deeper than personal level. For this reason, a magical
rite can never be placed on the level of a formal theatre-piece:
it is a part of the life-force flowing through the participants.
Further, the student is adjured that when he is privately
using a ritual, no matter how exactly it may have been prepared
by himself or by another, if when performing the actual
working he feels that another gesture or ritual movement
would be "right" he is to introduce it without hesitation.

From the nature of ritual working a number of further
principles can be deduced, which have to be considered with
a view to practical usage. The first of these concerns the place
of working itself.

Here we are concerned with the containing limits of the
magical action, the limits which must obtain for the conditions
created by the magician. Even supposing that he purposed to
influence the whole world by a single magical working
(we might in any given case question the wisdom of this, but
we cannot deny its possibility as a general hypothesis): still
his course of action should be to build up his force within a
limited space and to send it thence, rather than to allow it
from its beginning to disseminate among the myriad other
influences in the world, changing both in context and in
potency as the Hegelian processes of transformation affected
it. These processes must inevitably come into play: but the
Work should first be completed in security. In other words,
the Circle of Working is for true ceremonial magick a necessity:
whether for the protection of the magician and his work, or
for the simple conservation of energy, or for both purposes.
According to its use is the circle constructed and fortified: in

different rites we find the circumference traced with the sword-point for instance, or measured by "treading," while the working area may be fortified by Names of Power uttered or inscribed, and signs inscribed, or traced in the air, or framed within the visual imagination and thence projected forth.

Many magical operations involve one or more circumambulations of the area of working, within the limits of the circle. While purposeless circumambulation is to be avoided, it is suitable to introduce such a movement for the following reasons.

(1) To create a simple vortex of energy. It may be desired to perform a circumambulation, or a number as suitable for the rite, simply to stir the Light and to emphasise an intention of invoking or of banishing, of setting a current in motion or of inhibiting it. The operator may begin circumambulating from whatever quarter is most appropriate.

Where a "positive" intention has been implemented with the aid of a deosil circumambulation in the early part of a rite, it is very usual to balance this by an "unwinding" or widdershins circumambulation in the later part. This however is not a custom which should be observed except in cases where it has real purpose. In many instances it would be foolishness to "balance" the circlings in this manner and would simply annul the effect of the working: rather, the desired effect obtained, the forces involved in its production should be allowed to sink into quiescence.

There is among occultists a frequent reluctance to employ widdershins movements—that is, anti-clockwise movements—because of a popular belief that these are wholly or predominantly associated with the "Left-hand Path." This whole subject is very confused in the thoughts of many: for the peace of mind of our students we must state here that for purposes of invoking in rites of Luna or of the Chthonic Powers, or for banishing in any other rites, the left-hand turn or the widdershins circumambulation are altogether in order.

Those who would shun the Left-hand Path* should avoid
works for a selfish and debased end, including works which
border upon that description if the planetary association
thereof be Saturn, Mars or Luna; likewise avoiding any form
of blood sacrifice. The direction in which one turns in the
course of a rite cannot decide the matter.

(2) Circumambulation may validly be employed to
represent a cosmic orbit, on such principles as have already
been indicated.

(3) It may represent a systematic progress or pilgrimage,
particularly when the quarters or half-quarters, or some of
those points, can be used symbolically to represent stages
in the journey. The correspondences of the compass are for
the magician to employ and to bring out in his working if
they are appropriate thereto: any which are irrelevant may
simply be ignored, since they are not potent unless activated.†

(4) Aral or "closed" circumambulations to create a
simple vortex of energy. These occur in group-workings, and
are performed not in a processional manner, but with linked
hands, right hand palm downwards, left hand palm upwards:
the number of revolutions being suited to the working, or as
many as the circle leader feels to be right. Aral circumambulation is performed deosil: it is always positive and must *in
no circumstances* be countered.

(5) *Orthrochoros:*— a triple circumambulation deosil,
betokening the Triune Light, begun in the East, the arms
raised in the Ψ position. This circumambulation is only
used following high spiritual invocations. It is invariably to
be countered at the conclusion of the rite by:—

* This statement is made in context of the Western Mysteries, where "Left-hand
Path" is synonymous with anti-evolutionary processes. The term frequently has
other connotations in Eastern Traditions, denoting for instance the Vamacharya
school of Tantra, whose ritual involves the use of madya, māṁsa, matsya, mudrā,
and maithuna (wine, meat, fish, cereal, sexual congress), as sacramental means of
uniting the devotees with life-giving evolutionary forces.

† They can be ignored, but not brought in under false colours. For example, the
practice of denominating the principal focus of a chamber or temple as East,
regardless of its true bearings, is futile in ceremonial magick.

*Dyseochoros:*— a triple circumambulation widder-shins, betokening the withdrawal of the Triune Light: begun in the East, arms crossed on the breat left over right, head bowed.

Whenever possible, the operator should in his own mind assume a definite character, even where this is not specified in the rite. If he is simply "himself," it should be his magical personality of which he is aware: if the theme provides a specific enactment, then to assume for the time being a distinctive role will be far more satisfactory both from his own viewpoint and for the effectiveness of the rite. If the rite calls for one's taking on the character of the East Wind, it is better to be Eurus or Wabun or another manifestation of that wind, with whatever local identity is most apt to the working, than to remain faceless. If there is a lack of mythic material, one's ritual character should be built up from the imagination, as appositely as possible. This is not intended to imply the assumption of form, in the manner associated with god-forms: all that is intended here is a distinct characteriza-tion.\* These characters can be as vivid as the types of the Commedia dell'Arte, the "feel" of a particular role being the essence of the matter. For a group working, characterizations should be co-ordinated.

As to the actual movements and gestures which make up a rite, these should never lack in significance. If a rite is being constructed, long speeches should as a general rule be avoided, action should be interpreted by speech but should only minimally be replaced thereby; likewise it should be remembered that an action has besides its intrinsic significance, a significance deriving from the part of the circle in which it takes place, and the instrument (if any) with which it is performed. For example: the East is the place of light's origin.

---

\* Assuption of god-forms is preferred by the A.S. to be reserved to specific "theurgic moments," and not to be maintained throughout a working. As a general principle, "characterization" is otherwise considered more suitable.

To carry a lighted lamp to the East, therefore, is to offer it for identification with the Source of Light: thus to dedicate it and spiritualise its significance. To carry a lighted lamp to the West, however, is to carry light into darkness, to illumine the shadowed places, to carry enlightenment. In works involving aspiration to an Element or to the qualities signified thereby (as distinct from works involving invocation of Elemental forces) the natural zodiacal positions for the Elements are appropriate: East—Fire, South—Earth, West—Air, and North—Water.

To stamp the foot is an emphatic assertion of dominion over the lower powers, inner and outer. By implication, it is especially suited to the Adept in his aspect as the Grand Hermetic Androgyne, proclaiming victory over the lower elements. So the winged white steed Pegasus, Poseidon's emissary, stamped with his hoof upon the summit of Helicon to subdue that rebellious mountain: furthermore, from the apical hoofprint flowed Hippocrene, the sacred fount of the Muses. Thus the magician, whether in his magical personality simply, or in the character of Mithras, Heracles or other Heroic victor over the chthonic powers, may stamp his foot, either to signal his will to command them, or to indicate his freedom from their bondage and his right to drink of the nectar of inspiration.

To raise something upward is, generally, to bring it into operation as well as into manifestation. For example: in the A.S. Consecration of the Sword, before the act of consecration, the Sword is horizontal; after being consecrated it is raised up, the blade vertical, while the triumphant *Song of Iubar* is chanted.

The magical student should practice making broad, distinct gestures. Unless he is very young or else has some experience in costume drama, he may find difficulty in this; but these gestures are to belong to his magical personality, and self-consciousness must be put aside as it has been in developing the magical voice. The Astral Light is to be moved by the physical presence of the magician as well as by his expressed will. When once gesture has thus been made significant, it will be found that the direction and mode of every movement is as expressive as the glance of the eyes. Nor must the two-way action of expressive movement be forgotten. Quite apart from magical effects proper, to express a psychic state is to induce that psychic state, and care should be taken not unwittingly to induce a state liable to inhibit the effect of one's own ritual. For this reason, movements which express or suggest such inhibitive qualities as submission, inertia or dejection are generally to be avoided in magical working. The predominant tone of magical work is one of courage, generosity, and resolution. whether active or passive, and the major forces which the magician has to interpret are those of divine expansiveness and abundance. These are reflected in rite and gesture.

Thus when the goddess Ishtar (as an example) descends through the Underworld to reclaim Tammuz, and when at each portal of the seven adverse spheres she divests herself of a garment, her gesture in so doing is not one of abjection, or of submission to the demons of the sphere: she raises her arms upward and outward. Then she proceeds upon her way in divinity victorious. So when she reaches the seventh and deepest level, and renounces her final garment, entering to find Tammuz and to lead him thence to life renewed, she is her supernal and all-luminous self, the Star in effulgent nudity.

So also, to consider a different manifestation of the Goddess in a totally other region, cultural setting and emotional tone: when the gaiety and love and exquisiteness of Maitresse Erzulie are at last swept into a paroxysm of grief, the arms of the possessed in the Voudoun cult are flung wide and her trance passes into comatose sleep: the fact and the gesture have many witnesses. Here too the gesture is upward and outward. This is a grief neither selfish nor ephemeral: it is cosmic.

Our gesture when as the preliminary to a ritual it is necessary to bring power down from the Sacred Flame to sweep through the conscious personality, is the Calyx. In some measure, it may be said that the Calyx foreshadows the Formula of the Grail.

That the Holy Grail is associated in a manner with the Cauldron of Regeneration of Celtic lore, is a frequent statement among specialists in medieval legend. It is a statement whose profound truth goes far beyond any literary evidence, seeing into the very nature of Adepthood itself. The "Quest of the Grail" is indeed a distinct and recondite image of the task which lies before the risen Adept, the Knight, the Professed. Here, "that which he is to seek, he is to become": – the sacred vessel which is to receive the Wine of Inspiration. Nevertheless, this is but one level of the Grail's significance. It is also the specific and sacred symbol of the Goddess in her Binah Aspect, as receptacle of the power of the Supernal Father. The Grail thus represents a high spiritual reality: one of its co-symbols is the Universe. To raise up a magical instrument, as has been said, is to bring it into manifestation and into operation. He who elevates the Grail in solemn ritual, therefore, is making offering so far as he is able, of the universe itself as a receptacle and instrument of Divine Power. Not only that: he is also whether explicitly or implicitly offering himself as an instrument of that Power.*

When the Great Wand or Spear is ritually conjoined with the Grail, there is celebrated the supernal union of the Father with the Mother, the implanting of a seed of mighty significance. This is a theme of high import in the mysticism of the Stella Gloriosa; for when the new *Fiat* is uttered, and Adonis is conceived in the womb of Myrrha the King's Daughter, all has been prepared for the new equal-armed cross to come in due time to manifestation in the octagonal shrine of the centre. The Great Work is completed in one octave to recommence in another.

* Even thus does the Grand Master make offering of the Order, and of himself its representative before the Gods.

## ADDENDUM
### De Ture

Two types of censer are used by the Aurum Solis: the *thymiaterion* or standing vessel, and the *thurible*.

Incense should never be burned in excessive quantities, as this tends to detract from the potency of its valid use. In the first place, excessive burning of incense dulls the sense of smell and may in a limited space lead to stupefaction. In the second place, if censings occur too frequently in a ceremony they become a distraction, and a valuable instrument is reduced to banality. Incense should be used sparingly and purposefully.

Those who work within the A.S. system are bound by the following rules regarding the use of incense (general heads only are given).

The employment of incense is allowed:—

1.    *As a means of directing the mind to a particular modality.* This is the only use of incense which is invariably valid in any working soever. Thymiaterion.

2.    *As a symbolic purification, usually linked with lustration (symbolic cleansing).* A preparatory matter: cleansing and purification of materia, implements, aspirants. Also ambulatory cleansing and purification of an *unconsecrated temple*, preparatory to working. Thurible.

3.    *As an adjuvant in causing "movement within the Light."* As a means of attuning the ambience. Also specific ritual acts such as the censing of materia, implements, etc., at a crucial stage in a working, as a minor aid to modification of substance. Thymiaterion or thurible.

4.    *To aid the full materialisation of an evoked Spirit.* This is an exception to the rule regarding the sparing use of incense: it is recognised that considerable quantities *may* be needed to achieve the object. Thymiaterion.

5.    *As an act of worship.* An offering *per se* to the Gods. Also the offering of incense to a deity present under sacramental form. Thymiaterion or thurible.

The employment of incense is not allowed:—

1.    As a means of consecration in itself.

2.    As an equivalent of anointing, in whatever circumstances: for example, the censing of effectively charged implements, etc., at the culmination of consecration ceremonies.

3.    Ambulatory sprinkling and censing, with the intention of cleansing and purifying a *consecrated temple*.

4.    As an attempted reinforcement of astral defences.

5.    As an act of worship to less than divine beings.

## XVIII

### THE DANCE AS INSTRUMENT OF MAGICK
*"Of Woven Paces and of Waving Hands"*

In the study of magical ritual, the dance has an eminent place. If every magical act constitutes a deliberate stirring of the Light, the dance is a means *par excellence* of such stirring. It is not that dance is a sophistication of ceremonial movement or, for that matter, of mime:— dance as a means of expression is a spontaneous development, for the beginnings of which we have to look not only to primitive man, but even outside the human race. Many creatures, notably the feathered kind, have a courtship dance; some killers have a dance of fascination, of which even the cobra's rhythmic swaying would seem to be an example; the mongoose dances into battle, young animals of every description perform wild dances of sheer exuberance, while the honey-bee's marvellous dances of communication are still a subject of most exact research. The fact that these non-human forms of dancing must be governed entirely by instinct, emphasises the close relationship which still exists between the Nephesh and bodily movement in the dance, even when the dancers are human beings intellectually aware of at least a part of the significance of their actions.

Considering the dance as a human activity, we find that it is indeed basic to the race, and that any noteworthy occasion of any kind is likely to become an occasion for dancing. Courtship dances occur in all parts of the world, war-dances have been a conspicuous feature in many cultures, the funeral

117

processions of Egypt were accompanied by performers of acrobatic dances: unnumbered instances could be quoted of natural occasions for dancing.

These various motives for the dance and the corresponding modes thereof have mention in the present study because from earliest times, one sort or another of magical intention is bound up with them. The erotic dance was frequently linked with rites of fertility and with the forces of earth; the cosmic or seasonal dance frequently acquired a mystical interpretation which it did not initially possess. Initial motivation, however, can have been only a partial cause of development in the dance; there must also have been the work of experience when an effect, whether objective or subjective, was found to follow from the performance of certain dances in certain circumstances. The stirring of vibrations in the Light by a psychically united group, for instance, of young couples ritually performing erotic actions about the fields on a specified night when the new crop was germinating, would over a long period produce accumulated evidence for better harvests. Again, to take a different example, the vertigo produced by a whirling or circular dance (designed perhaps in the first instance simply to imitate the solar revolution) could be sufficient in the case of the more sensitive to induce a light hypnosis, leading easily into veritable ekstasis. In both these instances, the fertility dance and the dance of religious ecstasy, other factors would be introduced such as the selected occasion, suitable rhythms and music, and fitting movement, to achieve the specific purpose of the dance. It is true that not all agricultural dances are directly erotic and not all trance-producing dances are vertiginous; but the history of mankind shows these two groupings of concept, the erotic-geoponic and the cosmic-ecstatic, sufficiently often to make them important for our purpose.

When once the principle of magical dancing was established—and it must have been accepted at a very early period—the adaptation of so potent an instrument as "the charm of woven paces and of waving hands" to many matters had only to be qualified by time and need. The sorcerer depicted in the renowned early painting in the Cave of the Three Brothers at Ariège (France) is masked, and dancing: so is the central figure of a male group sculpted in rock in pre-dynastic times in Southern Egypt: success in the chase would seem plainly to be the purpose of both these represented acts of magick, several comparable figures existing elsewhere in early art. At a later epoch in Egypt, the blessings and divine favours of Hathor were dispensed to the people during her festivals, by means of dances performed by her priestesses; rather as in later England through many centuries the blessings of the Horned God were conveyed through the rural communities by the capering dance of the "Green Man" in his array of calf-skin and leafage, but probably in a manner more comparable to the stately progress of Salii and Saliae on the annual Roman festival of the First of March, when clad in brilliant garments they performed a processional dance of ritual gestures and attitudes to an accompaniment of musical instruments and of chanted hymns to Mars and to the three major Goddesses, Juno, Venus and Minerva.

It is noteworthy that although in modern speech the term "dancing" has especial reference to some movement of the feet, in the ancient world as it is recorded for us in literary references and in the visual arts, the idea of dancing had much more to do with movements of the arms and trunk. Although a special action of the feet is indicated in some Egyptian and Classical representations, it is not until the Middle Ages that the emphasis is transferred conspicuously to footwork. Associated in some tales with a cure for the medieval "dancing mania," in other tales with a mode of ritual progress or pilgrimage, the formula "two steps forward, one step back" took on at that time a curiously magical significance: it is indeed one of those rhythms which, by its action in bewildering the physical consciousness, can produce a degree of trance in the performers. Even in much earlier times, however, whatever the type of bodily movement, the insistence upon a very marked rhythm in a trance-producing movement is most noticeable. Thus in the First Book of Samuel, Ch. X, the encounter of Saul with a "company of the prophets" is foretold to him by Samuel—"thou shalt meet a company of prophets coming down from the high place *with a psaltery, and a tabret, and a pipe and a harp before them:* and they shall prophesy: and the Spirit of the Lord will come upon thee, and thou shalt prophesy with them, *and shalt be turned into another man."* Voudoun, of which an essential feature is possession by the Loa during the dance, works with drums consecrated to the cult. The rites of "the goddesse Syria" are described in *The Golden Asse* in very general and not too serious terms, Apuleius' purpose therein being satirical: but at one point he mentions a wild dance of "persons apparelled in divers colours, having painted faces, mitres on their heads, vestiments coloured like saffron, Surplesses of silk, and on their feet yellow shooes" who "began to hurle themselves hither and thither, as though they were mad," finally wounding their arms with knives as if insensible of pain. At other points in the episode there is "playing with Cimbals to get almes," "Tympany, Cymbals and instruments," and the company makes a processional progress through the villages "with Trumpets and Cymbals," so that we may surely conclude that the dancing also was accompanied by the typical music of the cult. This is also related to the dance in the cult of Cybele and Attis, as in Catullus' poetic description:— " . . . where the cymbals give voice and the timbrels reply, Where the curved flutes of the Phrygian sobbingly cry."

A quite different magical use of the dance is found in instances where the dance creates a focal point for the energies of a rite which otherwise tends to diffuseness in the time or the locale of the working. Such a focal point in the traditional English rites of Bealteinne was provided by the circular Maypole-dance, with its interweaving ribbons about the tall central pole. The ribbons, besides forming an adornment and a record of the course of the dance, besides ensnaring and making captive the force of the Fertility God in his emblem, compelled the dancers to follow a definite interwoven course, to tread within an exact circle about the Maypole. A purpose similar to that last was evidently served by the "mazes" or labyrinthine paths which from prehistoric times have been set out, in turf or stone or otherwise, across Europe; such as have been commemorated upon ancient coins of Crete, and known in Italy where Vergil two thousand years ago was at pains to explain (Aenid, Book V, lines 575 603) in legendary fashion why such intricate comings and goings were called "Troy games." It is not surprising to find that a maze whose remains were miscalled in medieval times "Rosamund's Bower," existed in London near the ancient temple which the Romans re-dedicated to Diana, and which in turn became the site of St. Paul's. It is however more startling to find just the traditional type of circular maze preserved in a cathedral: one such at Lucca purports to be a copy of the maze of Daedalus, with emphasis on the fact that Theseus only traversed it by the aid of Ariadne: another forms a floor-pattern at Chartres. Why they are there, none know, but a simple guess may surely be hazarded, that the mazes were there first, as part of a pre-Christian sacred site. The builders of the new religion would destroy much in the appropriation of the site—witness the adoption for Christian buildings of existing Holy Places everywhere—but of a beloved and mystical maze they would not dare destroy all trace. As to the original dedication of these sacred mazes, we have only to consider that the Romans assimilated the dedication of that in the city of London to Diana, that ancient Troy or Troia was a city of the Goddess, and that Crete was eminently a land of the Goddess and of the Moon-king, Minos, the Labyrinth appearing in myth as the abode of the Minotaur or Moon-Bull. Milton, too, seems to have known of this lunar association, for in a stanza which many editors asterisk out of his "Nativity Hymn" there is a description of sunrise—

> "And the yellow-skirted Fayes
> Fly after the night-steeds, leaving their moon-loved maze."

As to the purpose of such mazes, which are usually less of blind-alley puzzles than representations of an endless zigzag and roundabout progress to the centre—they exist surely for the purpose of guiding the feet of all who tread them in a fixed and inescapable way. Those who entered might move quickly or slowly, they might go alone or in procession, but their progress was always in that sense *a dance*, an established movement into the centre and out again. One such dance has survived to the present time, being employed notably in the sacred rites of Wicca, though it is no longer guided by the mazes of turf: the single or double spiral dance, either into the centre only, to form a globe of power, or into the centre and out again to proceed to another movement, the meaning in the latter case being of Rebirth. Carl Jung has somewhat to say also, as to the archetypal uterine significance of the spiral path.

The various functions of dancing in the history of Western magick have been but briefly outlined in the foregoing, yet the potentialities of this treasury are manifold.

Not only the major movements, but also the gestures of the dance must be linked to the mood of the work. The student with a flair for mime will readily improvise here, and such improvisation gives freshness and reality to a rite: but certain basic conventions exist, and help to simplify the task of planning a dance for a given purpose.

Unless some other specific interpretation is involved, it

can be taken that the hand extended with the palm upward is receiving but with the palm downward is giving. If persons are to link hands, this principle is adapted to facilitate transmission of energy or of psychic impressions among them: each participant turns the palm of the right hand downward, and the palm of the left hand upward, so that the more naturally transmissive hand of each transmits to the more naturally receptive hand of the next person. (In practice, the presence of a left-handed person in the line is not found to make any difference in the effect.) In the A.S. Dance of the Four Mills, derived from the Dervish dance, each individual uses the same principle in a different manner, by raising the *right* hand with palm uppermost to receive potency or blessing from above, the *left* hand being lowered, palm downwards, to transmit that potency or blessing to the Earth-sphere: here the dignity of the higher powers requires the use of the right hand to receive their bounty, while the left hand channels it forth. There is no contradiction. Man occupying a central position in the universal system, his more "positive" side is but receptive in relation to spiritual being, while even his more "negative" side is potent in regard to the passivity of the Earth-sphere. The Dance of the Four Mills is performed in a circle, the participants following one another deosil and each making a complete turn, also deosil, upon coming to each quarter successively.

The significance of deosil and widdershins circlings has been to some extent discussed in the preceding paper on ceremonial: quite often, however, it is desired merely to create energy without bias to solar or lunar, celestial or chthonic, and then the interwoven double circle is a method which commends itself. The participants face each other in pairs, males facing deosil, females facing widdershins, and move alternately outward and inward, passing each other progressively by right shoulder and by left shoulder.

Of the Spiral Dance, an important variant is the
Lampadephoria. This is performed on certain occasions
when a ritual restoration of light is required, and of its
nature the movement adds to that restoration its own
connotations of rebirth. Being also a slow and stately action,
it suits well with the Saturnian aspects of regeneration. It
begins in darkness: the participants carry unlighted torches
(candles or tapers). The line of dancers is led from a wide
circle in a widdershins spiral towards the centre: when the
leader reaches the centre, the procession halts. The leader
then kindles a flame with flint and steel, and lights his
torch from it. He then turns deosil and the line proceeds
outward, close to, and parallel to, the ingoing spiral, each
member lighting a torch from the central flame in passing.
The procession ultimately re-forms into a circumference of
lights.

In flame-dances, care and restraint impose themselves
upon the physical movements, but in magical dances this
is by no means the usual case. To a rite of the Sphere of
Jupiter, a square dance with music in common time may
be suited, being genial in mood and Jupiterian in rhythm.
The Sphere of Mars produces some dances of great dignity
and of rich pageantry (as instanced by the Salii) but also
strenuous and athletic forms such as Scottish Highland,
Cossack or other warlike dances. The Sphere of Venus
has graceful and fiery dances, whether as in ancient times
self-accompanied by the joyous sistrum, or in the modern
mode interpreting the music of the guitar. Mercurial dance
is light, swift-moving, serpentine and woven of conjoined
figures and forms: being essentially communicative it is
full of mime and also is closely associated with invocatory
song of undulant rhythm and intellectual flavour, like that
addressed to Sabrina in "Comus":—

"Listen and appear to us
In name of great Oceanus,
By the earth-shaking Neptune's mace
And Tethys' grave majestic pace,
By hoary Nereus' wrinkled look
And the Carpathian wizard's hook,
By scaly Triton's winding shell
And old soothsaying Glaucus' spell,
By Leucothea's lovely hands,
And her son that rules the strands,
By Thetis' tinsel-slipper'd feet
And the songs of Sirens sweet . . . "

But the spirit of dance cannot be contained in a book, or conveyed by description or diagram. Let the student watch dance of all kinds, classical ballet, folk dance, national dances and those entirely individual styles of which great exponents arise occasionally. Let him collect recorded music, of types and moods which seem to him typical of the Spheres, and for these types and moods let him create dances. Let him practise mime and callisthenics of every school that may be accessible to him. Let him develop both his personal style and his general proficiency. Bodily poise, deft and accurate movement of the feet and hands, are to be developed. Let him practice the expression of thought and emotion in physical action; and let him study the histories of the Gods and the significances of the Spheres so that he may find within himself the more to express.

Pursuing these matters, and so making his body more perfectly the instrument of his soul and his soul more perfectly the instrument of his spirit, he shall progress not only in the Sacred Dance but in all Magick.

*XIX*

*IMAGES*

I

*Archetypal Images, archangels and Archons*

3 CELESTIAL QUEEN
4 ENTHRONED PRIEST-KING
5 ARMED WARRIOR-KING
6 DIVINE CHILD, SOLAR KING,
          SACRIFICED GOD
7 NAKED AMAZON
8 HERMAPHRODITE
9 ITHYPHALLIC YOUTH
10 VEILED MAIDEN

In Chapter VI of Book III, two Magical or Archetypal Images are given in detail: those of the Sephiroth Geburah and Chesed, the Warrior-King and the Priest-King.

The details of these Images are worked out quite simply. The elements which compose the Image of the Warrior-King, for example, are all primary or secondary correspondences of Geburah, the Fifth Sephirah: the chariot, arms of war, red gold, emeralds and steel, the colours red, green and amber (with red predominating). At the same time, care has been taken that the overall effect is a united expression of Martian force.

The other Magical Images of the Sephiroth may be worked out similarly by reference to the correspondences in Volumes II and III: lineal figures (as the five-pointed figure for the Warrior-King, the lozenge or diamond-shape for the

127

Priest-King), colour symbolism, gems, metals, mythological considerations, attributions of weapons or other symbols, all these things and more are admissible. However, an Image thus worked out should not be cluttered with detail, and the significance of the Image as a whole should be taken into consideration. The Magical Images are capable of a wide range of interpretation, and can be rendered according to any chosen art-style.*

Figures may be worked out in like manner to represent the Archangels and Archons of the World of Briah; but whereas in the case of the Magical Images the figures are such particularised characters as *Celestial Queen* or *Veiled Maiden*, the figure devised by this general method to represent an Archon or an Archangel should express more broadly the nature of the Sephirah to which it is referred. As an example let us take the Archangel of Binah:—

The Archangel Tzaphqiel could be depicted in colours belonging to the Sphere of Binah, that is in *indigo*, with traces of *flashing white* and highlights of *dove-grey;* holding aloft a cup, the attribute of Binah, in his left hand, or holding it in his right hand and pouring from it. The expression of the face should be strong and pensive. The Archangel may be seen as standing upon rock beneath a dark, wild sky, or as above a mighty swelling ocean in twilight.

Whereas the Archetypal Images are necessarily formulated by this general method, Images of Archons and Archangels may alternatively be worked out from the attributions and colour correspondences of the letters of their names, according to the method which is exemplified below.

* Concerning Archetypal Images, see also Book III, Chapter VIII.

## II
### *Theurgic images formulated by letter correspondences (for Briatic and Yetziratic names)*

It is frequently required that a form should be devised by which to know and recognise some certain being, which is not by tradition or by nature limited to any specific form. One of the most usual methods by which a form can be devised for such a being is to build up an image from the letters of its name.

The basis on which this method is founded is the attribution of a clearly individualised character to each letter of the Hebrew alphabet; this character takes into account to some extent the name-signification—Ox, House, Camel, and so on—more usually the elemental, planetary or zodiacal attributions—Air, Mercury, Moon—and also the position on the Tree of Life of the Path to which the letter is associated. Other considerations apply in individual cases. The form of the letter Aleph, for example, is traditionally said to represent "an Ox." As is well known, however, what we essentially have here is an upright, like the simple stroke of the Arabic letter Alif, but "winged." The "wings" not only give a more identifiable form to the letter, which was probably their original purpose, but were in time emphasised by rabbinical authors and illuminators as expressing the unfettered spirituality which is of the nature of Aleph.

The qualities thus associated with each letter of the Hebrew alphabet are summarised below. Some of the qualities are such as relate directly to a visual image, while others, more abstract, can suitably be indicated in posture, for example, or in countenance; the method of building up entire figures from these indications is subsequently described. The Greek letters also prefixed to the attributions are equated with the juxtaposed Hebrew letters solely for the purpose of forming magical images; they cannot in some instances be considered equivalent for other purposes such as Gematria. (For numerical values, see separate tables for Greek and Hebrew alphabets in the paper *Sigils*.)

N.B. The formulation of images by letter correspondences is not considered by the A.S. to be valid for names drawn from the Enochian hierarchies.

## Theurgic Telesmatic Qualities*

א   A   Dynamic, winged, bright and vibrant, of the essential quality of Air, and having an affinity with the activity of the Ruach. This letter is also to be considered as a catalyst, strengthening the patterns of relationship established by other letters in a name: thus the wings will be such as to increase the unity of the whole form. *Eleventh Path.*

ב   B   Unresting, of variable aspect, dual in nature but expressive of truth. A bodily character dark, sinewy, nervous and eloquent; additions of color are especially brilliant. *Twelfth Path.*

ג   Γ   Gracefully formed and pale, but resilient, indicating strength concealed in beauty; placid and confident in aspect, gently curved in contour. *Thirteenth Path.*

ד   Δ   Etherial loveliness, inviting and passively serene, with an appearance of perfect balance, rhythm and harmony expressed in warmth and tenderness. Shapely and with suitable adornments. *Fourteenth Path.*

ה   E   Amazonian, potent, expressive of leadership and of an affinity with the element of Fire, fluent, not abrupt. Alert and proud, with a tendency to heraldic forms. *Fifteenth Path.*

ו   Υ   Strong, generous in proportions and in nature, slow-moving, unassuming, with a hint of the grotesque or even of the whimsical. Ponderousness concealing a degree of hidden fire. *Sixteenth Path.*

ז   Z   Animated, youthful, having much that suggests movement, and that quality of fascination which arises from

---

* Originally, the word *telesma* signifies an outlay or payment (Liddell & Scott) and has a venerable magical tradition as used for a consecrated object placed (for example) in the foundation of a new building. The use of the adjective telesmatic to denote images or qualities existing in the World of Yetzirah is less correct, but is here retained by us as being currently accepted.

a subtle ambiguity of character or of effect. *Seventeenth Path*.

ח   H X   The masked, veiled or withdrawn countenance, every kind of disguise or camouflage, the Mannerist style, clear-cut precision of detail, exquisitely decorative elements often evocative of marine forms. *Eighteenth Path*.

ט   Θ   Grand, noble, but potentially menacing: like smouldering embers which glow genially but could leap to sudden flame; having the brooding strength which is suggested by a volcano, massive and of great dignity. *Nineteenth Path*.

י   I   Pensive, slight, but without weakness, having an intrinsic dynamism only less than that of Aleph but perhaps tinged by the sadness of early spring or of immaturity. Clear of outline, tending to create division rather than to unite. *Twentieth Path*.

כ   K   Mystical, contemplative, showing physical force combined with spiritual receptivity, or justice tempered by benevolence. The symbolism is of the chivalric legends, or of the Eagle and Cup as associated with Ganymede or with St. John the Divine. *Twenty-first Path*.

ל   Λ   Poised, dancing or whirling, arms outflung or posture otherwise symmetrical, the form agile and beautiful: harmony and balance may be shown in vorticist or kaleidoscope effects. *Twenty-second Path*.

מ   M   Of the essential quality of Water, and having an affinity with the action of the Nephesh. Infinitely mysterious, powerful, maternal, veiled as to form, merging into shadow. *Twenty-third Path*.

נ   N   Dark complexion, brooding, morose aspect, deep-set eyes, thick body, movement torpid. Sharp weapons of gleaming steel or similar emblems of menace are in evidence, as appropriate. *Twenty-fourth Path*.

ס   Ξ Σ   Of prophetic and inspired aspect, as for instance a harp-player: athletic, hardy physique, light colouring, spiritual force. *Twenty-fifth Path*.

ע   O Ω   Primitive, resolute, upsurging: the consciousness in the root-stock which strives upwards in growth toward the light: the stark will-to-live in absence of all refinements. Barbaric treasures symbolise sustenance drawn from the deeps. *Twenty-sixth Path.*

מ   Π Φ   Clamorous, rushing, with dishevelled hair, with whip and blazing torch. Body strong, well-developed but not tall, complexion ruddy. The trumpet or the mailed shoe (gauntlet, kneecap) are also symbols here. *Twenty-seventh Path.*

ע   Ψ   Sincere, smiling, communicative, human, with indications of deep understanding: there is a tendency to simplification of forms, with a fearless juxtaposition of significant colours in disregard of aesthetic convention, but all is intellectually controlled and flowing in effect to avoid heaviness. *Twenty-eighth Path.*

פ          Receptive and recessive, not showing marked individuality of character but mobile, graceful, rhythmic and undulating. *Twenty-ninth Path.*

ר   P   Strong and vital, intrinsically free, courageous but not aggressive: forming a natural focal point of attention, and showing harmonious beauty, pride, and generosity. *Thirtieth Path.*

ש          Wild, invincible, of the essential quality of Fire: expressive of spirit rather than of form or emotion, of change rather than of static condition. *Thirty-first Path.*

ת   T   Silent, vigilant, negating movement, literal and material in interpretation of concepts, tending to isolation, to darkness, to weight. Melancholy and inert in aspect. *Thirty-second Path.*

Each letter, as characterised in the foregoing list, shows an essential nature which could be represented as a complete figure. Generally however this is not required, and only so much of the character of each letter is employed as is appropriate to its place in the name and to the figure which is desired to be derived from that name. A great deal of latitude is allowed in the composition of these figures; the strict requirements are only that the composition should begin at the head and should proceed in sections not necessarily equal to one another but apportioned so as to correspond in number to the number of letters in the name. A letter is thus allotted to each section of the intended figure, in as nearly as possible the correct order as the letters occur in the name; and each section is endowed with some of the attributions of its allotted letter.

Figures may, if desired, be given frankly zoomorphic characteristics where the letters Heh, Vau, Cheth, Teth, Nun, Samekh, Ayin, Qoph, occur;* these will be derived from the zodiacal attributions of the letters, as for instance Heh—Aries—Ram. As the initial letter of a name, Heh would be represented by a ram's head; as the final letter of a name, Heh would be represented by ram's hooves, and so on. (With the Hebrew hierarchy this practice is best restricted to Yetziratic names. With other hierarchies, other customs. Even with the Hebrew, however, the telesmatic quality of Aleph is a different matter, and wings for Briatic forms may be symbolic or actual.)

The animal correspondences of letters which have planetary attributions—Beth, Gimel, Daleth, Kaph, Peh, Resh, Tau†—are not to be used as integral parts of images for theurgic names; but they may be used as emblems, crests, etc., this mode of use being applicable to Briatic as well as Yetziratic names.

In the planning of each figure, before an analysis is made of the letters of the name, it is necessary that the *Determinant Influence* be studied: that is, the cosmic or contingent force to which the entity bearing the name is referred. The Determinant Influence being kept in mind throughout, so that it may govern the whole form as well as

* This applies equally to the Greek letters E, H, Θ, N, Ξ and O; and, for the present purpose, Υ, Χ, Σ and Ω.
† Likewise the Greek letters B, Γ, Δ, K, Π; and, for the present purpose, Φ, P, and T.

the choice of particulars, the individual letters are then allocated
to the respective parts of the figure and the details of the parts
worked out to accord with the telesmatic qualities of those
letters.

With regard to zodiacal beings there is an especial
complexity, the zodiacal nature showing multiple factors.
The Zodiacal Determinant Influences are therefore considered
below. The Planetary and Elemental Determinant Influences
are relatively simple and need no comment here, and the
student will find ample material in Volumes II and III.

*Theurgic Determinant Influences*

♈ is frank and bold, single-minded, the youthful champion
and enthusiast, inclining to the spectacular and colourful, but
with a certain gracefulness and good taste. A female form may
be represented here, as Brunhilde, Britomart, Pallas Athene.

♉ is not a Sign which imposes an individual character,
but emphasises force, breadth, and weight in the aggregate of
qualities: there is also an aesthetic finesse in their unification,
perhaps involving a subtle quality of caricature as in the work
of Goya.

♊ is not greatly concerned to appear consistent throughout. There may be an intellectually-controlled element of
glamour or illusion, as in the proportions of Greek classical
art and architecture, while (as in the same examples) all is
maintained in lightness, brightness, and incisive clarity.

♋ is idealistic. There is a tendency to adjust proportions,
or to dwell upon ornament, for the sake of conveying a beautiful impression or submerging logical incongruities, as in a
harlequinade or a masked ball; at the same time, all really
harmonious qualities are displayed in loving detail. In these
tendencies and in the marine affinities of the Sign, Minoan
art-forms may be recalled.

♌ emphasises whatever is high, noble, dignified in the
subject-matter to be represented. There is no softness, but
considerable restraint and formality: a great richness of effect

is however desirable. If the lunar Cancer reminds us of Minoan art, the solar Leo may recall the Egyptian.

♍ shows excellent organisation and design with the purpose of giving each part of the whole a just and intelligible place. The unity of the whole may appear to be subordinated to the exposition of the parts, but it is precisely in preserving the parts as a well-studied and valid series that the character of Virgo is reflected throughout.

♎ Balance and compensation are leading principles in the Libran form. If grotesque aspects must appear, a symbolic or fanciful interpretation assists the harmony of the general effect: aesthetic considerations are here vital. Outline may be lost to give movement.

♏ is resolute, energetic, purposeful and relentless: he dominates turbulence, whether in the mode of the armed and armoured Scorpion or in that of the tempest-riding Eagle.

♐ Symbols and images drawn from the cycle of agricultural life, or from the natural universe, keep sanity in the context of this Sign's soaring spirituality. In forming a figure for Sagittarius, the main characteristic and tendency of the indicated attributes should be carefully considered and forcefully followed out, no matter whether it seems Sagittarian or not: considerable freedom can be taken in bringing out the naturally arising character of the figure, for to work in this way is to express the true spirit of Sagittarius.

♑ is serious, literal-minded and authoritarian: it is not only a matter here of the cumulative effect, there is a tendency to require wherever possible a Capricornian bias in every distinct part of the figure, whether it expresses Capricorn by sombreness, by intensity, by vigilance, by inhibition of movement, or otherwise as suitable.

♒ is human and humane: Abelard's *homo risibilis, navigabilis*. Here the laws of limitation themselves are the means of progress, whether it be the worlds of the psyche or the worlds of science and nature which are to be explored.

Thus clear definition (not of mere accidental fact, but of the underlying principles thereof as far as these can be perceived) is the criterion in the expression of Aquarius. This permits a harmonious interpretation of the attributes to be achieved, where a mere transcription of external forms would bring discord.

♓ has an especial tendency to geometric or other impersonal symbols in preference to living forms as adjuncts to the main figure, which should be represented as simply and as directly as possible. Crudity or abruptness are both however out of place here, as are all exaggerated gestures or show of emotion: where these occur, they should be minimised as far as possible.

---

An examination of the examples of analysed names which we give below should enable the student to understand the matter more effectively than any further explanation: the essential elasticity of the system cannot be too often or too plainly stated. The student must use his own initiative and creative sense.

*TzPhQIAL, Archangel of Binah*

(Considerations)

*Determinant Influence:—*
   Saturn.
*Letters and Qualities:—*
   Tzaddi (Path 28).
      Sincere, smiling, communicative, human, with indications of
      deep understanding: there is a tendency to simplification of
      forms, with a fearless juxtaposition of significant colours in
      disregard of aesthetic convention, but all is intellectually
      controlled and flowing in effect to avoid heaviness.
   Peh (Path 27).
      Clamorous, rushing, with dishevelled hair, with whip and blazing
      torch. Body strong, well-developed but not tall, complexion
      ruddy. The trumpet or the mailed shoe (gauntlet, kneecap) are
      also symbols here.
   Qoph (Path 29).
      Receptive and recessive, not showing marked individuality of
      character but mobile, graceful, rhythmic and undulating.
   Yod (Path 20).
      Pensive, slight, but without weakness, having an intrinsic
      dynamism only less than that of Aleph, but perhaps tinged by
      the sadness of early spring or of immaturity. Clear of outline,
      tending to create division rather than to unite.
   Aleph (Path 11).
      Dynamic, winged, bright and vibrant, of the essential quality
      of Air, and having an affinity with the activity of the Ruach.
      This letter is also to be considered as a catalyst, strengthening
      the patterns of relationship established by other letters in a
      name: thus the wings will be such as to increase the unity of
      the whole form.
   Lamed (Path 22).
      Poised, dancing or whirling, arms outflung or posture otherwise
      symmetrical, the form agile and beautiful: harmony and
      balance may be shown in vorticist or kaleidoscope effects.

*Colour Scale:—*
  Prismatic.

(The Image)

*TZADDI.* Thick and flowing *purple* hair, streaming out against an indigo
    sky. Face pale, features lean and somewhat harsh but with
    expression of intellectual perception and deep understanding.
*PEH.* The shoulders of the strong, spare figure are covered by a wide
    collar of *red;* the sleeves have deep borders of the same colour.
    The right arm of the figure is raised to about shoulder level, the
    hand grasping a trumpet as in the act of raising it to the lips.
*QOPH.* The robe itself is *magenta*, with loose and undulating folds, and
    wide sleeves, concealing the form. The left hand of the figure
    holds a golden cup, just above the level of the waist.
*YOD.* A narrow girdle of *yellow-green* stands out sharply.
*ALEPH.* The figure's mighty wings, radiant *yellow* with lights of gold,
    are folded about it so that the pinions cross in front at the level
    of the knees.
*LAMED.* The lower border of the robe is *green*, whirling and widespread
    above the rock on which the figure stands.

KShNIOIH, Angel Ruling the Sign of Capricorn

*(Considerations)*

Determinant Influence:—
    Capricorn is serious, literal-minded and authoritarian: it is not only
        a matter here of the cumulative effect, there is a tendency to
        require wherever possible a Capricornian bias in every distinct
        part of the figure, whether it expresses Capricorn by sombre-
        ness, by intensity, by vigilance, by inhibition of movement, or
        otherwise as suitable.
*Letters and Qualities:—*
    Kaph (Path 21).
        Mystical, contemplative, showing physical force combined
        with spiritual receptivity, or justice tempered by benevolence.
        The symbolism is of the chivalric legends, or of the Eagle and
        Cup as associated with Ganymede or with St. John the Divine.
    Shin (Path 31).
        Wild, invincible, of the essential quality of Fire: expressive
        of spirit rather than of form or emotion, of change rather than
        of static condition.
    Nun (Path 24):
        Dark complexion, brooding, morose aspect, deep-set eyes,
        thick body, movement torpid. Sharp weapons of gleaming steel
        or similar emblems of menace are in evidence, as appropriate.

Yod (Path 20).
> Pensive, slight, but without weakness, having an intrinsic dynamism only less than that of Aleph, but perhaps tinged by the sadness of early spring or immaturity: clear of outline, tending to create division rather than to unite.

Ayin (Path 26).
> Primitive, resolute, upsurging: the consciousness in the root-stock which strives upwards in growth towards the light: the stark will-to-live in absence of all refinements. Barbaric treasures symbolise sustenance drawn from the deeps.

Yod (Path 20).
> As above.

Heh (Path 15).
> Amazonian, potent, expressive of leadership and of an affinity with the element of Fire, fluent, not abrupt. Alert and proud, with a tendency to heraldic forms.

*Colour Scale:* —
Contingent.

(The Image)

This being stands as a sentinel barring the way in a dark, wild landscape.

*KAPH.* Upon the head is a helmet, *delphinium-blue,* with a crest in the form of an eagle: this shadows the face, or the visor is lowered.

*SHIN.* A cloak of *cadmium scarlet,* shimmering as silk, covers the shoulders then falls behind the figure. It gives an impression as of actual flame.

*NUN.* Beneath the cloak, a tunic of metallic *prussian-blue,* as of scale-armour, covers the broad torso to the waist. In one hand the figure holds a javelin.

*YOD.* The lower limbs are slender as compared to the torso, but muscular and strong. They are clad in hose of *deep olive-green;* the hose covering the thighs but not united at the crutch, being extended upwards to points which are tied to a waistcord, thus exposing the genitals. The penis, of somewhat youthful appearance, is fully erect.

*AYIN.* About each thigh is a broad band of *raw umber,* as leather, having upon it, wrought in small black and white pearls, the symbolic device of an eye.

*YOD.* Below these bands, the *olive-green* hose appear again covering the knees and the lower legs.

*HEH.* The ankles and feet are clad in wide-topped boots of soft leather, of the colour of *scarlet madder,* of fine workmanship and elegant appearance.

## XX

## *SIGILS*

The word *sigil* is the basic form of the Latin word *sigillum*,
meaning a sign. In occult usage, a sigil is specifically a sign
representing the name or the nature of a spiritual entity. A
sigil can be an actual signature, exacted from a spirit in the
course of negotium, for instance; but most usually it is a sign
derived by one or another system from the letters of the name
of a being, and may have additions designating aspects of
that being's nature and power.

In the A.S. method of deriving sigils from names, a sigil
is composed of several parts: the presigillum, the sigillic line,
the terminal, and if necessary, the circle. The following are
examples of sigils formed according to this method:—

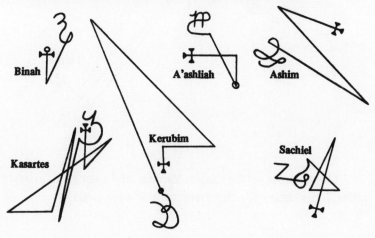

Binah    A'ashliah    Ashim

Kasartes    Kerubim    Sachiel

141

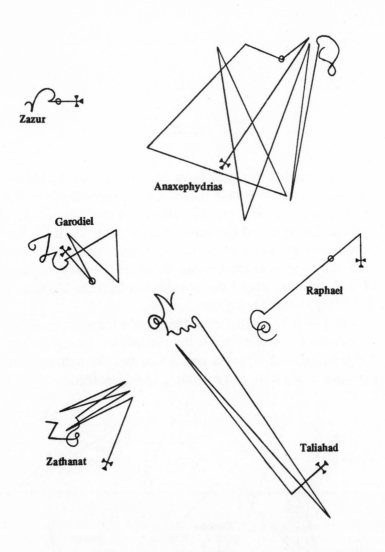

Zazur

Anaxephydrias

Garodiel

Raphael

Zathanat

Taliahad

The ensuing letter-values, kameas and presigilla, provide material necessary for the formation of such sigils.

## *Values of the Hebrew Letters*

| | | | | | | | |
|---|---|---|---|---|---|---|---|
| א | Aleph | = 1 | | ל | Lamed | = 30 |
| ב | Beth | = 2 | | מ | Mem | = 40 |
| ג | Gimel | = 3 | | נ | Num | = 50 |
| ד | Daleth | = 4 | | ס | Samekh | = 60 |
| ה | Heh | = 5 | | ע | Ayin | = 70 |
| ו | Vau | = 6 | | פ | Peh | = 80 |
| ז | Zain | = 7 | | צ | Tzaddi | = 90 |
| ח | Cheth | = 8 | | ק | Qoph | = 100 |
| ט | Teth | = 9 | | ר | Resh | = 200 |
| י | Yod | = 10 | | ש | Shin | = 300 |
| כ | Kaph | = 20 | | ת | Tau | = 400 |

| | | |
|---|---|---|
| ך | final Kaph | = 500 |
| ם | final Mem | = 600 |
| ן | final Nun | = 700 |
| ף | final Peh | = 800 |
| ץ | final Tzaddi | = 900 |

*Values of the Greek Letters*

| A | Alpha | = 1 | | N | Nu | = 50 |
|---|-------|-----|---|---|-----|------|
| B | Beta | = 2 | | Ξ | Xi | = 60 |
| Γ | Gamma | = 3 | | O | Omikron | = 70 |
| Δ | Delta | = 4 | | Π | Pi | = 80 |
| E | Epsilon | = 5 | | P | Rho | = 100 |
| Z | Zeta | = 7 | | Σ | Sigma | = 200 |
| H | Eta | = 8 | | T | Tau | = 300 |
| Θ | Theta | = 9 | | Y | Upsilon | = 400 |
| I | Iota | = 10 | | Φ | Phi | = 500 |
| K | Kappa | = 20 | | X | Chi | = 600 |
| Λ | Lambda | = 30 | | Ψ | Psi | = 700 |
| M | Mu | = 40 | | Ω | Omega | = 800 |

## Kameas

**(15)\***

| | | |
|---|---|---|
| 4 | 9 | 2 |
| 3 | 5 | 7 |
| 8 | 1 | 6 |

Planetary ♄

**(34)**

| | | | |
|---|---|---|---|
| 4 | 14 | 15 | 1 |
| 9 | 7 | 6 | 12 |
| 5 | 11 | 10 | 8 |
| 16 | 2 | 3 | 13 |

♃

**(65)**

| | | | | |
|---|---|---|---|---|
| 11 | 24 | 7 | 20 | 3 |
| 4 | 12 | 25 | 8 | 16 |
| 17 | 5 | 13 | 21 | 9 |
| 10 | 18 | 1 | 14 | 22 |
| 23 | 6 | 19 | 2 | 15 |

♂

**(175)**

| | | | | | | |
|---|---|---|---|---|---|---|
| 22 | 47 | 16 | 41 | 10 | 35 | 4 |
| 5 | 23 | 48 | 17 | 42 | 11 | 29 |
| 30 | 6 | 24 | 49 | 18 | 36 | 12 |
| 13 | 31 | 7 | 25 | 43 | 19 | 37 |
| 38 | 14 | 32 | 1 | 26 | 44 | 20 |
| 21 | 39 | 8 | 33 | 2 | 27 | 45 |
| 46 | 15 | 40 | 9 | 34 | 3 | 28 |

☿

**(111)**

| | | | | | |
|---|---|---|---|---|---|
| 6 | 32 | 3 | 34 | 35 | 1 |
| 7 | 11 | 27 | 28 | 8 | 30 |
| 19 | 14 | 16 | 15 | 23 | 24 |
| 18 | 20 | 22 | 21 | 17 | 13 |
| 25 | 29 | 10 | 9 | 26 | 12 |
| 36 | 5 | 33 | 4 | 2 | 31 |

☉

\* The key-number shown, bracketed, at top right of each of the kameas indicates the total to which each horizontal and vertical adds up; likewise (with one exception) each of the two diagonals. The exception is the kamea of Mercury, which properly has two key-numbers:— 260 relating to each of the horizontals and verticals and the diagonal top left to bottom right, and 257 relating to the diagonal top right to bottom left.

*Kameas*

(260 & 257)

| 8  | 58 | 59 | 5  | 4  | 62 | 63 | 1  |
|----|----|----|----|----|----|----|----|
| 49 | 15 | 14 | 52 | 53 | 11 | 10 | 56 |
| 41 | 23 | 22 | 44 | 48 | 19 | 18 | 45 |
| 32 | 34 | 35 | 29 | 25 | 38 | 39 | 28 |
| 40 | 26 | 27 | 37 | 36 | 30 | 31 | 33 |
| 17 | 47 | 46 | 20 | 21 | 43 | 42 | 24 |
| 9  | 55 | 54 | 12 | 13 | 51 | 50 | 16 |
| 64 | 2  | 3  | 61 | 60 | 6  | 7  | 57 |

☿

(369)

| 37 | 78 | 29 | 70 | 21 | 62 | 13 | 54 | 5  |
|----|----|----|----|----|----|----|----|----|
| 6  | 38 | 79 | 30 | 71 | 22 | 63 | 14 | 46 |
| 47 | 7  | 39 | 80 | 31 | 72 | 23 | 55 | 15 |
| 16 | 48 | 8  | 40 | 81 | 32 | 64 | 24 | 56 |
| 57 | 17 | 49 | 9  | 41 | 73 | 33 | 65 | 25 |
| 26 | 58 | 18 | 50 | 1  | 42 | 74 | 34 | 66 |
| 67 | 27 | 59 | 10 | 51 | 2  | 43 | 75 | 35 |
| 36 | 68 | 19 | 60 | 11 | 52 | 3  | 44 | 76 |
| 77 | 28 | 69 | 20 | 61 | 12 | 53 | 4  | 45 |

☽

## Kameas

**(65)**

| 17 | 24 | 1 | 8 | 15 |
|----|----|----|----|----|
| 23 | 5 | 7 | 14 | 16 |
| 4 | 6 | 13 | 20 | 22 |
| 10 | 12 | 19 | 21 | 3 |
| 11 | 18 | 25 | 2 | 9 |

Supernal ♄

**(671)**

| 68 | 80 | 92 | 104 | 116 | 7 | 19 | 31 | 43 | 55 | 56 |
|----|----|----|----|----|----|----|----|----|----|----|
| 81 | 93 | 105 | 117 | 8 | 20 | 32 | 44 | 45 | 57 | 69 |
| 94 | 106 | 118 | 9 | 21 | 33 | 34 | 46 | 58 | 70 | 82 |
| 107 | 119 | 10 | 22 | 23 | 35 | 47 | 59 | 71 | 83 | 95 |
| 120 | 11 | 12 | 24 | 36 | 48 | 60 | 72 | 84 | 96 | 108 |
| 1 | 13 | 25 | 37 | 49 | 61 | 73 | 85 | 97 | 109 | 121 |
| 14 | 26 | 38 | 50 | 62 | 74 | 86 | 98 | 110 | 111 | 2 |
| 27 | 39 | 51 | 63 | 75 | 87 | 99 | 100 | 112 | 3 | 15 |
| 40 | 52 | 64 | 76 | 88 | 89 | 101 | 113 | 4 | 16 | 28 |
| 53 | 65 | 77 | 78 | 90 | 102 | 114 | 5 | 17 | 29 | 41 |
| 66 | 67 | 79 | 91 | 103 | 115 | 6 | 18 | 30 | 42 | 54 |

⊗ (Malkuth)

## Theurgic Presigilla

(\* indicates the commencement of the presigillum, when this is traced either to lead into a sigil, or independently with an invoking or banishing heptagram.)

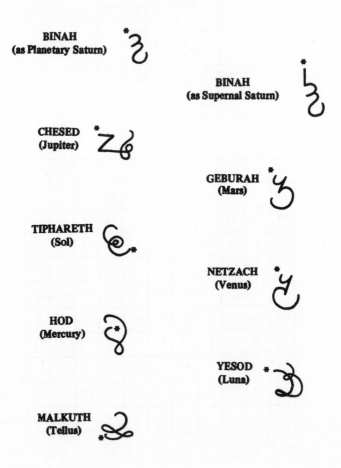

**BINAH**
(as Planetary Saturn)

**BINAH**
(as Supernal Saturn)

**CHESED**
(Jupiter)

**GEBURAH**
(Mars)

**TIPHARETH**
(Sol)

**NETZACH**
(Venus)

**HOD**
(Mercury)

**YESOD**
(Luna)

**MALKUTH**
(Tellus)

## *Theurgic Presigilla*

ARIES

LIBRA

TAURUS

SCORPIO

GEMINI

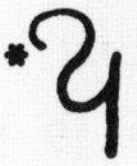

SAGITTARIUS

CANCER

CAPRICORN

LEO

AQUARIUS

VIRGO

PISCES

*Theurgic Presigilla*

AIR                    WATER

EARTH                    FIRE

---

To continue. Initially, the sigil must be established upon tracing paper. The first part to be drawn is the presigillum, which must be correctly chosen according to the Sephirah (or planetary sphere), the zodiacal Sign, or the Element of the operation. The presigillum initiates and intensifies the force which is carried by the sigillic line. The presigilla must not be confused, for they are by no means arbitrary symbols.

The presigillum commences at that end which is shown by an asterisk in our tables; the sigillic line continues from the other end of the presigillum, as shown in our examples of sigils. To obtain the sigillic line from the name under consideration, the relevant kamea* and table of letter-values are required. The tracing paper is placed over the kamea, the continuation end of the presigillum being over the square

---

* The word *kamea* signifies "a bond." Of the nine kameas given in this paper, the first seven are traditional, the last two are A.S. work and are drawn up in accordance with traditional method. To form the sigil of a zodiacal being, the zodiacal presigillum is used, but the sigillic line is formed from the kamea of the ruling planet of that sign.

For various reasons the student should make his own copies of the kameas from which to work. The kamea designs may also be engraved on metal (or wax) tablets, so that these may be displayed in appropriate rites.

which is numbered with the numerical value of the first letter of the name. From that point, a straight line is ruled to a chosen point within the square which has the numerical value of the second letter; and so on. When this tracing of the sigillic line is accomplished, the terminal should be drawn as a single bar across it at right angles, just before its end.

Although the relevant square for each letter-value in a kamea is fixed, the choice of an exact point within that square remains for each student to determine. Regard should be had in all cases to both the appearance and the intelligible drawing of the sigil, and the personal judgment must be the guide in this matter.

Where two or more successive positions in a name are occupied by one letter, as for instance in יההאל (Yod, Heh, Heh, Aleph, Lamed) or, similarly, where numerical reduction brings two consecutive letters to the same value; or where the position of a letter is not indicated by an angle upon the sigillic figure because with the previous and the succeeding point it makes a straight line: in all these cases a circle is to be formed upon the sigillic line at the point of the concealed letter or letters. When a concealed letter is to be indicated at the extreme end of a sigillic line, the circle is to be formed at that position; see the sigil of Binah above.

In obtaining a sigillic line, numerical reduction is sometimes a necessary device. The numerical value of a letter may be higher than the value shown in any square of the kamea appropriate to the name in which the letter occurs, as in the Aquarian name GARODIEL. This name is made up of the letters Gimel, Resh, Vau, Daleth, Yod, Aleph, Lamed, which have the values 3, 200, 6, 4, 10, 1, 30. The kamea appropriate to this name, however, is that of planetary Saturn (the ruler of Aquarius) in which the highest number is 9. The values of the letters Resh, Yod, and Lamed, are therefore reduced, so that the series for the purpose of forming the sigil becomes

3, 2, 6, 4, 1, 1, 3. This in turn illustrates the case above referred to, "where numerical reduction brings two consecutive letters to the same value."

For the tables of letter-values given in this paper, it will be found that in any instance where reduction becomes necessary, only zeros will be involved. Further, it should be observed that in no instance is a value to be reduced further than is needful. While the kamea of planetary Saturn necessitates the reduction of 200 to 2, the kamea of Mars would require its reduction only to 20.

When a sigil is prepared for a working, a fair copy should be made either in the text of the rite or on a separate sheet. As may be seen in the sigils given as examples herewith, when set out on paper a sigil is meticulously drawn: customarily the arms of the terminal are broadened into small serifs, the end of the sigillic line being similarly treated unless a circle occurs at that position.

---

When a sigil is being traced in the air, that is, when it is being "cut", as we say, the action begins with the forming of the presigillum and is carried through the sigillic line in one continuous motion of weapon or of right hand. The terminal bar is then added. Where a circle occurs upon the sigillic line, at that point a simple loop is to be made while forming the line, or a more elaborate flourish may be used. Should a circle occur at the end of the sigillic line — as in the sigil of Binah shown at the beginning of the paper — the line itself is concluded with the requisite loop or flourish, and the terminal bar is then traced to conclude the sigil. Always, in action, the terminal will be represented by a single definitive stroke across the sigillic line.

N.B. In forming sigils for names from the Enochian elemental hierarchies (see *De Rebus Enochianis 1, Texts f, g, h, i)* the elemental presigilla are employed, the sigillic line being plotted in every such instance from the kamea of Malkuth. The numerical values of the Enochian letters (A.S. usage) are shown in *De Rebus Enochianis 2, part I.*

## XXI

### OF THE CONJURATIONS OF THE ART

#### I

*General*

To have sight or speech of beings of other orders of life, to win knowledge or aid or the pure delight of unfailing wonder from their manifest presence, is no small part of the magician's recompense for much study and intense application to his art. Yet study, earnestly though it is commended to the aspirant, is by no means the major factor for achievement in this regard. Knowledge, however extensive, cannot avail without the developed magical sense which enables the magician to think and to act in a manner wholly harmonious to the powers which concern him in any given rite: and this inner touchstone, though it may be in a considerable degree innate, is only to be brought to its full development by reflection upon all that can be garnered both from reading and from practical experience.

The principle of magical evocation is, up to a point, very simple. A congenial channel having been prepared, the spiritual force flows through it. Nevertheless, the simplicity of this concept should not prevent us from perceiving the great subtlety which may be required to put it into effect. The spiritual force which we contemplate is not an impersonal energy of the type of an electric current: it is a living and conscious force, differing from our human personality in that it lacks the complications and limitations of a physical nervous system, but having instead a directness of apprehension and a delicacy of awareness which may well tax our human imagination unless we have brought ourselves truly into full harmony with it. This harmony will not mean that our attitude will be subservient to the spiritual being: the magician must, on the contrary, maintain always his complete individuality, even while he accords full recognition to the dignity and power of the other.

The formulation of a rite, either spontaneously or with meticulous thought, which shall fulfill these various requirements, will inevitably be the fashioning of a thing of beauty; whether we define beauty as entire fitness for purpose, or as a mingling of the traditionally accepted with the moment's unique freshness, or as the satisfaction of certain abstruse mathematical formulae unconsciously perceived but productive of perfect equilibrium. The definition itself is not relevant here, for intrinsic to the very nature of beauty is its conveyance of excellences beyond those purposed for it: and this quality is its greatest commendation here, since it gives to the magician a means of transcending his actual knowledge in choosing or in creating a rite. Let the rite contain all the fitness he can consciously assess, and let it be beautiful; he can then be assured that it carries other harmonies which he has not yet perceived, and is linked to its purpose in ways which he may hope to discern more clearly in time. This can be true even of a rite of his own composition: many a poet has found in his own earlier lines hidden truths of which he had no conscious knowledge when he wrote the words.

This power of beauty to convey a greater significance than we could have set forth in plainer terms, is referred to by the Master Therion in his declaration on the potency of Art in "calling forth true Gods to visible appearance." In these present considerations, however, the spoken utterance of a rite is chiefly in question.

There is frequently perceptible a certain idiom of address
to inhabitants of the non-material spheres: a lyricism rather
than any fixed system of metre or rhyme, a tradition persistent
because effective in circumstances and surroundings widely
differing; from the medieval Exorcism of Benedictbeuern—

"Omne genus demoniorum
Cecorum, claudorum, sive confusorum,
Attendite iussum meorum
Et vocationem verborum—"

to extant invocations such as, "Come in a form intelligible
to us and not terrible to us: and in speech that is known
to us and manifest to us, be your true answers addressed
to us." Many series of "barbarous names", too, show
similarly broken rhythms and assonances, which thereby, even
apart from their other associations, build up a strangely
compelling atmosphere when vibrated with power. In ancient
poetry, truly, there are certain rhythms and metres with
which for special purposes experiment may be made, to
bring back the potency of dithyrambus and choriambus,
of bacchius and paean, whether with the freedom of Greek
or the drum-beat precision of Latin verse: for most usages
these ancient forms are too remote from our modes of
speech, but for that very reason their competent use on
rare occasions can be the more effective. Again, it may be
possible to introduce into the words of an invocatory speech
one of the traditional Qabalistic patterns, if that is suitable:—
of Gematria, or of Notaricon, or of other kindred device.
Of Gematria, sufficient has already been said in Book III in
connection with *The Song of Praises*. Notaricon is the
formation of a word from the initials of a sentence, or,
equally, the formation of a sentence whose initial letters
spell out a significant word. Two examples shall be given,
one Hebrew, one Greek. The first example is the word
AGLA, so often used from medieval times as a powerful

word of defence, and derived from the initials of

אתה גבור לעלם אדני

*(Thou, Lord, art powerful to eternity!)*

The second example is the first line of Cleanthes' Hymn to Zeus,

ΚΥΔΙΣΤ' ΑΘΑΝΑΤΩΝ, ΠΟΛΥΩΝΥΜΕ ΠΑΓΚΡΑΤΕΣ ΑΙΕΙ,–
*(O thou most glorious, many-named omnipotent Immortal!)*

of which the initial letters of the Greek spell out the name of
the letter Kappa; this letter is the equivalent of the Hebrew
letter Kaph, and shares its correspondence to ♃* therefore
to Zeus.

In the adoption for magical use, however, of any form
in which the choice of words is to be influenced by considerations of rhyme, rhythm, alliteration, assonance or other
structures, the greatest care must be taken that no ambiguity
or obscurity of meaning results from the use of these devices.
For the same reason, any deliberate archaism of language
should be avoided unless its author be thoroughly at home
with it. It is futile to expect that of two possible meanings, a
spiritual entity will naturally perceive and follow that which
the magician intends. Although the being upon which one
lays a command may have and may be suspected to employ a
very keen ability to scan one's unconscious mind, to perceive
the buried wish, the motive which is disguised even from oneself, nevertheless an imperfectly declared intention of the
mind's conscious level is very differently treated. Given any
chance of placing a wrong interpretation upon one's spoken
command, or of misconstruing one's manifest wish, even the
most unmalicious of spirits is liable to act upon and to

---

* In view of the reluctance of scholars to credit the Qabalah, and especially the
Greek Qabalah, with earlier than medieval origins, this Greek example of Qabalistic
method and correspondence is most worthy of remark. The authenticity of the
hymn is undisputed: its author, Cleanthes, was born A.D. 331 in Mysia. References
for the text of the hymn:– C. Pearson, *The Fragments of Zeno and Cleanthes*,
London 1891. I. U. Powell, *Collectanea Alexandrina*, Oxford 1925.

implement that error. If Freudian theory would tend to suggest that the cause in such cases lies in the subconsciousness of the operator, which planted the ambiguity in words of such vital importance, this gives all the more reason to examine our work critically for any such lapses.

## II
### *A note on hierarchical conjurations*

A matter to which attention must be given is the manner of addressing spiritual beings of the different levels of existence. This is a vitally important consideration because the terms of address will naturally reflect the relationships which exist, or which are to be established, between the conscious personality of the magician and the beings of the various worlds. A misunderstanding of these relationships would be either damaging to the psychological welfare of the magician, or disruptive of the Work.

Atziluthic Powers are never commanded; neither are Briatic beings, since these are as it were ambassadors of the Divine. It may be added, in fact, that Atziluthic Powers and Briatic beings *cannot* be commanded. At the same time, the magician will realise that in presenting to these (as he will take care to do) a proposed work and a rite which are both entirely conformable to their nature, he is giving them a channel of realisation which, all being as it should be, they will not refuse. His address to them therefore, although charged with a rightful reverence and awe, will never be either servile or imploring. The Work is requisite to be done, that the nature of these particular forces may be manifested in the matter in hand: else this invocation would not be made. The magician also fulfils a necessary purpose of his existence in making the invocation, so that to make it accords completely with the dignity of both the invoker and the Invoked. The magician therefore exults in the power and splendour of the Atziluthic and Briatic names which occur in his rite, and this exultation is reflected in the magnificence of language which he applies to them. Considering his speech from this viewpoint, the magician will perceive that terms of respect are to be accorded to high beings, not in fear but in rejoicing. Requests addressed to Atziluthic and Briatic Powers are frequently softened by the use of such expressions as "Vouchsafe" or "Deign" or "I pray thee," which are not at all rendered insincere by the considerations put forward at the beginning of this paragraph: these expressions convey our recognition that the power invoked is a living force which functions by choice rather than mechanically, and that it is higher to a vast degree in the scale of existence than is the consciousness, however elevated, of the magician himself.

Yetziratic beings, in contrast, if invoked must be addressed with authority, no matter how beautiful or how noble they may be in appearance or in truth. Any weakness in this regard is bad magical practice; no comparable act in other fields of action—from throwing the reins upon a horse's neck to leaving an intelligent five-year-old in charge of the house—comes close to it for peril. At the same time, the presence of many different types of beings in the World of Yetzirah must not be overlooked, nor are all to be addressed alike. Those higher Yetziratic spirits which in Hebrew, Enochian, and cognate systems are designated as Angels, and the beings comparable to them in other systems, are conjured in a manner consistent with their especial elevation: likewise the Intelligences, although hierarchically of less elevation than the angels, yet are that which their name implies, and are to be addressed with reverence albeit with entire authority. With regard to those which are nearest to the Earth-sphere, and which in general are termed simply "spirits", here the most unquestionable commands are given by the magician, since from their proximity to Matter these spirits are the most difficult to control and also are likely to

have the most direct effect upon any material results of the
rite: but at the same time it is true that all the superior
names and powers of their hierarchy can and should be
brought to focus upon the ultimate Yetziratic level.

# PART IV

# ENOCHIAN STUDIES

**Paper XXII**

**De Rebus Enochianis 1**

## DE REBUS ENOCHIANIS 1
### Texts

(a)  The Four Enochian Tablets

(b)  Characteres Symmetrici:  Air

(c)  Characteres Symmetrici:  Water

(d)  Characteres Symmetrici:  Earth

(e)  Characteres Symmetrici:  Fire

(f)  Hierarchical Table:  Air

(g)  Hierarchical Table:  Water

(h)  Hierarchical Table:  Earth

(i)  Hierarchical Table:  Fire

(j)  48 Claves Angelicae

(k)  Liber Scientiae

**(a)**

## THE FOUR ENOCHIAN TABLETS

| | | | | | | | | | | | | | | | | | | | | | | | |
|---|---|---|---|---|---|---|---|---|---|---|---|---|---|---|---|---|---|---|---|---|---|---|---|
| r | Z | i | l | a | f | A | y | t | l | p | a | e | T | a | O | A | d | v | p | t | D | n | i m |
| u | r | d | Z | a | i | d | p | u | L | a | m | a | a | b | c | o | o | r | o | m | e | b | b |
| c | 3 | o | n | s | a | r | o | Y | a | v | b | x | T | o | g | c | o | n | x | m | a | l | G m |
| T | o | i | T | t | 3 | o | P | a | c | o | C | a | n | h | o | d | D | i | a | l | e | a | o c |
| S | i | y | a | s | o | m | r | b | 3 | n | h | r | p | a | t | A | x | i | o | V | s | P | s N |
| f | m | o | n | d | u | T | d | i | a | r | i | p | S | a | a | i | x | a | a | r | V | r | o i |
| o | r | v | i | b | A | h | a | o | 3 | p | i | | m | p | h | a | r | s | l | g | a | i | o l |
| t | N | a | b | r | V | i | x | g | a | s | d | h | M | a | m | g | l | o | i | n | L | i | r x |
| O | i | i | i | t | T | p | a | l | O | a | i | | o | l | a | a | D | n | g | a | T | a | p u |
| A | b | a | m | o | o | o | a | C | u | c | a | C | f | a | L | c | o | i | d | x | P | a | c n |
| N | a | o | c | O | T | t | T | n | p | r | n | T | o | n | d | a | 3 | N | 3 | i | V | a | a s u |
| o | c | a | n | m | a | 3 | o | t | r | o | i | | m | i | i | d | P | o | n | s | d | A | s p i |
| S | h | i | a | l | r | a | p | m | 3 | e | x | a | x | r | i | n | h | t | a | r | n | d | i l |

m o t i b ... a T n a i i ... n a n T u ... b i t o m

| | | | | | | | | | | | | | | | | | | | | | | | |
|---|---|---|---|---|---|---|---|---|---|---|---|---|---|---|---|---|---|---|---|---|---|---|---|
| b | O | a | Z | a | R | o | p | h | a | R | a | | d | o | n | p | a | T | d | a | n | V | a a |
| u | N | n | a | x | o | P | S | o | n | d | n | | o | l | o | a | G | e | o | o | b | a | u a |
| a | i | g | r | u | n | o | o | m | a | g | g | m | O | P | a | m | n | o | V | G | m | d | n m |
| o | r | p | m | n | i | n | g | b | e | a | l | o | a | p | l | s | T | e | d | e | c | a | o p |
| r | s | O | n | i | 3 | i | r | l | e | m | v | C | s | c | m | i | o | o | n | A | m | l | o x |
| i | 3 | i | n | r | C | 3 | i | a | M | h | l | h | V | a | r | s | G | d | L | b | r | i | a p |
| M | O | r | d | i | a | l | h | C | t | G | a | | o | i | P | t | e | a | a | p | D | o | c e |
|  | C | a | n | c | h | i | a | s | o | m | t | p | p | s | u | a | c | n | r | Z | i | r | Z a |
| A | r | b | i | 3 | m | i | i | l | p | i | 3 | | S | i | o | d | a | o | i | n | r | 3 | f m |
| O | p | a | n | a | L | a | m | S | m | a | P | r | d | a | b | t | T | d | n | a | d | i | r e |
| d | O | L | o | P | i | n | i | a | n | b | a | a | d | i | x | o | m | o | n | s | i | o | s p |
| r | x | p | a | o | c | s | i | 3 | i | x | p | x | O | o | D | p | 3 | i | A | p | a | n | L i |
| a | x | t | i | r | V | a | s | t | r | i | m | e | r | g | o | a | n | n |  | A | C | r | a r |

(b)

CHARACTERES SYMMETRICI

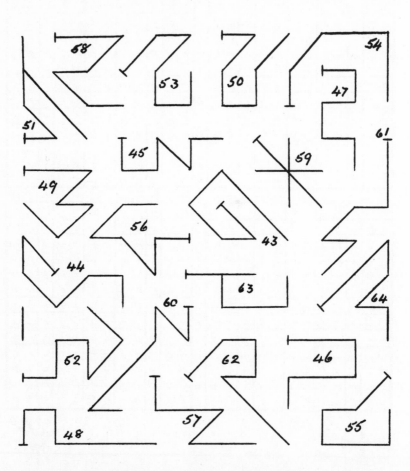

N.B. The *characteres symmetrici* shown here, and on the three pages following, are as in BM Sloane MS 3191; the numerals added by us to the *characteres* are for reference in connection with the Order of Invocation of Forces of the Liber Scientiae (see *De Rebus Enochianis 2*, part IV).

## (c)

CHARACTERES SYMMETRICI

## (d)

✚ *CHARACTERES SYMMETRICI* ∇

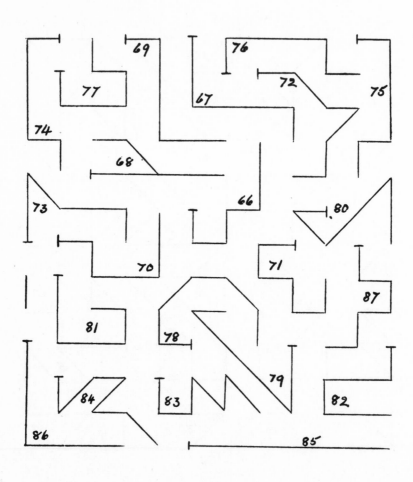

(e)

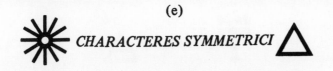

CHARACTERES SYMMETRICI

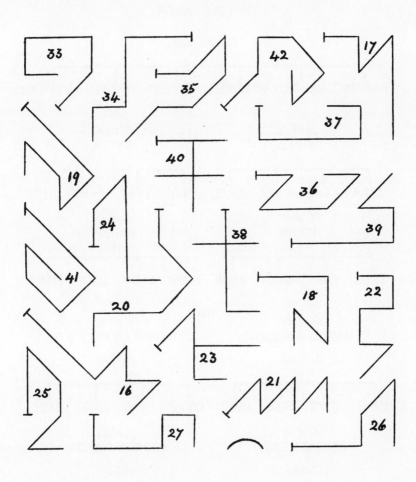

(f)

HIERARCHY

I

ORO IBAH AOZPI

BATAIVAH

HABIORO  AAOZAIF  HTMORDA  AHAOZPI  HIPOTGA  AVTOTAR

II

△ of △
ERZLA

RZLA  ZLAR  LARZ  ARZL

▽ of △
EYTPA

YTPA  TPAY  PAYT  AYTP

▽ of △
HTNBR

TNBR  NBRT  BRTN  RTNB

△ of △
HXGSD

XGSD  GSDX  SDXG  DXGS

III

△ of △
IDOIGO & ARDZA
(RZLA)

CZNS  TOTT  SIAS  FMND

▽ of △
LLACZA & PALAM
(YTPA)

OYVB  PAOC  RBNH  DIRI

▽ of △
AIAOAI & OIIIT
(TNBR)

ABMO  NACO  OCNM  SHAL

△ of △
AOURRZ & ALOAI
(XGSD)

ACCA  NPNT  OTOI  PMOX

N.B. This table and the three following are after Dee, with names conformed to the *tabula recensa* (the 1587 revision of the Enochian Tablets.)

(g)

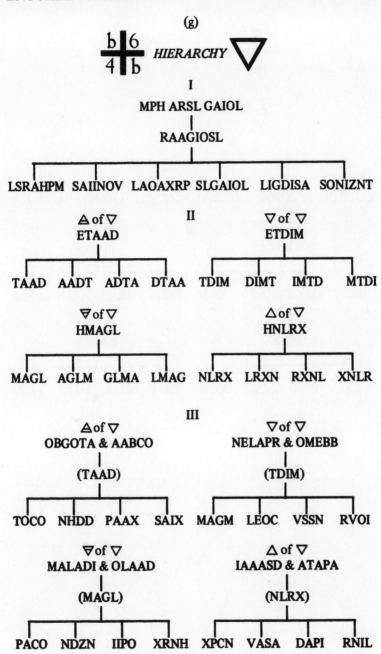

b 6
4 b

*HIERARCHY* ▽

I

MPH ARSL GAIOL

RAAGIOSL

LSRAHPM    SAIINOV    LAOAXRP    SLGAIOL    LIGDISA    SONIZNT

II

△ of ▽
ETAAD

TAAD    AADT    ADTA    DTAA

▽ of ▽
ETDIM

TDIM    DIMT    IMTD    MTDI

▽ of ▽
HMAGL

MAGL    AGLM    GLMA    LMAG

△ of ▽
HNLRX

NLRX    LRXN    RXNL    XNLR

III

△ of ▽
OBGOTA & AABCO

(TAAD)

TOCO    NHDD    PAAX    SAIX

▽ of ▽
NELAPR & OMEBB

(TDIM)

MAGM    LEOC    VSSN    RVOI

▽ of ▽
MALADI & OLAAD

(MAGL)

PACO    NDZN    IIPO    XRNH

△ of ▽
IAAASD & ATAPA

(NLRX)

XPCN    VASA    DAPI    RNIL

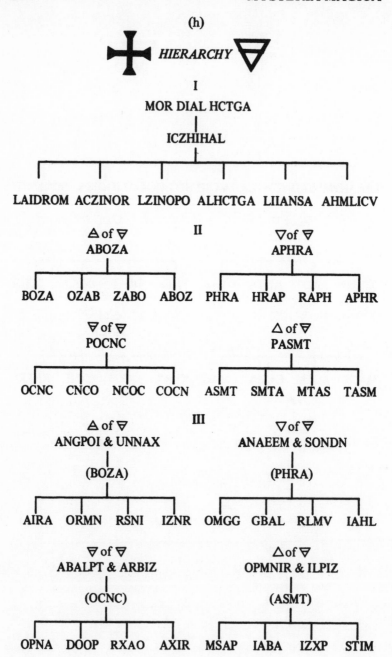

(h)

HIERARCHY

**I**

MOR DIAL HCTGA

ICZHIHAL

LAIDROM   ACZINOR   LZINOPO   ALHCTGA   LIIANSA   AHMLICV

**II**

△ of ▽
ABOZA

BOZA   OZAB   ZABO   ABOZ

▽ of ▽
APHRA

PHRA   HRAP   RAPH   APHR

▽ of ▽
POCNC

OCNC   CNCO   NCOC   COCN

△ of ▽
PASMT

ASMT   SMTA   MTAS   TASM

**III**

△ of ▽
ANGPOI & UNNAX

(BOZA)

AIRA   ORMN   RSNI   IZNR

▽ of ▽
ANAEEM & SONDN

(PHRA)

OMGG   GBAL   RLMV   IAHL

▽ of ▽
ABALPT & ARBIZ

(OCNC)

OPNA   DOOP   RXAO   AXIR

△ of ▽
OPMNIR & ILPIZ

(ASMT)

MSAP   IABA   IZXP   STIM

(i)

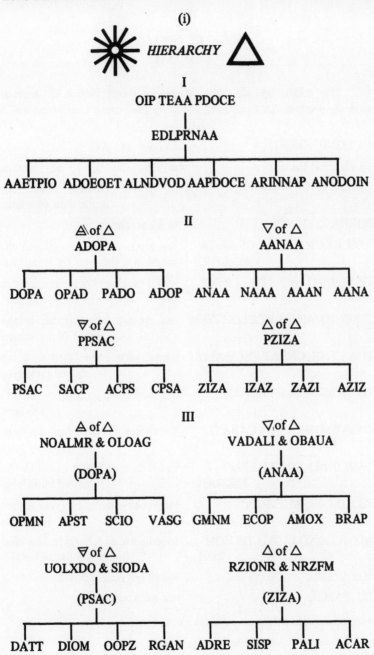

*HIERARCHY*

I

OIP TEAA PDOCE

EDLPRNAA

AAETPIO   ADOEOET   ALNDVOD   AAPDOCE   ARINNAP   ANODOIN

II

△\of △
ADOPA

DOPA   OPAD   PADO   ADOP

▽ of △
AANAA

ANAA   NAAA   AAAN   AANA

▽ of △
PPSAC

PSAC   SACP   ACPS   CPSA

△ of △
PZIZA

ZIZA   IZAZ   ZAZI   AZIZ

III

△ of △
NOALMR & OLOAG

(DOPA)

OPMN   APST   SCIO   VASG

▽\of △
VADALI & OBAUA

(ANAA)

GMNM   ECOP   AMOX   BRAP

▽ of △
UOLXDO & SIODA

(PSAC)

DATT   DIOM   OOPZ   RGAN

△ of △
RZIONR & NRZFM

(ZIZA)

ADRE   SISP   PALI   ACAR

## (j)

### 48 CLAVES ANGELICAE
### Anno 1584

The text of the 48 Claves Angelicae which follows is verbatim
with the original, BM Sloane MS 3191: the punctuation has been revised.

(Key 1)

| | |
|---|---|
| OL SONF VORSG, | I rayng ouer you, |
| GOHO IAD BALT, | sayeth the God of Iustice, |
| LONSH CALZ VONPHO: | in powre exalted above the firmaments of wrath: |
| SOBRA Z–OL | in whose hands |
| ROR I TA NAZPSAD GRAA TA MALPRG: | the Sonne is as a sword and the Mone as a throwgh thrusting fire: |
| DS HOLQ QAA NOTHOA ZIMZ, | which measureth your garments in the mydst of my vestures, |
| OD COMMAH TA NOBLOH ZIEN: | and trussed you together as the palms of my hands: |
| SOBA THIL GNONP PRGE ALDI, | whose seats I garnished with the fire of gathering, |
| DS VRBS OBOLEH GRSAM. | and bewtified your garments w$^{th}$ admiration. |
| CASARM OHORELA CABA PIR | To whome I made a law to govern the holy ones |
| DS ZONRENSG CAB ERM IADNAH. | and deliuered you a rod with the ark of knowledg. |
| PILAH FARZM ZNRZA* | Moreouer you lifted vp your voyces and sware |
| ADNA GONO IADPIL DS HOM TOH, | [obedience and faith to him that liueth and triumpheth]† |
| SOBA IPAM, | whose begynning is not, |
| LU IPAMIS, | nor ende can not be, |

* Marginal note in MS indicates this word to be ZURZA.

† This clause occurs as a marginal note in the MS.

| | |
|---|---|
| DS LOHOLO VEP ZOMD POAMAL, | which shyneth as a flame in the myddst of your pallace, |
| OD BOGPA AAI | and rayngneth amongst you |
| TA PIAP PIAMOL OD VOOAN | as the ballance of righteousnes and truth. |
| ZACARe CA OD ZAMRAN: | Moue, therfore, and shew yo$^r$ selues: |
| ODO CICLE QAA: | open the Mysteries of your Creation: |
| ZORGE: | Be frendely vnto me: |
| LAP ZIRDO NOCO MAD, | for I am the servant of the same yo$^r$ God, |
| HOATH IAIDA. | the true wurshipper of the Highest. |

(Key 2)

| | |
|---|---|
| ADGT VPAAH ZONGOM FAAIP SALD, | Can the wings of the windes vnderstand yo$^r$ voyces of wunder, |
| VIIV L, | O you the second of the first, |
| SOBAM IALPRG IZAZAZ PIADPH: | whome the burning flames haue framed within the depth of my Iaws; |
| CASARMA ABRAMG TA TALHO PARACLEDA, | whome I haue prepared as Cupps for a Wedding, |
| QTA LORSLQ TURBS OOGE BALTOH. | or as the flowres in their beawty for the Chamber of righteousnes. |
| GIUI CHIS LUSD ORRI, | Stronger are your fete then the barren stone, |
| OD MICALP CHIS BIA OZONGON, | and mightier are your voices then the manifold windes. |
| LAP NOAN TROF CORS TAGE, | For you are become a buylding such as is not, |
| OQ MANIN IAIDON. | but in the mynde of the All powrefull. |
| TORZU GOHEL: | Arrise, sayth the First: |
| ZACAR CA CNOQOD: | Move therfore vnto his Servants: |
| ZAMRAN MICALZO: | Shew your selues in powre: |
| OD OZAZM VRELP: | And make me a strong Seething: |
| LAP ZIR IOIAD. | for I am of him that liueth for euer. |

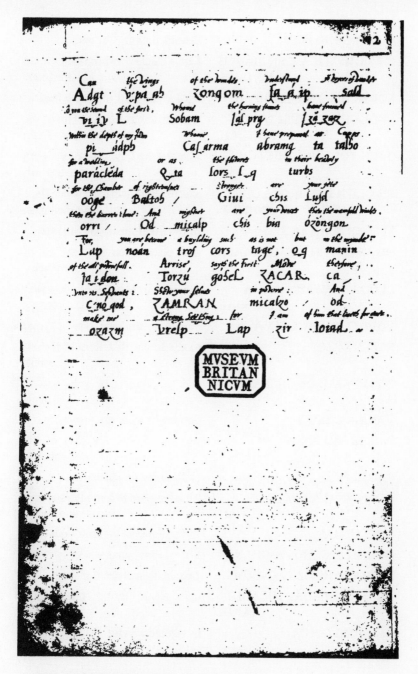

Can    the kings    of the lands    vnderstand    & voyces of lamet

**Adgt   vpa_ah   zongom   fa_a_ip   sall**

ô you the Second of the first,   Whome   the burning flames   haue framed

**vi_iv L   Sobam   Ial_prg   Izã_zaz**

within the depth of my Iawe   whome   I haue prepared   as   Cuppes

**pi_adpb   Cafarma   abramg   ta   talbo**

for a wedding   or as   the flowers   in their beauty

**paracleda   Qta   lors   I_q   turbs**

for the Chamber   of righteousnes   stronger   are   your fete

**ooge   Baltoh /   Giui   chis   Lusd**

then the barren stone: And   mightier   are   your voices   then the manifold winds

**orri /   Od   micalp   chis   bia   ozongon**

For,   you are become   a buylding such   as is not   but   in the mynde

**Lup   noan   trof   cors   tage,   o_q   manin**

of the all potentfall.   Arrise,   sayth the First   Moue   therefore,

**fa_i_don   Torzu   gofel   ZACAR   ca**

vnto us Seruants:   Shew your selues   in power.   And

**C_no_qod,   ZAMRAN   micalzo   od**

make me'   a strong Seething:   for   I am   of him that liueth for euer

**ozazm   vrelp   Lap   zir   Ioiad ~**

MVSEVM
BRITAN
NICVM

Folio 3v, BM Sloane MS 3191
By Courtesy of the Board of the British Library

179

(Key 3)

| | |
|---|---|
| MICMA GOHO PIAD, | Behold, sayeth your god, |
| ZIR COMSELH A ZIEN BIAB *OS* LONDOH: | I am a Circle on whose hands stand 12 Kingdoms: |
| NORZ CHIS OTHIL GIGIPAH: | Six are the seats of Liuing Breath: |
| VNDL CHIS TA PUIM Q MOSPLEH TELOCH, | the rest are as sharp sickles or the horns of death, |
| QUIIN TOLTORG CHIS I CHIS GE | wherein the Creatures of $y^e$ earth are to are not, |
| EM OZIEN DST BRGDA OD TORZUL. | except myne own hand which slepe and shall ryse. |
| I LI E OL BALZARG | In the first I made you Stuards |
| OD AALA THILN *OS* NETAAB, | and placed you in seats 12 of government. |
| DLUGA VOMSARG LONSA CAPMIALI | giving vnto euery one of you powre successively |
| VORS *CLA* HOMIL COCASB: | ouer 456, the true ages of tyme: |
| FAFEN IZIZOP | to the intent that from $y^e$ highest vessells |
| OD MIINOAG DE GNETAAB | and the corners of your governments |
| VAUN NA NAEEL, | you might work my powre, |
| PANPIR MALPIRGI | powring downe the fires of life and encrease |
| CAOSG PILD: | continually on the earth: |
| NOAN VNALAH BALT OD VOOAN. | Thus you are become the skirts of Iustice and Truth |
| DOOIAP MAD, | In the Name of the same your God, |
| GOHOLOR GOHUS AMIRAN. | lift vp, I say, your selues. |
| MICMA IEHUSOZ CACACOM | Behold his mercies florish |
| OD DOOAIN NOAR MICAOLZ AAIOM. | and Name is become mighty amongst vs. |
| CASARMG GOHIA: | In whome we say: |

ZACAR VNIGLAG OD          Moue, Descend, and apply your
           IMUAMAR,                                    selues vnto vs,

PUGO PLAPLI                    as vnto the partakers

ANANAEL QAAN.           of the Secret Wisdome of your
                                      Creation.

(Key 4)

| | |
|---|---|
| OTHIL LASDI BABAGE | I haue set my fete in the sowth |
| OD DORPHA, GOHOL, | and haue loked abowt me, saying, |
| G CHIS GE AUAUAGO CORMP *PD* | are not the Thunders of encrease numbred 33 |
| DSONF VI VDIV? | which raigne in the Second Angle? |
| CASARMI OALI *MAPM* | vnder whome I haue placed 9639 |
| SOBAM AG CORMPO CRPL, | whome none hath yet numbred but one, |
| CASARMG CROODZI CHIS OD VGEG, | in whome the second beginning of things are and wax strong, |
| DST CAPIMALI CHIS CAPIMAON: | which allso successively are the number of time: |
| OD LONSHIN CHIS TA LO *CLA.* | and their powres are as the first 456. |
| TORGU NOR QUASAHI OD F CAOSGA: | Arrise, you Sonns of pleasure, and viset the earth: |
| BAGLE ZIRENAIAD DSI OD APILA. | for I am the Lord yo$^r$ God which is, and liueth. |
| DOOAIP QAAL, | In the name of the Creator, |
| ZACAR OD ZAMRAN OBELISONG | Move and shew your selues as pleasant deliuerers, |
| RESTEL AAF NORMOLAP. | That you may praise him amongst the sonnes of men. |

(Key 5)

| | |
|---|---|
| SAPAH ZIMII DUIB | The mighty sownds haue entred in y$^e$ 3$^{th}$ Angle |
| OD NOAS TAQUANIS ADROCH, | and are become as oliues in y$^e$ oliue mownt, |
| DORPHAL CAOSG | looking w$^{th}$ gladnes vppon the earth |
| OD FAONTS PERIPSOL | and dwelling in the brightnes of the heuens |
| TABLIOR. | as contynuall cumforters. |
| CASARM AMIPZI NAZARTH *AF* | vnto whome I fastened pillers of gladnes 19 |
| OD DLUGAR ZIZOP ZLIDA CAOSGI TOL TORGI: | and gaue them vessels to water the earth w$^{th}$ her creatures: |
| OD ZCHIS ESIASCH L TAVIU | and they are the brothers of the first and second |
| OD IAOD THILD | and the beginning of their own sea [ts] |
| DS HUBAR *PEOAL* | which [are garnished with continuall burning lamps] * 69636 |
| SOBA CORMFA CHIS TA LA VLS OD QCOCASB. | whose numbers are as the first, the endes, and y$^e$ contents of tyme. |
| CA NIIS OD DARBS QAAS: | Therfore come you and obey yo$^r$ creation: |
| FETHARZI OD BLIORA: | viset vs in peace and cumfort: |
| IAIAL EDNAS CICLES: | Conclude vs as receiuers of yo$^r$ mysteries: |
| BAGLE? GEIAD I L. | for why? Our Lord and M$^r$ is all One. |

(Key 6)

| | |
|---|---|
| GAH SDIU CHIS EM, | The spirits of y$^e$ 4$^{th}$ Angle are Nine, |
| MICALZO PILZIN: | Mighty in the firmament of waters: |
| SOBAM EL HARG MIR BABALON | whome the first hath planted a torment to the wicked |
| OD OBLOC SAMVELG: | and a garland to the righteous: |
| DLUGAR MALPRG ARCAOSGI | [g]iving vnto them fyrie darts to vanne the earth |
| OD *ACAM* CANAL | and 7699 continuall Workmen |
| SOBOL ZAR T-BLIARD* CAOSGI | whose courses viset with cumfort the earth |
| OD CHIS ANETAB OD MIAM | and are in government and contynuance |
| TA VIV OD D. | as the second and the third. |
| DARSAR SOL PETH BIEN: | Wherfore harken vnto my voyce: |
| BRITA OD ZACAM G MICALZO: | I haue talked of you and I move you in powre and presence: |
| SOBHAATH TRIAN LUIAHE | whose Works shalbe a song of honor |
| ODECRIN MAD QAA ON. | and the praise of your God in your Creation. |

---

* F-BLIARD is shown as an alternative in the MS, and is clearly to be preferred.
Compare "viset with cumfort" here, with "viset the earth" (F CAOSGA) in Key 4.

(Key 7)

| | |
|---|---|
| RAAS ISALMAN PARADIZOD | The East is a howse of virgins |
| OECRIMI AAO IALPIRGAH | singing praises amongst the flames of first glory |
| QUIIN ENAY BUTMON: | wherein the Lord hath opened his mowth: |
| OD INOAS *NI* PARADIAL | and they are become 28 liuing dwellings |
| CASARMG VGEAR CHIRLAN, | in whome the strength of man reioyseth, |
| OD ZONAC LUCIFTIAN | and they are apparailed w$^{th}$ ornaments of brightnes |
| CORS TA VAUL ZIRN TOLHAMI. | such as work wunders on all creatures. |
| SOBA LONDOH OD MIAM | Whose Kingdomes and continuance |
| CHIS TAD ODES VMADEA | are as the Third and Fowrth Strong Towres |
| OD PIBLIAR, | and places of cumfort, |
| OTHIL RIT OD MIAM. | The seats of Mercy and Continuance. |
| CNOQUOL RIT: | O you Servants of Mercy: |
| ZACAR, ZAMRAN: | Moue, Appeare: |
| OECRIMI QADAH OD OMICAOLZ AAIOM. | sing prayses vnto the Creator and be mighty amongst vs. |
| BAGLE PAPNOR IDLUGAM LONSHI | For to this remembrance is given powre |
| OD VMPLIF VGEGI BIGLIAD. | and our strength waxeth strong in our Cumforter. |

(Key 8)

| | |
|---|---|
| BAZMELO ITA PIRIPSON | The Midday, the first, is as the third heaven |
| OLN NAZAVABH *OX:* | made of Hiacynet Pillers 26: |
| CASARMG VRAN CHIS VGEG | in whome the Elders are become strong |
| DSABRAMG BALTOHA | w<sup>ch</sup> I haue prepared for my own righteousnes |
| GOHO IAD: | sayth the Lord: |
| SOLA\* MIAN TRIAN TA LOLCIS | whose long contynuance shall be as bucklers |
| ABAIUONIN | to the stowping Dragon |
| OD AZIAGIER RIOR. | and like vnto the haruest of a Wyddow. |
| IRGIL CHIS DA DS PAAOX | How many ar there which remayn |
| BUFD† CAOSGO, | in the glorie of the earth, |
| DS CHIS, ODIPURAN TELOAH, | which are, and shall not see death, |
| CACRG O ISALMAN LONCHO OD VOUINA CARBAF? | vntyll this howse fall and the Dragon synck? |
| NIISO, BAGLE AUAUAGO GOHON: | Come away, for the Thunders haue spoken: |
| NIISO, BAGLE MOMAO SIAION | Come away, for the Crownes of the Temple |
| OD MABZA IAD O I, AS MOMAR, POILP. | and the coat of him that is, was, and shalbe crowned, are diuided. |
| NIIS, ZAMRAN CIAOFI CAOSGO | Come, appeare to the terror of the earth |
| OD BLIORS | and to our cumfort |
| OD CORSI TA ABRAMIG. | and of such as are prepared. |

\* A marginal note in the MS suggests SOBA, which is plainly the correct reading.

† A marginal note in the MS suggests BUSD, which is evidently correct; compare "in the glorie of the earth" here, with "hast thy begynning in glory" (ACROODZI BUSD) in Key 16.

(key 9)

MICAOLI BRANSG PRGEL — A mighty garde of fire

NAPTA IALPOR — w^th two edged swords flaming

DS BRIN EFAFAFE *P* VONPHO OLANI OD OBZA: — (which haue Viols 8 of Wrath for two tymes and a half:

SOBCA VPAAH CHIS TATAN OD TRANAN BALYE, — whose wings are of wormwood and of the marrow of salt,)

ALAR LUSDA SOBOLN — haue setled their feete in the West

OD CHIS HOLQ CNOQUODI *CIAL.* — and are measured with their Ministers 9996.

VNAL ALDON MOM CAOSGO — These gather vp the moss of the earth

TA LAS OLLOR GNAY LIMLAL: — as the rich man doth his threasor:

AMMA CHIIS SOBCA MADRID Z CHIS: — cursed ar they whose iniquities they are

OOANOAN CHIS AUINY DRILPI CAOSGIN, — in their eyes are milstones greater then the earth,

OD BUTMONI PARM ZUMVI CNILA: — and from their mowthes rune seas of blud:

DAZIS ETHAMZ A CHILDAO, — their heds are covered with diamond,

OD MIRC OZOL CHIS PIDIAI COLLAL. — and vppon their heds* are marble sleues.

VLCININ A SOBAM VCIM. — Happie is he on whome they frown not.

BAGLE? — For why?

IAD BALTOH CHIRLAN PAR! — The God of righteousnes reioyseth in them!

NIISO, OD IP OFAFAFE, — Come away, and not your Viols,

BAGLE A COCASB ICORSCA VNIG BLIOR. — for the tyme is such as requireth cumfort.

---

* In the 1st Key, the translation of ZOL is given as *hands*.

(Key 10)

| | |
|---|---|
| CORAXO | The Thunders of Iudgment and Wrath |
| CHIS CORMP OD BLANS LUCAL | are numbred and are haborowed in the North |
| AZIAZOR PAEB, | in the likenes of an oke, |
| SOBA LILONON CHIS VIRQ *OP* | whose branches are Nests 22 |
| EOPHAN OD RACLIR | of Lamentation and Weaping |
| MAASI BAGLE CAOSGI, | layd vp for the earth, |
| DS IALPON DOSIG OD BASGIM: | which burn night and day: |
| OD OXEX DAZIS SIATRIS | and vomit out the heds of scorpions |
| OD SALBROX CYNXIR FABOAN. | and live sulphur myngled with poyson. |
| VNAL CHIS CONST DS *DAOX* COCASG | These be the Thunders that 5678 tymes |
| *OL* OANIO YOR | in y$^e$ 24$^{th}$ part of a moment rore |
| VOHIM *OL* GIZYAX OD EORS | * |
| COCASG PLOSI MOLUI | tymes as many surges |
| DS PAGEIP | which rest not |
| LARAG OM DROLN MATORB COCASB EMNA. | neyther know any [    ]† tyme here. |
| L PATRALX YOLCI *MATB*, | One rock bringeth furth 1000, |
| NOMIG MONONS OLORA GNAY ANGELARD. | euen as the hart of man doth his thowghts. |
| OHIO, OHIO, OHIO, OHIO, OHIO, OHIO, | Wo, Wo, Wo, Wo, Wo, Wo, |
| NOIB OHIO CAOSGON! | yea Wo be to the earth! |
| BAGLE MADRID I ZIROP CHISO DRILPA. | For her iniquitie is, was and shalbe great. |
| NIISO: | Come awaye: |
| CRIP IP NIDALI. | but not your noyses. |

* See plate facing.

† Word untranslated in MS.

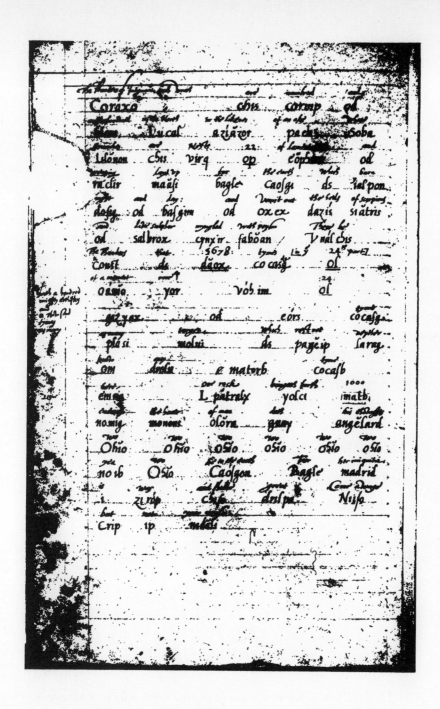

189

(Key 11)

| | |
|---|---|
| OXIAYAL HOLDO OD ZIROM *O* CORAXO | The Mighty Seat groaned and they were 5 thunders |
| DS ZILDAR RAASY: | which flew into the East: |
| OD VABZIR CAMLIAX OD BAHAL, | and the Egle spake and cryed w[th] a lowde voyce, |
| NIISO: | Come awaye: |

\*

| | |
|---|---|
| SALMAN TELOCH CASARMAN HOLQ | the howse of death of whome it is measured |
| OD TI TA Z CHIS, SOBA CORMF I *GA*. | and it is as they are, whose number is 31. |
| NIISA BAGLE ABRAMG NONCP. | Come away, for I haue prepared† for you. |
| ZACARe CA OD ZAMRAN: | Moue, therfore, and shew your selues: |
| ODO CICLE QAA: | open the Mysteries of your Creation: |
| ZORGE: | be frendely vnto me: |
| LAP ZIRDO NOCO MAD, | for I am the servant of y[e] same yo[r] God, |
| HOATH IAIDA. | the true wurshipper of the Highest. |

---

\* A marginal note in the MS indicates an omission at this point but supplies only the English words *and they gathered themselues together and became.*

† The words *haue prepared* are given in the MS as a textual alternative to *prepare*, but the above is plainly the correct version.

(Key 12)

NONCI DSONF BABAGE OD
      CHIS *OB,*

HUBAIO TIBIBP,

ALLAR ATRAAH OD EF.

DRIX FAFEN *MIAN* AR ENAY
      OVOF,

SOBA DOOAIN AAI I VONPH.

ZACAR GOHUS OD ZAMRAN:

ODO CICLE QAA:

ZORGE:

LAP ZIRDO NOCO MAD,

HOATH IAIDA.

O you that rayng in the Sowth
      and are 28,

The Lanterns of Sorrow,

bynde vp yo$^r$ girdles and viset vs.

Bring down your trayn 3663 that
     the Lord may be magnified,

whose name amongst you is Wrath.

Moue, I say, and shew yo$^r$ selues:

open y$^e$ Mysteries of yo$^r$ Creation:

be frendely vnto me:

for I am the servant of the same
      yo$^r$ God,

the true wurshipper of the Highest.

(Key 13)

NAPEAI BABAGEN                         O you swords of the Sowth

DS BRIN *VX* OOAONA LRING              which haue 42 eyes to styr vp
      VONPH DOALIM,                         the wrath of synn,

EOLIS OLLOG ORSBA DS CHIS              making men drunken which are
      AFFA.                                         empty.

MICMA ISRO MAD OD                      Behold the promise of God and
      LONSHITOX                              his powre

DS IVMD AAI GROSB.                     which is called amongst you A
      Bitter Sting.

ZACAR OD ZAMRAN:                       Moue and shew your selues:

ODO CICLE QAA:                         open the Mysteryes of yo$^r$
      Creation:

ZORGE:                                 be frendely vnto me:

LAP ZIRDO NOCO MAD,                    for I am the servant of y$^e$ same
      yo$^r$ God,

HOATH IAIDA.                           the true wurshipper of the Highest.

(Key 14)

NOROMI BAGIE PASBS OIAD,  O you sonns of fury, the dowghters
of the Iust,

DS TRINT MIRC *OL* THIL,  which sit vppon 24 seats,

DODS TOLHAM CAOSGO  vexing all creatures of the earth
HOMIN,  with age,

DS BRIN OROCH *QUAR:*  which haue vnder you 1636:

MICMA BIAL OIAD,  behold the Voyce of God,

AISRO TOX DSIVM AAI  the promys of him which is called
BALTIM.  amongst you Furye or Extreme
Iustice.

ZACAR OD ZAMRAN:  Moue and shew yo$^r$ selues:

ODO CICLE QAA:  open the Mysteries of yo$^r$
Creation:

ZORGE:  be frendlely vnto me:

LAP ZIRDO NOCO MAD,  for I am the servant of the same
your God,

HOATH IAIDA.  the true wurshipper of the Highest.

(Key 15)

ILS TABAAN LIALPRT          O thow the governor of the first
                                                            flame

CASARMAN VPAAHI CHIS *DARG*  vnder whose wyngs are 6739

DSOCIDO CAOSGI ORSCOR:      which weaue the earth w$^{th}$ drynes:

DS OMAX MONASCI BAEOUIB     which knowest the great name
                                                    Righteousnes

OD EMETGIS IAIADIX.         and the Seale of Honor.

ZACAR OD ZAMRAN:            Moue and shew yo$^r$ selues:

ODO CICLE QAA:              open the Mysteries of yo$^r$
                                                        Creation:

ZORGE:                      be frendely vnto me:

LAP ZIRDO NOCO MAD,         for I am the servant of the same
                                                        your God,

HOATH IAIDA.                the true wurshipper of the High[e]st.

(Key 16)

| | |
|---|---|
| ILS VIUIALPRT, SALMAN BALT, | O thow second flame, the howse of Iustice, |
| DS ACROODZI BUSD | which hast thy begynning in glory |
| OD BLIORAX BALIT: | and shalt cumfort the iust: |
| DSINSI CAOSG LUSDAN *EMOD* | which walkest on the eart[h] with feete 8763 |
| DSOM OD TLIOB: | that vnderstand and separate creatures: |
| DRILPA GEH YLS MAD ZILODARP. | great art thow in the God of Stretch Furth and Conquere. |
| ZACAR OD ZAMRAN: | Moue and shew yo$^r$ selues: |
| ODO CICLE QAA: | open the Mysteries of yo$^r$ Creation: |
| ZORGE: | be frendely vnto me: |
| LAP ZIRDO NOCO MAD, | for I am the servant of the same your God, |
| HOATH IAIDA. | the true wurshipper of the Highest. |

(Key 17)

ILS DIALPRT                          O thow third flame

SOBA VPAAH CHIS NANBA                whose wyngs are thorns to styr
        ZIXLAY DODSIH                                    vp vexation

OD BRINT *FAXS* HUBARO               and hast 7336 Lamps Liuing going
        TASTAX YLSI,                                     before the,

SOBAIAD I VONPOVNPH,                 whose God is Wrath in Angre,

ALDON DAX IL OD TOATAR.              gyrd vp thy loynes and harken.

ZACAR OD ZAMRAN:                     Moue and shew yo$^r$ selues:

ODO CICLE QAA:                       open the Mysteries of yo$^r$
                                                      Creation:

ZORGE:                               be frendely vnto me:

LAP ZIRDO NOCO MAD,                  for I am the servant of the same
                                                      your God,

HOATH IAIDA.                         the true wurshipper of the Highest.

(Key 18)

| | |
|---|---|
| ILS MICAOLZ OLPIRT | O thow mighty Light |
| IALPRG BLIORS | and burning flame of cumfort |
| DS ODO BUSDIR OIAD | which openest the glory of God |
| OUOARS CAOSGO, | to the center of the erth, |
| CASARMG LAIAD *ERAN* BRINTS CAFAFAM, | in whome the Secrets of Truth 6332 haue their abiding, |
| DS IVMD AQLO ADOHI | which is called in thy kingdome |
| MOZ OD MAOFFAS; | Ioye and not to be measured: |
| BOLP COMOBLIORT PAMBT. | be thow a wyndow of cumfort vnto me. |
| ZACAR OD ZAMRAN: | Moue and shew your selues: |
| ODO CICLE QAA: | open the Mysteries of your Creation: |
| ZORGE: | be frendely vnto me: |
| LAP ZIRDO NOCO MAD, | for I am the servant of the same your God, |
| HOATH IAIDA. | the true wurshipper of the Highest. |

(The Key of the Thirty Ayres)

| | |
|---|---|
| MADRIAX DS PRAF *LIL*, | O you heuens which dwell in the First Ayre, |
| CHIS MICAOLZ SAANIR CAOSGO, | are mightie in the partes of the Erth, |
| OD FISIS BALZIZRAS IAIDA! | and execute the Iudgment of the Highest! |
| NONCA GOHULIM, MICMA ADOIAN MAD, | To you it is sayd, Beholde the face of your God, |
| IAOD BLIORB, | the begynning of cumfort, |
| SABA* OOAONA CHIS LUCIFTIAS PERIPSOL: | whose eyes are the brightnes of the hevens: |
| DS ABRAASSA NONCF NETAAIB CAOSGI | which prouided you for the gouernment of the Erth |
| OD TILB ADPHAHT DAMPLOZ, | and her vnspeakable varietie, |
| TOOAT NONCF GMICALZOMA | furnishing you w$^{th}$ a powr vnderstanding |
| LRASD TOFGLO | to dispose all things |
| MARB YARRY IDOIGO | according to the providence of Him that sitteth on the Holy Throne, |
| OD TORZULP IAODAF, GOHOL: | and rose vp in the begynning, saying: |
| CAOSGA TABAORD SAANIR | the Earth let her be gouerned by her parts |
| OD CHRISTEOS YRPOIL TIOBL, | and let there be diuision in her, |
| BUSDIR TILB NOALIR PAID ORSBA | that the glory of hir may be allwayes drunken |
| OD DODRMNI ZYLNA. | and vexed in it self. |
| ELZAP TILB PARM GI PERIPSAX | Her course, let it ronne w$^{th}$ the hevens, |
| OD TA QURLST BOOAPIS. | and as an handmayd let her serve them. |
| LNIBM OVCHO SYMP, | One season let it confownd an other, |

---

* A textual variant shown here gives SOBA, which is the acceptable reading.

| | |
|---|---|
| OD CHRISTEOS AG TOLTORN MIRC Q TIOBL LEL: | and let there be no creature vppon or within her the same: |
| TON PAOMBD DILZMO AS PIAN, | all her members let them differ in their qualities, |
| OD CHRISTEOS AG L TORTORN PARACH A SYMP: | and let there be no one creature aequall w<sup>th</sup> an other: |
| CORDZIZ | the reasonable Creatures of the Erth* |
| DODPAL OD FIFALZ LSMNAD, | let them vex and weede out one an other, |
| OD FARGT BAMS OMAOAS: | and the dwelling places let them forget their names: |
| CONISBRA OD AUAUOX TONUG: | the work of man, and his pomp, let them be defaced: |
| ORSCATBL NOASMI TABGES LEUITHMONG. | his buyldings let them become caves for the beasts of the feeld. |
| VNCHI OMP TILB ORS. | Confownd her vnderstanding with darknes. |
| BAGLE? MOOOAH OL CORDZIZ. | For why? It repenteth me I made Man. |
| L CAPIMAO IXOMAXIP | One while let her be known |
| OD CACOCASB GOSAA: | and an other while a stranger: |
| BAGLEN PII TIANTA A BABALOND, | bycause she is the bed of an Harlot, |
| OD FAORGT TELOC VO VIM. | and the dwelling place of Him that is Faln. |
| MADRIIAX TORZU: | O you heuens arrise: |
| OADRIAX OROCHA ABOAPRI. | the lower heuens vnder neath you, let them serve you! |
| TABAORI PRIAZ ARTABAS: | Gouern those that govern: |
| ADRPAN CORSTA DOBIX. | cast down such as fall! |
| YOLCAM PRIAZI ARCOAZIOR, | Bring furth with those that encrease, |

---

\* A textual note in the MS adds, specifically, *Men.*

| | |
|---|---|
| OD QUASB QTING. | and destroy the rotten! |
| RIPIR PAAOXT SAGACOR: | No place let it remayne in one number: |
| VML OD PRDZAR CACRG AOIVEAE CORMPT. | ad and diminish vntill the stars be numbred! |
| TORZU, ZACAR, | Arrise, Move, |
| OD ZAMRAN ASPT SIBSI BUTMONA, | and Appere before the Couenant of his mowth, |
| DS SURZAS TIA BALTAN. | which he hath sworne vnto vs in his Iustice. |
| ODO CICLE QAA: | Open the Mysteries of your Creation: |
| OD OZAZMA PLAPLI IADNAMAD. | and make vs partakers of Vndefyled Knowledg. |

### (The Thirty Ayres)*

| | | | | | |
|---|---|---|---|---|---|
| 1 | *LIL* | 11 | ICH | 21 | ASP |
| 2 | ARN | 12 | LOE | 22 | LIN |
| 3 | ZOM | 13 | ZIM | 23 | TOR |
| 4 | PAZ | 14 | VTA | 24 | NIA |
| 5 | LIT | 15 | OXO | 25 | VTI |
| 6 | MAZ | 16 | LEA | 26 | DES |
| 7 | DEO | 17 | TAN | 27 | ZAA |
| 8 | ZID | 18 | ZEN | 28 | BAG |
| 9 | ZIP | 19 | POP | 29 | RII |
| 10 | ZAX | 20 | CHR | 30 | TEX |

* In the MS these are listed in the margin of the first of two folios on which the Key of the Thirty Ayres is given.

(k)

## LIBER SCIENTIAE, AUXILII, ET VICTORIAE TERRESTRIS
### ANNO 1585
*The Book of Knowledge, of Might, and of Terrestrial Victory*

Of the ten columns of the Liber Scientiae, six only are treated here. These are described in the original MS as follows (A.S. translations).

Column I - *Nonaginta et unius partium, series continua.* The unbroken succession of 91 parts.

Column II - *Partium terrae nomina ab hominibus imposita.* Names of the parts of the earth as given by mankind.

Column III - *Partium terrae nomina divinitus imposita.* Names of the parts of the earth as divinely given.

Column V - *Bonorum principum aereorum ordines sphaerici.* Spheral Orders of Good Aerial Princes.

Column VI - *Bonorum ministrorum uniuscuiusque ordinis numerus tripartitus.* Threefold number of Good Ministers in each of the Orders.

Column VIII - *Angeli reges ipsis 30 ordinibus praedominantes.* Angel Kings ruling the said thirty Orders.

The text of these columns, given below, is verbatim with Sloane MS 3191, save that Column III is conformed to the 1587 revision of the Enochian Tablets.

| I | II | III | V | VI | VIII |
|---|---|---|---|---|---|
| 1 | Aegyptus | OCCODON | Ordo 1 LIL | 7209 | ZARZILG |
| 2 | Syria | PASCOMB | | 2360 | ZINGGEN |
| 3 | Mesopotamia | VALGARS | | 5362 | ALPVDVS |
| 4 | Cappadocia | DONGNIS | Ordo 2 ARN | 3636 | ZARNAAH |
| 5 | Tuscia | PACASNA | | 2362 | ZIRACAH |
| 6 | Parua Asia | DIALOIA | | 8962 | ZIRACAH |
| 7 | Hyrcania | SAMAPHA | Ordo 3 ZOM | 4400 | ZARZILG |
| 8 | Thracia | VIROOLI | | 3660 | ALPVDVS |
| 9 | Gosmam | ANDISPI | | 9236 | LAVAVOTh |

| I | II | III | V | VI | VIII |
|---|---|---|---|---|---|
| 10 | Thebaidi | THOTANP | Ordo 4 PAZ | 2360 | LAVAVOTh |
| 11 | Parsadal | AXXIARG | | 3000 | LAVAVOTh |
| 12 | India | POTHNIR | | 6300 | ARFAOLG |
| 13 | Bactriane | LAZDIXI | Ordo 5 LIT | 8630 | OLPAGED |
| 14 | Cilicia | NOCAMAL | | 2306 | ALPVDVS |
| 15 | Oxiana | TIARPAX | | 5802 | ZINGGEN |
| 16 | Numidia | SAXTOMP | Ordo 6 MAZ | 3620 | GEBABAL |
| 17 | Cyprus | VAUAAMP | | 9200 | ARFAOLG |
| 18 | Parthia | ZIRZIRD | | 7220 | GEBABAL |
| 19 | Getulia | OPMACAS | Ordo 7 DEO | 6363 | ZARNAAH |
| 20 | Arabia | GENADOL | | 7706 | HONONOL |
| 21 | Phalagon | ASPIAON | | 6320 | ZINGGEN |
| 22 | Mantiana | ZAMFRES | Ordo 8 ZID | 4362 | GEBABAL |
| 23 | Soxia | TODNAON | | 7236 | OLPAGED |
| 24 | Gallia | PRISTAC | | 2302 | ZARZILG |
| 25 | Illyria | ODDIORG | Ordo 9 ZIP | 9996 | HONONOL |
| 26 | Sogdiana | CRALPIR | | 3620 | LAVAVOTh |
| 27 | Lydia | DOANZIN | | 4230 | ZARZILG |
| 28 | Caspis | *LEXARPH* | Ordo 10 ZAX | 8880 | ZINGGEN |
| 29 | Germania | *COMANAN* | | 1230 | ALPVDVS |
| 30 | Trenam | *TABITOM* | | 1617 | ZARZILG |
| 31 | Bithynia | MOLPAND | Ordo 11 ICH | 3472 | LAVAVOTh |
| 32 | Graecia | VSNARDA | | 7236 | ZVRCHOL |
| 33 | Licia | PONODOL | | 5234 | HONONOL |
| 34 | Onigap | TAPAMAL | Ordo 12 LOE | 2658 | ZVRCHOL |
| 35 | India Maior | GEDOONS | | 7772 | CADAAMP |
| 36 | Orchenii | AMBRIOL | | 3391 | ZIRACAH |

| I  | II              | III         | V         | VI      | VIII      |
|----|-----------------|-------------|-----------|---------|-----------|
| 37 | Achaia          | GECAOND     |           | 8111    | LAVAVOTh  |
| 38 | Armenia         | LAPARIN     | Ordo 13   | 3360    | OLPAGED   |
| 39 | Cilicia         | DOCEPAX     | ZIM       | 4213    | ALPVDVS   |
|    | Nemrodiana      |             |           |         |           |
| 40 | Paphlagonia     | TEDOOND     |           | 2673    | GEBABAL   |
| 41 | Phasiana        | VIUIPOS     | Ordo 14   | 9236    | ALPVDVS   |
| 42 | Chaldei         | VOANAMB     | VTA       | 8230    | ARFAOLG   |
| 43 | Itergi          | TAHAMDO     |           | 1367    | ZARZILG   |
| 44 | Macedonia       | NOTIABI     | Ordo 15   | 1367    | LAVAVOTh  |
| 45 | Garamantica     | TASTOZO     | OXO       | 1886    | ARFAOLG   |
| 46 | Sauromatica     | CUCNRPT     |           | 9920    | ZIRACAH   |
| 47 | Aethiopia       | LAVACON     | Ordo 16   | 9230    | HONONOL   |
| 48 | Fiacim          | SOCHIAL     | LEA       | 9240    | ARFAOLG   |
| 49 | Colchica        | SIGMORF     |           | 7623    | ZIRACAH   |
| 50 | Cireniaca       | AYDROPT     | Ordo 17   | 7132    | OLPAGED   |
| 51 | Nasamonia       | TOCARZI     | TAN       | 2634    | ZARZILG   |
| 52 | Carthago        | NABAOMI     |           | 2346    | GEBABAL   |
| 53 | Coxlant         | ZAFASAI     | Ordo 18   | 7689    | ALPVDVS   |
| 54 | Idumea          | YALPAMB     | ZEN       | 9276    | ARFAOLG   |
| 55 | Parstauia       | TORZOXI     |           | 6236    | ARFAOLG   |
| 56 | Celtica         | ABRIOND     | Ordo 19   | 6732    | CADAAMP   |
| 57 | Vinsan          | OMAGRAP     | POP       | 2388    | ZINGGEN   |
| 58 | Tolpam          | ZILDRON     |           | 3626    | GEBABAL   |
| 59 | Carcedoma       | PARZIBA     | Ordo 20   | 7629    | HONONOL   |
| 60 | Italia          | TOTOCAN     | CHR       | 3634    | ALPVDVS   |
| 61 | Brytania        | CHIRZPA     |           | 5536    | ARFAOLG   |
| 62 | Phenices        | TOANTOM     | Ordo 21   | 5635    | CADAAMP   |
| 63 | Comaginen       | VIXPALG     | ASP       | 5658    | ZVRCHOL   |
| 64 | Apulia          | OSIDAIA     |           | 2232    | ARFAOLG   |
| 65 | Marmarica       | *PAOAOAN*   | Ordo 22   | 2326    | OLPAGED   |
| 66 | Concaua Syria   | CALZIRG     | LIN       | 2367    | ARFAOLG   |

| I | II | III | V | VI | VIII |
|---|---|---|---|---|---|
| 67 | Gebal | RONOOMB | Ordo 23 TOR | 7320 | ZARNAAH |
| 68 | Elam | ONIZIMP | | 7262 | LAVAVOTh |
| 69 | Idunia | ZAXANIN | | 7333 | ZINGGEN |
| 70 | Media | ORANCIR | Ordo 24 NIA | 8200 | ZARNAAH |
| 71 | Arriana | CHASLPO | | 8360 | LAVAVOTh |
| 72 | Chaldea | SOAGEEL | | 8236 | ZINGGEN |
| 73 | Serici Populi | MIRZIND | Ordo 25 VTI | 5632 | ZARNAAH |
| 74 | Persia | OBUAORS | | 6333 | ZIRACAH |
| 75 | Gongatha | RANGLAM | | 6236 | ARFAOLG |
| 76 | Gorsin | POPHAND | Ordo 26 DES | 9232 | ARFAOLG |
| 77 | Hispania | NIGRANA | | 3620 | CADAAMP |
| 78 | Pamphilia | LAZHIIM | | 5637 | ARFAOLG |
| 79 | Oacidi | SAZIAMI | Ordo 27 ZAA | 7220 | ZIRACAH |
| 80 | Babylon | MATHVLA | | 7560 | ZARNAAH |
| 81 | Median | CRPANIB | | 7263 | GEBABAL |
| 82 | Idumian | PABNIXP | Ordo 28 BAG | 2630 | LAVAVOTh |
| 83 | Foelix Arabia | POCISNI | | 7236 | ZARZILG |
| 84 | Metagonitulian | OXLOPAR | | 8200 | ZVRCHOL |
| 85 | Assyria | VASTRIM | Ordo 29 RII | 9632 | HONONOL |
| 86 | Affrica | ODRAXTI | | 4236 | ZARNAAH |
| 87 | Bactriani | GMTZIAM | | 7635 | ARFAOLG |
| 88 | Afnan | TAAOGBA | Ordo 30 TEX | 4632 | ARFAOLG |
| 89 | Phrygia | GEMNIMB | | 9636 | ZARNAAH |
| 90 | Creta | ADVORPT | | 7632 | HONONOL |
| 91 | Mauritania | DOXMAEL | | 5632 | ZVRCHOL |

**Paper XXIII**

**De Rebus Enochianis 2**

# (The Enochian Alphabet)*

| | | | | | |
|---|---|---|---|---|---|
| ᛈ | B | (1) | ᛣ | L | (20) |
| ᛒ | C | (2) | ᛒ | P | (30) |
| ᛔ | G | (3) | ᛏ | Q | (40) |
| ᛪ | D | (4) | ᛲ | N | (50) |
| ᛉ | F | (5) | ᚵ | X | (60) |
| ᛔ | A | (6) | ᛈ | O | (70) |
| ᛇ | E | (7) | ᛊ | R | (80) |
| ᛖ | M | (8) | ᛈ | Z | (90) |
| ᛉ | I,Y | (9) | ᛈ | U,V | (100) |
| ᛟ | H | (10) | ᛈ | S | (200) |
| | | | ᛈ | T | (300) |

* With transliteration, and with numerical values as employed in the A.S.

## DE REBUS ENOCHIANIS 2
## (PRACTICAL COMMENTARY)

### I

### *Preparation*

The Four Enochian tablets are set out, two above, two below, and are united by the names EXARP, HCOMA, NANTA and BITOM.

Two schemes of the Tablets are given in BM Sloane MS 3191. The original plan shows the Tablet of △ top left, that of ▽ top right, that of △ bottom left, that of ▽ bottom right; but a revised arrangement shows △ top left, ▽ top right, ▽ bottom left, △ bottom right. In addition to this rearrangement of the Tablets, certain of the letters shown thereon also underwent alteration; and on another folio of the MS appears Dee's finalisation of the whole, bearing the note "Die , 20 Aprilis, 1587, thus reformed by Raphael." This latter scheme is the one we use, which we refer to as the *tabula recensa.*

To have the Tablets by him for use in his workings, the student should fashion them in metal, engraving the mystical letters of each on four separate sheets of brass or of copper (wax or parchment may be substituted) approximately 6" wide by 6½" deep. He should engrave the letters in the original Enochian alphabet (shown facing), but he may for convenience simplify these letters somewhat if he finds it necessary.

For these individual Tablets, the names EXARP, HCOMA, NANTA and BITOM are, naturally, not added.

On the reverse of each Tablet, in the centre, is to be engraved, in outline, the Character associated with that Tablet:—

207

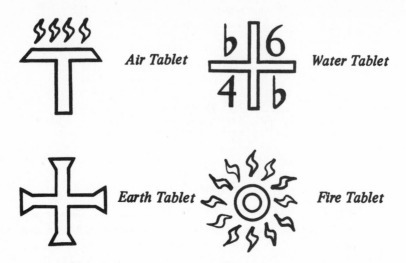

Air Tablet

Water Tablet

Earth Tablet

Fire Tablet

At the corners, and smaller in size, are to be set the Characters for all four Tablets: one Character to a corner, and arranged in this sequence:— Character for the Tablet of Air, top right; for that of Water, top left; for Earth, bottom right; and for Fire, bottom left. Thus the four smaller Characters in the corners will appear precisely the same on the reverse of all four Tablets, only the large central Character varying from one Tablet to another.

Each tablet is to be kept in a burse: that for the Tablet of △ being red, that for ▽ being green, for ▽ black, for △ white. (The attribution of these colours to the quarters in the Enochian system has the authority of Edward Kelly's seership: witness the vision of June 30, 1584.)

Each burse is to be of silk damask (or artsilk), lined with plain silk of the same colour, and having an interlining to give it firmness: each is to be hand sewn. Upon each burse there should be embroidered in gold (or in colours complimentary to the silk used), solely the appropriate Character, fully worked, not outlined.

## II
### *The Four Characters*

Concerning these Characters it is written:– "The seals and authorities of those Houses [the Tablets or Watchtowers] are confirmed in the beginning of the world. Unto every one of them be 4 Characters, tokens of the presence of the Son of God: by whom all things were made in creation Ensignes, upon the Image whereof is death: whereon the Redemption of mankind is established, and with which he shall come to judge the earth."*

By a rather elaborate system, these Characters, in conjunction with the *Sigillum Aemeth*, can be made to yield four names: those of the Great Elemental Kings.† (The A.S. does not, however, make use of these names, and prefers a more general invocation of the Kings in the Latin of the Vulgate.) These Mighty Princes are "bound" by the Four Characters, the "tokens of the presence of the Son of God," the symbols of the rulership of Spirit over the Four Elements.

The Kings appear in Chapter VI of the Johannine *Book of Revelation*, and they are, of course, none other than "the four dread Horsemen of the Apocalypse."

*The King of Air.* "And I saw, and lo, a white horse: and his rider held a bow, and a crown was given to him and he went forth conquering, that he might overcome."

*The King of Earth.* "And another went forth, a red horse, and a rider thereon: to him it was assigned that he should take away peace from the earth, so that men might destroy one another: and a great sword was given to him."

* A True and Faithful Relation . . . . 1659.

† For the system, see *The Golden Dawn*, Volume IV, Book Nine. For the Sigillum Aemeth, see Crowley's *Liber LXXXIX vel Chanokh*.

*The King of Water.* "And lo, a black horse: and his rider held a balance in his hand. And I heard as it were a voice amid the Four Beasts saying, Two pounds weight of wheat for a penny, and thrice two pounds weight of barley for a penny: and you shall not harm the wine nor the oil."

*The King of Fire.* " And lo, a pale horse, and his rider whose name was Death: and the Lower World followed him. And power was assigned to these over the four parts of the earth, to slay by the sword, by hunger, by death, and by the beasts of the earth."

It is worthy of note that even as the Characters which contain the key to the names of the Kings, and which "bind" the Kings, are "tokens . . . of the Son of God", so, in context of the Johannine mythology, it is only the Lamb slain yet upright, whose emblem in art has ever been the banner with the equal-armed cross, who has power over the seals which restrain the Four Horsemen. For it is traditionally held that the Four Characters are the first four seals of the Book Sealed with Seven Seals.*

(For further on the Great Elemental Kings, see part III following.)

### III

#### *Names and Calls*

The four Enochian Tablets, the Watchtowers, consist each of a grid of letters from which can be drawn many names, Divine, Archangelic, Angelic and Aerial; with the names of the Spirits of the Elements properly so called, and also of Goetic potencies. With the two last-mentioned classes of names we are not concerned in this paper.

The general principles by which names are drawn forth from the Tablets are too well known to need comment here,

---

* Thus the Four. Let him who has the wit perceive the Three, so to understand, with hardihood, the Seven.

and in any case, comparison of the hierarchies to the Tablets will enable those interested to "crack" the system. The hierarchies listed in "De Rebus Enochianis 1" (Texts f, g, h, i) are set out in a manner adapted to practical working, and all are based upon the authentic work of John Dee.

The first name in section I of each of these hierarchiacal tables is the God-name of 3 plus 4 plus 5 letters, as ORO IBAH AOZPI for △, MOR DIAL HCTGA for ▽. These triune names are, collectively, *Quater tria, nomina Dei ... quae, omnes super terram creaturas gubernant (tam invisibiles, quam visibiles), duodecim gestata vexillis:* * "the four times three Names of God . . . which govern all creatures on earth (those invisible, even as those visible), displayed upon the Twelve Banners". These, the Great Names of the Tablets, are Atziluthic.

The second name in section I of each of the hierarchical tables is the *numen divinum*, "the Divine Presence", obtained from the centre of each Tablet by a whirling construction ◉ , as BATAIVAH for △, RAAGIOSL for ▽. Each of these names, of 8 letters, is *angelicum* and *sanctum Dei nomen*, which is to say they are names both Divine and Angelic, their function being Briatic. Even as these names are obtained by the whirling construction, so do they go forth from God to inform the Mighty Seniors, whose thrones (to take up again the imagery of the Apocalypse) are set in a circle about the Throne of God.

The names of the third line of section I of each table are those of the Briatic Seniors (six names to each table), each of 7 letters. These are the Twenty-four Seniors *de quibus in Apocalypsi Beati Ioannis est mentio,* "concerning whom mention is made in the Apocalypse of Blessed John":—

AND AROUND THE THRONE WERE THRONES TWENTY-FOUR: AND THEREON SEATED, TWENTY-FOUR SENIORS

* Dee's Latin, as this, is italicised throughout this part III. The purpose is to avoid confusion, Latin of other authorship being also quoted herein.

## CLOTHED IN WHITE GARMENTS, WITH CROWNS OF GOLD UPON THEIR HEADS

*Revelation IV, 4. Trans. from Vulgate.*

Section II of each table comprises four sub-elemental groups, each of one Atziluthic and four Briatic names. In each of these groups, the Atziluthic or Divine Name consists of 5 letters, as ERZLA for △ of △, the related Briatic names each having 4 letters: as, in the same instance, RZLA, ZLAR, LARZ, ARZL.

The Briatic beings for the Airy sub-element of section II of each of the four hierarchical tables (△ of △, △ of ▽, △ of ▽, and △ of △) are titled *Fideles veracesque Dei omnipotentis nostri creatoris ministri.* Thus this title, "Ministers faithful and true of Almighty God our creator", attaches to the Briatic beings named in section II, for the Airy sub-element on each hierarchical table equally:— on the hierarchical table of △, it applies to RZLA, ZLAR, LARZ, ARZL: on the table of ▽ it applies to TAAD, AADT, ADTA, DTAA: on the table of ▽, to BOZA, OZAB, ZABO, ABOZ: on the table of △, to DOPA, OPAD, PADO, ADOP.

Thus, also in section II, the Briatic beings for the Watery sub-element on each of the four hierarchical tables (▽ of △, ▽ of ▽, ▽ of ▽, ▽ of △) are titled *Fideles nobilesque nostri omnipotentis creatoris angeli ac ministri,* "Faithful and noble Angels and Ministers of our omnipotent creator". The Briatic beings for the Earthy sub-element on each of the four hierarchical tables (▽ of △, ▽ of ▽, ▽ of ▽, ▽ of △) are titled *Sancti veracesque Dei onmipotentis creatoris nostri ministri,* "Holy and true Ministers of Almighty God our creator". In this same section, the Briatic beings for the Fiery sub-element of each of the hierarchical tables (△ of △, △ of ▽, △ of ▽, △ of △) are titled *Angeli sagaces veracesque omnipotentis Dei (eiusdemque creatoris nostri) ministri,* "Angels wise and true, Ministers of Almighty God (the same our creator)".

Section III of each table again comprises four sub-elemental groups. However, each group here gives two Atziluthic names, of 6 and 5 letters respectively, as LLACZA and PALAM for ▽ of △; one Briatic name, as YTPA for ▽ of △; and four Yetziratic names, as OYUB, PAOC, RBNH, DIRI in the same instance.

The Yetziratic beings for the Airy sub-element of section III of each of the four hierarchical tables (△ of △, △ of ▽, △ of ▽, △ of △) are titled *Angeli lucis*. Thus this title, "Angels of Light", attaches to the Yetziratic beings named in section III, for the Airy sub-element on each hierarchical table equally:— on the hierarchical table of △ it applies to CZNS, TOTT, SIAS, FMND: on the table of ▽ it applies to TOCO, NHDD, PAAX, SAIX: on the table of ▽, to AIRA, ORMN, RSNI, IZNR: on the table of △, to OPMN, APST, SCIO, VASG,

Thus also in section III, the Yetziratic beings for the Watery sub-element on each of the four hierarchical tables are titled *Angeli lucis fideles Dei (creatoris nostri) ministri*, "Angels of Light, faithful Ministers of God (our creator)". The Yetziratic beings for the Earthy sub-element on each of the four hierarchical tables are titled *Boni veracesque Dei (creatoris nostri) angeli*, "Good and true Angels of God (our creator)". The Yetziratic beings for the Fiery sub-element on each of the four hierarchical tables are titled *Angeli Dei veritatis et bonitatis pleni*, "Angels of God full of goodness and truth."

## *The Enochian Hierarchies in A.S. Working*

Section I of each hierarchy comprises the ruling names for the Element in question.

The triune God-name of 3 plus 4 plus 5 letters, with the Divine and Angelical name of 8 letters, is used in general invocations of the Spirits of the Element ("Elementals" specifically) whose names can be drawn from the relevant Tablet although the method is not herein treated: in such a case, hierarchical names from sections II or III are not included, nor are the names of the Seniors. An invocation of the Seniors collectively, without naming them, is however appropriate for this purpose.

All names in section I, including those of the Six Seniors, are to be invoked whenever it is intended to proceed to section II or to section III. It is to be noted at this juncture that sections II and III are never *both* employed in a working, but the one or the other according to the nature and purpose of the operation.

Section II, following section I, is to be employed on occasions when it is intended to invoke a hierarchy to Briatic level only. The God-name ruling one of the sub-elements is invoked, as HXGSD for △ of △, then all the four Briatic names governed thereby, as XGSD, GSDX, SDXG, DXGS, in the same instance. It will be observed that the God-name in every group of section II consists of the same succession of letters as the first of the four Briatic names, with a prefixed letter. This prefix, following Dee's system, is drawn from the vertical column which stands between the Tablets as they are set out two above two below: but using the "tabula recensa." Furthermore, the second, third and fourth Briatic names are permutations of the first: because the hierarchy is not being invoked to Yetziratic level, all these four names are to be invoked in succession, in order to stabilise the force in Briah.

For a particular working, it may well be sufficient and appropriate to use the group of names relating to a pure sub-element, for example △ of △, or again △ of △.* However, it may be considered that all the sub-elements of the Element of the working should be employed for greater force, and this is also a valid use: in this case, the names of section I should be uttered once only, to be followed by the four sequences

---

* Although classed as sub-elements, the Pure Sub-elements indicate the purest form of the Elements: each of them represents the essential quiddity of its Element, infusing the other sub-elements and thereby the whole of the Elemental hierarchy encyphered in its particular Tablet.

of sub-elemental names (Atziluthic with Briatic) in section II.

Section III, to follow section I, should only be considered for major works: it brings into action the "big guns" of a hierarchy, for our invocation is to Yetziratic level. Here, the *Claves Angelicae** are employed, as prescribed within *The Theban Angelic Formula* given below: neither the *Claves* nor the *Formula* should be employed with section II. (In contra-distinction to section II, section III permits of the employment of only one sub-element in any working.)

| Angelic Key | Attribution | Angelic Key | Attribution |
|---|---|---|---|
| 1 | ⊕ | 10 | △ of ▽ |
| 2 | ⊕ | 11 | ▽ of ▽ |
| 3 | △, and △ of △ | 12 | △ of ▽ |
| 4 | ▽, and ▽ of ▽ | 13 | △ of 🜃 |
| 5 | 🜃, and 🜃 of 🜃 | 14 | ▽ of 🜃 |
| 6 | △, and △ of △ | 15 | △ of 🜃 |
| 7 | ▽ of △ | 16 | △ of △ |
| 8 | 🜃 of △ | 17 | ▽ of △ |
| 9 | △ of △ | 18 | 🜃 of △ |

Of the two Divine Names in each sub-elemental group of section III, that of 6 letters awakens the forces of the Yetziratic beings of its group, the Name of 5 letters controls them.

The Briatic name, bracketed in our lists, is not to be permuted here as we have shown it to be for use in section II. Neither is the 5-letter Divine Name of section II to be employed, an entirely different descent of power and governance now being in operation.

Within the appropriate sub-elemental group of section III, *one only* of the four Yetziratic Angels is determined upon for the working. (A preponderance of Atziluthic and Briatic names is evident in the association of sections I and III: this

---

* With the exception of the Second Angelic Key, and the Key of the Thirty Ayres. See below, *The First and Second Keys, the Keys of Spirit.*

focusing of mighty forces to a precise point constitutes a main reason for the great deliberation which is necessary to a safe and effective working of the Enochian system). Reading left to right, these four Yetziratic names indicate successive levels of function in the Astral Light, the fourth functioning most closely to the material world, as for example PMOX, $\triangle$ of $\triangle$, or again, SAIX, $\triangle$ of $\nabla$. It is to be understood that all these Angels are equal to one another in power and in authority, and have no hierarchical dominion the one over the other: the factor guiding the magician's choice is simply that of the suitability of a more or a less material vehicle for the Yetziratic phase of the bringing down of power in the particular working.

In each of these sub-elemental groups of section III, the four Yetziratic Angels are in A.S. working accorded the titles respectively (left to right), Excellent Angel, Luminous Angel, High Angel, Shining Angel. Dee indicates these forms of address—*praeclare, illustris, insignis, fulgide*—only in the case of that one group from every Tablet which is attributed to a Fiery sub element: but they can validly be applied to the appropriate Yetziratic beings of every sub-element.

When an actual working employing sections I and III is performed, whatever magical utterances or acts may be devised for the development of the rite will be introduced as suitable: this will include rehearsal of the names of the Enochian Hierarchy of the working to Yetziratic sub-elemental level, with whatever styles of address, declarations, adjurations, conjurations, commands, the particular working may require. The following sequence, *The Theban Angelic Formula,* forms the pre-climactic procedure of the rite, and is a special formulation not to be departed from, but to be encapsuled within the rite as a whole; of which the form is otherwise entirely and completely adaptable to purpose and occasion. The Angelic Keys necessary to be employed in the pre-climactic sequence should be reserved, in the rite, to that sequence, even though the Enochian hierarchical names may and should be given a wider application. The austere pre-climactic sequence itself should be followed by a jussive declaration to the Yetziratic Angel of the working, with, if necessary, further reiteration of hierarchical names.

### The Theban Angelic Formula*

A  (i)  The operator faces, across the Bomos, the quarter of the Element of working. Upon the Bomos is displayed the appropriate Enochian Tablet, letters uppermost.

(ii)  Raising the Tablet in both hands, he holds it vertically before him. Thus standing, he vibrates the relevant one of the four Divine Names which unite the Tablets, and which are referred to Spirit, the mystical Fifth Element:— EXARP if the working be of △, HCOMA if it be of ▽, NANTA if it be of ▽, BITOM if it be of △. In the same posture he proceeds to the vibration of the First Angelic Key.†

B  (i)  The Tablet is replaced on the Bomos, letters uppermost as before.

(ii)  A cross is traced above the face of the Tablet and in parallel to it, the first movement being from left to right of the Tablet, the second from top to bottom of the Tablet.

(iii)  The triune Divine Name of 3 plus 4 plus 5 letters, ruling the Element, is vibrated.

(iv)  The Divine Presence is invoked:— the Divine and Angelical name of 8 letters is vibrated, and at

---

\* Named of the Boeotian exemplar of the power of sound and teacher of the use of letters.

† Invariably, the use of any one or more of the Elemental Angelic Keys (Third to Eighteenth Keys inclusive) is to be preceded by the First Key, to ensure that the elemental force shall be always under the presidency of Spirit. This has been found an indispensable precaution.

the same time a whirl ✑ is traced above the centre of the Tablet and in parallel to the surface.

(v)   The names of the Six Seniors of the Element are vibrated.

C   (i)   Dependent upon the Element of working, the Major Elemental Key is vibrated:— the Third Key for △, the Fourth Key for ▽, the Fifth for ▽, or the Sixth for △, as appropriate.

(ii)   Dependent upon the particular sub-element of the working, the related sub-elemental Key is intoned; as, the Ninth Key for △ of △, the Eleventh Key for ▽ of ▽.

In the case of the pure sub-elements, △ of △, ▽ of ▽, ▽ of ▽, △ of △, no such Key is at this point required, the Major Elemental Key alone sufficing.

It is emphasised that in the employment of any one of the mixed sub-elements (the sub-elements properly so called), the sub-elemental Key is always to be preceded by vibration of the Major Elemental Key:* this is an invariable rule of working.

(iii) The Divine Name of 6 letters which stands at the head of the sub-elemental group is vibrated: simultaneously, a perpendicular line is described in the air above the Tablet, downwards but not to touch its surface. The Divine Name of 5 letters is next vibrated, simultaneously with which a horizontal is traced, cutting the perpendicular so as to form with it a cross. The vibration of these two Divine Names should proceed without a hiatus, so that the tracing of the two beams of the cross may form one smooth succession of movements.

---

* To ensure that the student perfectly understands the relationship between the sub-element and the Element of the working, a few examples are offered:— if the sub-element is △ of △, the Element is △. If the sub-element is ▽ of △, the Element again is △. If the sub-element is △ of ▽, the Element is ▽. If the sub-element is △ of △, the Element is △.

(iv)  The Briatic name is vibrated.

(v)  The name of the Angel of the working is vibrated.

N.B. The Yetziratic force is banished by means of the triune Divine Name of its Element. If pentagrams are employed, the relevant Spirit Name (Exarp, Hcoma, Nanta or Bitom), with the banishing Pentagram of Spirit, will precede the triune Divine Name and Elemental Pentagram.

Pentagrams must not be incorporated into the Theban Angelic Formula, which is complete in itself; but they may form part of the magical action leading up to that Formula, and in the jussive declaration following it.

### The First and Second Keys, the Keys of Spirit

Although the elemental Keys (Third through Eighteenth) should always be preceded by the First Key, the First Key may be used without these elemental Keys when an invocation of spiritual force is required in a working. In this case, immediately after vibration of the First Key, an invocation is made of the Archangels LEXARPH, COMANAN and TABITOM. These Archangels are never invoked when the First Key precedes elemental Keys in hierarchical working. Their names, which occur in column III of the Liber Scientiae, are formed from a synthesis of the four Spirit Names which unite the Tablets, together with the letter L which is one of the "free letters" not incorporated in the *characteres symmetrici*. In A.S. working, these Archangels are held to be Powers respectively of The Son and Transcendent One; The Great Mother; The Father.

The Second Angelic Key, like the First, is an invocation of the forces of Spirit, but its purpose is different. In working it is principally used to precede the Key of the Thirty Ayres. It is noteworthy that this combination of the Second Key and the Key of the Thirty Ayres may if desired be used in a rite which employs elemental Keys, though never in direct

association with them, but solely to introduce the forces of
the Liber Scientiae as set forth in part IV of this paper: the
Liber Scientiae having its own integral structure and working.

The Second Key can, furthermore, be used independently
of the Key of the Thirty Ayres: this independent use of the
Second Key, however, should on no account be undertaken
in a rite which uses elemental Keys. It may be introduced at
a fitting moment in a high rite when the role of the operator
is one of complete receptivity to spiritual force: following
vibration of the Second Key, an invocation is made of the
Archangel PAOAOAN. This Archangel is never invoked when
the Second Key precedes the Key of the Thirty Ayres. Its
name, which occurs in column III of the Liber Scientiae, is
formed from all the remaining "free letters" not incorporated
in the *characteres symmetrici*. In A.S. working, this Archangel
is held to be a Power of The Lower Mother.

The Second Key has in our system no other uses than
those here indicated.

### The Great Elemental Kings

The Four Kings represent great Briatic energies, the pure
and unmodified potential of their respective Elements in that
World. Any effective Enochian working, even when the relevant
King is not invoked, engages by nature the power of that King,
to be manifested in the normal action and according to the
normal potency of the Beings named. However, if in process of
such a working the King concerned is invoked, then the normal
energies of the operation will be tremendously magnified, and
the Light stirred to an intense degree of activity.

A King is in general only to be invoked in operations
wherein the Enochian hierarchy down to Yetziratic sub-
elemental level is invoked, and wherein the great resultant
increase of energy can be completely and harmoniously
assimilated in the resolution of the working, without either
running wild as an unassimilable residue (thus becoming

Goetic), or countering the operation itself. *Where there is any doubt of the wisdom of making such an invocation, it should not be attempted.* (It is to be noted that a different purpose in the invocation of a King may occur in the much more favourable circumstances of invocation of the forces of the Liber Scientiae: see part IV below).

The invocation of the King, if needed, should follow the Angelic Formula and Jussive Declaration, and it is to be made once only. If the working is not entirely Enochian (employing perhaps Hebrew names associated with the Elements), those names which belong to other systems should not replace any part of the Enochian hierarchy, but should be additional to it.

The following are the invocations customarily used in the A.S. for the Great Elemental Kings. In rehearsing one of these invocations, nothing whatever is added verbally; nor is the mind of the operator directed to the purpose of his rite, but entirely and simply to the invocation itself. The Latin texts herein are in the words of the Vulgate: translations of which are given (in the same order) in part II above.

To make the invocation the operator faces the quarter of the Element of the working. Upon the Bomos before him is set the Tablet of the working, the Characters uppermost. Placing the fingers of his left hand upon the central Character of the Tablet, he raises his right hand to about six inches from his eyes, as if to shield them, the palm being turned outward. In this posture, he vibrates the invocation.

### (Air)

O thou mighty Prince, majestic Governor of the Eastern Watchtower of the Universe, behold me, and behold the First Seal whereon my hand is set.

ET VIDI ET ECCE EQUUS ALBUS, ET QUI SEDEBAT SUPER ILLUM HABEBAT ARCUM, ET DATA EST EI CORONA, ET EXIVIT VINCENS UT VINCERET.

*(Earth)*

O thou mighty Prince, majestic Governor of the Northern
Watchtower of the Universe, behold me, and behold the Second
Seal whereon my hand is set.

ET EXIVIT ALIUS EQUUS RUFUS: ET QUI SEDEBAT SUPER
ILLUM, DATUM EST EI UT SUMERET PACEM DE TERRA, ET UT
INVICEM SE INTERFICIANT, ET DATUS EST EI GLADIUS
MAGNUS.

*(Water)*

O thou might Prince, majestic Governor of the Western
Watchtower of the Universe, behold me, and behold the Third
Seal whereon my hand is set.

ET ECCE EQUUS NIGER: ET QUI SEDEBAT SUPER ILLUM,
HABEBAT STATERAM IN MANU SUA. ET AUDIVI TANQUAM
VOCEM IN MEDIO QUATUOR ANIMALIUM DICENTIUM: BILIBRIS
TRITICI DENARIO ET TRES BILIBRES HORDEI DENARIO, ET
VINUM, ET OLEUM NE LAESERIS.

*(Fire)*

O thou mighty Prince, majestic Governor of the Southern
Watchtower of the Universe, behold me, and behold the fourth
Seal whereon my hand is set.

ET ECCE EQUUS PALLIDUS: ET QUI SEDEBAT SUPER EUM,
NOMEN ILLI MORS, ET INFERNUS SEQUEBATUR EUM, ET DATA
EST ILLI POTESTAS SUPER QUATUOR PARTES TERRAE, INTER-
FICERE GLADIO, FAME, ET MORTE, ET BESTIIS TERRAE.

These Four Kings are imaged for us, in the mystical
symbolism of the Apocalypse, as Four Horsemen. This is
scarcely in itself a formulation: the "White Horses" of the
ocean's breakers are a familiar image, and so are those forces
of storm, the "Wild Riders" of the sky. Scott, in *The Lay of
the Last Minstrel*, gives a variation of this widespread feeling
when he declares that in a vivid display of the Aurora Borealis,
"spirits were riding the Northern Light." Dream analysis and

kindred explorations frequently show such animals as horses to be symbols of natural energies, the "rider" being that which directs the force: in the matter we are considering, the "horsemen" are the names and attributive identities of the Four Kings.

## IV
### *Liber Scientiae*

To comprehend the A.S. use of the Liber Scientiae, it is necessary first to understand something of the intrinsic concept of that Book. The Key of the Thirty Ayres moves the mighty forces of the Book of Terrestrial Victory. In the Key of the Thirty Ayres, the powers of the Ayres are saluted as divinely provided with "a powr Understanding to dispose all things according to the providence of Him that sitteth on the Holy Throne . . . " This provision "for the government of the Erth and her unspeakable varietie" is shown as dependent on the complexity and division inherent in Earth's very nature: of which changeful imbalance the magician can avail himself in pursuit of his purpose.

This continual flux and reflux in earthly conditions is indicated to be the result of a divine decree:—

"One season let it confownd an other and let there be no creature uppon or within her the same . . . "

Many great powers exist which are associated with earthly conditions, each having its own distinctive character. Any one of these great powers, when the circumstances naturally occurring or ritually created are fully harmonious to its action, will upon invocation pour into the channel thus formed a torrent of energy to further the work. The magician, giving focus and pattern to their operation as he employs the Liber Scientiae within the structure of his work, thereby sends forward his work in unity with the purpose of the Liber: which purpose is the implementation of natural law.

The power of this combination derives from the fact that the magician's purpose is likewise to fulfill one aspect or

another of natural law. This statement may at first glance
cause surprise: but in truth every work which the magician
wills to undertake, proves upon examination to be, for him, a
necessary manifestation of natural law, else he could neither
will it, nor perceive it as desirable. If this proposition should
seem on any occasion open to doubt, the magician would do
well to reconsider the intended operation altogether: usually
the lines of necessity converging upon the magical purpose
will be almost instantly discernible. Thus do we invoke
blessing upon that which is already blessed, while upon that
which is already cursed do we call a curse. Thus is that which
is inordinate helped to its impending dissolution, while that
which brings promise into manifestation is nurtured and sped
forward upon its way. Terrible, inexorable, yet an essential
condition of effective being, the spirit of this guided development is totally magical in its intent.

Before giving the procedure for the use of the Liber
Scientiae, we subjoin a table condensed from A.S. documentation. This documentation has evolved over the years from
the Order's practical magical work with the Enochian system.
It is to be noted that the Yetziratic Order of "Good Ministers"
inhabiting each Ayre is in fact made up of three divisions or
sub-orders (col. VI of the Liber), save for the Order inhabiting
the lowest Ayre, which is made up of four sub-orders. In the
following table, the names of the "Good Ministers" of these
Yetziratic sub-orders are given, and the nature of the works
under their care. The sequence of the table follows "the
unbroken succession of 91 parts:" thus 1, 2, and 3 are the
sub-orders of LIL, the First Ayre; 88, 89, 90 and 91 are the
sub-orders of the lowest, the Thirtieth Ayre, TEX.

### THE GOOD MINISTERS OF THE AYRES

1    *Rainbow-vestured Guardians of the Limbeck of Blood.*
▽    Thy blood and thine, ye slain of earth, thy blood and thine ye
     sufferers, is in the limbeck: yet behold, hour by hour it diminisheth
     for the flame is set beneath and the spirit riseth up thence. Rejoice

now with the keepers thereof! In all works of celebration shall they aid: in those also which seek understanding, courage, and joy of spirit.

2    *The Dwellers in the Lake of Sapphires.*
▽    In perfect harmony and unity these inhabit, and in most sincere truth: wan are they and fair of form, and in their dark hair they twine as it were garlands of clear blue reeds. All that they may, they weave together: all works of integration will they make their care.

3    *The Flame-clad Amethysts which adorn the North.*
▽    Now like to the lightning, now like to misty rain are these as they dance: their music is as of cymbals ringing from a great distance. These will aid in rites to inspire followers for the Work, to charm away opposition, to win allies: but to win love to thine own self invoke them not.

4    *Lords of the Plain of Chrysoleth.*
▽    In feasting and gladness, in music and mirth are they seen, who are all human of aspect. They hear and know strange and far things, and the thoughts of men. Of their dominion are works of consecration, and the making of the Magical Link: also operations inaugurating a new enterprise to influence others.

5    *The Angers of the Olive Mount, Captains of Ruin.*
▽    These are seen as giants, vast of form and slow in movement. Yet do they swiftly hear when any calls their aid, if on three successive nights before that of his rite he will but take olive oil, mingle this with sand of the sea-shore, and macerate leaves of bindweed therewith: and this burning fumigate his place of working at the tenth hour of the night. Their aid is of high avail in works intended to preserve continuity in conditions of change, to perpetuate tradition, to mitigate the effects of vicissitude: or to promote loyalty.

6    *The Dwellers in the Pillared City.*
▽    These have their abode upon a hill in shape as a cone, and builded from foot to summit upon a broad spiral terrace. Each round is the like of each, and each side differs from other: so on foot move the Dwellers through variety, or move they by flight upward and downward in one aspect. Call thou upon these winged pilgrims if thy rite be for productive journeying whether earthly or astral, or if the art of bilocation be thine aim.

7      *The Whispering Ones, Spirits of the Basalt Forest.*
▽      Forms of gleaming emerald, dwellers among dark boughs and
       shadowy leaves, they are but slightly hidden yet oft go unknown.
       Most bounteous are they, if thy works be of their kind:— formation
       of an artificial elemental for benevolent purposes, or any other
       work to further the interests of other people.

8      *The Comfort of the Just, the Woes of Hyssop, Rue and Wormwood.*
▽      These move in knots and in rings, armed with scourges: ever and
       anon they howl, as they were smitten. Yet is their movement a
       dance, and their howling an oblation. These will assist in all
       operations intended to control the Lower Watcher or Dweller at
       the Threshold: likewise all works concerned with the fulfilment
       of natural responsibilities or with the furtherance of a mature
       attitude to life.

9      *Samite-robed Ministers of the Wave-carven Altar.*
▽      These appear as maidens, with flowing hair and with eyes down-
       cast: yet do they carry rods of power and commandment. They
       will aid in works performed to attain understanding of human
       needs, or in works dependent upon such an understanding: they
       will give assistance also in any work involving telepathy.

10     *The Lords Invincible, Leaders of the Silent Ones.*
▽      These appear as young women, vigorous and laughing of aspect.
       They will give assistance in all works of protection, likewise in
       operations relating to any aspect of the upbringing of children:
       those to whose aid they are called will be victors.

11     *The Mighty Spirits, Voices of the Throne.*
▽      Fast thou three days and call upon their aid in any works of
       thaumaturgy, any works to be produced as "signs" or "evidence."

12     *Lissome Ones of the Habitations of Twilight.*
▽      Their teeth and claws are marble white as milk, yet will they offer
       no harm to the pensive or the solitary. If by Art Magick thou dost
       strive to find congenial fellowship, or to gain from natural forces
       (as by gambling, or by agriculture) these are for thee. Yet, to
       keep their aid, all that thou doest must be free from undue haste
       and from greed.

13     *The Panoplied Horsemen of the River of Dreams.*
▽      These have the aspect of young horsemen, armoured as knights,

having over their armour surcoats of green and gold. Pennons of gold with devices of green they bear also upon their lances. The mists about the river part at a shallow ford: the knights make the crossing in joyous companies. The aid of these is to be invoked in the high consecration of the Grail, and in all works of the Grail. Most potent and benign are they: yet are the mists of that river filled with strange images, and if thou dost undertake this work and make this invocation, look guardedly that thou forsake it not for aught else that may appear within thy fancy until this work be well concluded.

14 *Princes of the Waters of Death.*
▽  Changing winds and currents alike serve their advance. Call then upon their name for aid in operations to explore emotional experience, or to develop the imagination.

15 *The Governors of Continuance.*
▽  These blue-robed recline upon couches of alabaster, and discourse of the unity of past and future: for to them past and future are one, and are ever-present. They are to be called upon in works intended to nullify a force, or to affirm contentment and stillness, or for negation in any form.

16 *Guardians of the Wells of Pharphar.*
△  These watch over the unfailing sources of a torrent of swift radiance amidst dunes of crystalline fragments: they dip their hands to give drink of living flame to all who come to them. Works of fulfilment and of equilibrium are theirs: they are sought also in New Sowing, and for the transcending of Time.

17 *Children of the Seven Thunders, Oracles of the Undefiled.*
△  Voices of the sword of lightning are these, terrible to hear: and for each voice shineth the face of a child of splendour, golden and ruddy. And these are their works that they will aid: To rule indirectly, to show the way, to teach, to heal, to nourish, to protect, to foster.

18 *Host of the Amber Ships, the Lamps of Awe.*
△  Many and many are these, many and glorious. Their bodies are as flames of great stillness, and in each a most lofty and potent countenance. These will forward such works as to find entrance to other spheres: they are apt to aid such as would command wonders or would be instructed by oracles.

19  *Princes of the Salt of Wisdom.*
△   Slight of form and placid of countenance, these are all golden in
    hue, golden is their vesture and very luminous are their eyes. Their
    aid should be sought in works of healing, whether of diseases or
    of injuries: also in works wrought to strengthen the Nephesh: also
    for rites inaugurating a new enterprise in a just cause.

20  *The Flame-bearers, the Mighty Crowned Spirits.*
△   Each sits enthroned beside each, at the circumference of a space
    proportionable to the shadow of the Earth. Their countenances
    may not be seen for bright-shining: for each wears a crown having
    64 points, and each point is a fire of radiance. Let thy voice go
    forth to them when thou wilt perform such mighty works as
    those which culminate in, or involve, resurrection or regeneration.

21  *Swift Ones of the Portals of Flame.*
△   Deepest blackness is the visible aspect of these, but too rapidly
    do they move for the eye to dwell upon them. Theirs is the solution
    of specific problems: they will aid also in ceremonial methods of
    occult research, or in solemn dedication of thy studies.

22  *The Diamond-helmed Lords of Vexation.*
△   Keen are their blades, a multitude: they guard the secret fords of
    Hakirath, and keep the last of the Seven Bridges, which is the
    drawbridge. Thou canst win their aid in works for sundering the
    magical link, likewise for works undertaken to achieve indepen-
    dence of environment or of associates.

23  *The Mighty Ones, Breastplates of Fire.*
△   As a great company of free warriors mounted upon wyverns, these
    go forward silently, one flame encompassing all. Their delight is
    in operations of transmutation: seek then their aid in such, or in
    operations for the realisation of a paramount wish, or for the
    fulfilment of an ambition. To any one of these will they assist: be
    certain therefore that it is thy true desire.

24  *Princes of the Torch-lit Labyrinth.*
△   Mail-clad and helmed are these, and seated each before his banner:
    white and green, scarlet, azure and black tremble the sacred
    emblems. Ask thou the help of these in no work save one: the
    consecration of the Spear.

25  *Iron-shod Lords of Splendor.*

△   Horned helmets these bear, and cloaks of scarlet. The times of
    their full power are in the far past, and in the time yet to come:
    but in all ages are they awake to earthward. One word they heed
    from all who call upon them for aid: the name of friend. If they
    seem to defend the bonds of blood and of marriage, it is but as
    the parties therein are also friend and friend: all duty they laugh
    to scorn, the self-seeker also do they laugh to tenfold scorn. Yet
    in works undertaken for friendship's sake, or for furtherance of a
    friend's interests, but call upon them and they will heed instantly:
    no offering they seek, and no promised veneration.

26  *The Governors of the Blackened Waters.*

△   These appear in form terrible, even as that which tradition
    averreth of sea-bishops: their bodies green and scaled, their wings,
    beards and the webs of their feet crimson, and having upon their
    heads seeming mitres of violet and gold. If thou be so earnest to
    obtain somewhat that thou wilt have it at whatever cost, then
    before thy rite burn to them upon glowing charcoal a lock freshly
    cut from thy hair, with 5 drops of thine own blood drawn from
    thy right thumb, and sprinkled with some grains of salt of the sea:
    while this burns call upon these Governors, and state clearly thy
    desire.

27  *The Ministers of Glory, Summoners of the Harps of Iron.*

△   These keep their beacon-fires upon the highest summits: vast are
    the flames thereof. Seek their aid in works to influence public
    opinion, to propagate ideas and ideals.

28  *The Clarions of Orichalc, Ministers of Dissension.*

29  *The Princes of Justice, Millstones of the Mighty.*

30  *The Ministers of Guerdon, the Blue Flames of the Last.*

31  *Tresses of Myrrh and of Asadulcis, Voices of Persuasion.*

▽   Tall and supple are they, with limbs of youth, but their garments
    are heavy and dim as night and their faces are not seen. Some bear
    vessels of various shape, wrought of marble and of agate: some
    speak strange words of counsel. Their care is for works that would
    bring equilibrium out of unrest: also for works of transubstanti-
    ation, and for the art of talismanic consecration.

**32**    *The Noises of the Lower World, the Sighing Rumour of the Waters.*

▽    Hardly are these to be seen, whether by sight earthly or spiritual: a sighing are they and a laughter, and a calling amid a wind: else are they like forms of glass that turn and move in endless swayings. Yet the heart of each is as it were a thin flame of changeful blue. Pour to them, before thy rite's beginning, a libation of white wine mingled with salt: upon barren earth pour it, or upon sand. They will aid in works of transformation, and in all works designated to produce change of circumstances.

**33**    *The Implacable Ministers, Living Lamps of the Concealed Shrine.*

△    As heads graven of limestone seen in the midst of a furnace, so fiercely and so brilliantly glow these in whiteness. Their asssistance may be sought for works of levitation, teleportation, or any magical work with the object of transcending an obstacle or passing a barrier: only before calling their name, look thou dwell for seven days poorly, eat no cooked food, and speak no needless word.

**34**    *Wielders of the Blades of Division.*

△    These inhabit a fair garden, wherein the leaves and blossoms are of light. Their name should be called for aid in magical operations to explore philosophic concepts, or to increase capacity therein.

**35**    *Dark Governors of the Powers of Pestilence.*

△    These are seen under the aspect of winged heads, their countenances expressive of most acute intelligence, their wings of lapis lazuli, gliding swiftly. They will aid thee for works performed during adverse tides, if there is need that such be done: also in operations seeking success in diplomacy.

**36**    *Princes of the Sanctuary, Rulers of the Forces of Conquest.*

△    All ruddy with sparkles of light are these, their faces and their vesture, as if they were of iron heated to redness. That which they try, they touch: if it be worthy it is transformed to brightness, if it be not worthy they leave upon it blackness as of burning. Theirs is the Red Work: theirs also are all works to attain renown and dominion.

37    *Keepers of the Mystery wherein are the Swords 600,000 of length.*
△     Sandals they have of bronze, tunics of flashing crystal: in ranks
and files are they seen, and each looks upon each with one
countenance: also that which one of them does, they all do the
like. The aid of these may be called for all works of Art Magick
performed by means of a mirror, for all works dependent upon
the powers of sex, and for all works effected to increase psychological perception or insight into matters touching the Astral World.

38    *Spirits of the Incensory of Confoundment.*
△     Wild are their whirlings and their hissings, these many-headed,
these many-handed, with tearing fangs of steel and flinty claw. As
scarlet and livid flames mingled with grey smoke they leap and
writhe, and seek to draw all that they can within their clutch.
Theirs are all works of malediction, of cursing and of destruction.

39    *The Daughters of Death, Guardians of the Secrets 8987.*
△     These go in majesty, with tall crowns upon their hair: winged are
they, with pinions of changeful flame. Deep counsel is theirs: if
thine be a work to attain the powers of interpretation, or to open
a means of progress whether of the mind or in earthly things, or
to find the keys of lost knowledge, these be for thee. Seek their
aid too, if thy work be to prepare the Hand of Glory.

40    *Builders of the Wine-press, Foundations of Zeal.*
△     Small are they of stature, mighty of limb, and their countenance
is as the setting sun. Theirs is the pool of purple and the wall of
hewn rock: huge works have they made, huge works shall make
without speech thereof. To them commend works undertaken to
gain leadership in social affairs, to defend a lawsuit or a matter of
reputation.

41    *The Priestesses of Wrath, the Daughters of Storm.*
△     Swarthy are these of hue, jewelled with splendours: they move,
they leap with potent flashings: they rend the vapours. Before thy
rite, in a wild and secret place make offering to these of red wine
mingled with honey, if thy purpose in working be to obtain good
fortune in love, or toward the ceremonial making of a Love
Charm. Do likewise for all works concerned with increase in
personal attractiveness or in popularity.

42    *The Lords of the Column of Flame.*
△    Very powerful be these in high matters that touch upon the earth:—
in consecration of a new building or temple, or magical works
undertaken to obtain such a building: or rites to purify a location of
adverse spirits or influences. But if thou dost see the form in which
these Lords appear, tell not of it lest confusion be multiplied.

43    *Veiled Sentinels of the Onyx Causeway.*
△    As white smoke rising, beheld in a vertical and immobile shaft
of light, so vibrant and so unmoving shine these. They celebrate
established unity, even of the highest: their power confirms the
works of Unity Attained.

44    *The Pale Queens Mighty in Sorrow, the Tears of Flame.*
△    Their faces are of crystal, their robes are burning rubies, as with
loud wailing they pass across a purple air. Before thy rite, call unto
these in the dawn softly, and in some high place: so the work be to
meet spiritual challenge, or to make assault upon enemies, to
inspire them with terror, to rule them through their discords.

45    *The Mighty Sons, Reapers of the Harvest of Firedrakes.*
△    Who would stir the forces of abundance: who is for honour,
riches, health: seek ye these strong ones who exult with laughter,
who gather and bind the terrible sheaves of destiny.

46    *Spirits of the 24th Part of a Moment: Timeless Movers.*
△    These show themselves as men, or as lizards that go upright; but as
figures seen across bare rocks in burning sunlight do they tremble
and quiver, seeming for less space than a second to be gone. Thus
instant by instant they go and return: and in the instant when they
are gone, they are departed a vast distance to another place, even so
to return. Thus do they almost dwell presently in two regions of
the universe: thus test they knowledge by knowledge and truth
by truth. Great is their aid for works of evocation, for works that
require a very high degree of activity in the Light: or of veracity.

47    *Calling Voices of the Bright Wilderness.*
△    These are of a region of whiteness, which cloudlike builds to any
form. They themselves appear most often in likeness of whirlwinds
or waterspouts that sway and move with a gliding motion: but
changeful and melodious is their song. They stir the minds and
bodies of those who seek them with fitting rites, to the magical
dance and to mystical drama in all its modes: any magical use of
the creative arts is of their nature.

48   *The Smiling Brothers, the Sentinels of the Silver Castle.*

△   In tunics of pearl, in surcoats of manifold hue, they guard walls of strong shining: their laughter is a lash of more avail than many arrows. Potent allies are they if thy work seeks converse with beings of the Higher Light, or if it be thy design to promote acuteness of intellect.

49   *Laughing Children of the Arrows of Cimah.*

△   These appear as white mares rearing and plunging, casting from their shining flanks the purple and peacock breakers of a level shore. Seek their aid for all works of blessing, or for any works or rites undertaken in a spirit of devotion to tradition.

50   *The Princes of Power, Voices of Thunder.*

△   Upon thrones of majesty these are established, each in his own hall: in heavy mantles of grey are they enwrapped, their hair and their beards are as black smoke curling upon itself. Their aid is given to those who seek it for works pertaining to leadership in high projects, or to magical direction of human affairs: but they will not answer to the first entreatment nor yet to the second: utter then the Call of the Ayre three times for these Princes.

51   *The Garlanded Ones, Knowers of the Mind that Shall Be.*

△   These appear in the likeness of sphynges that have the faces of young boys, but old in wisdom: their garlands be of serpents, which speak to them, and to which they give drink of yellow wine in goblets of alabaster. These Garlanded Ones will aid in works performed to attain an understanding of living creatures, or in works dependent upon such an understanding: they will guide also in magical explorations of the realms of Nature.

52   *The Shields of the Sky, the Wings of Mail.*

△   Strong is the song of these, as the voices of trumpets or of the organ: at the sound of their coming, the columns of granite quail and lean one to another. Seek their aid if thou wouldst have any work that thou desirest, performed by the hands of others: likewise for any work that is to be done in partnership.

53   *The Mercies of Everlastingness, the Vessels of Salt and of Honey.*

△   Pale Spirits are these, appearing in wide robes of whiteness: and in the midst of the brow of each, a shining flame. With them an odour as of myrrh, and of opoponax, and of lavender and of many sweet and bitter herbs. Many of them bear flasks of tears, and jars with offerings to the Shadowed Ones, that all be done in due measure. Seek therefore their aid in celebration of all rites of the dead, whether funerary or commemorative, whether Samhuinn also or Parentalia.

54   *Empalled Regents of Splendor, Governors of the Glittering Fane.*
△   These are seen as tall and stately forms swathed about in great mantles of azure, some light, some deeper in hue, some as the midnight. Their aid is meet for any operation that is performed to win ability to counsel wisely: if thou wilt call upon them for this work, on the eve of thy rite sleep thou upon a hill-top where is no human habitation, and on arising make obeisance to the place of sunrise.

55   *Keepers of the Mouths of the Winds.*
△   The habitations of these are as craggy islands in a lake of silver. Their aid is sought in works for the development of practical wisdom, and in works generally of an austere nature or purpose.

56   *Shadow-mantled Sages of the White Mountain beyond the Shores*
△   *of Mist.*
    Wouldst thou travel in thy flesh or in spirit to the foot of the sheer cliff-face which underlies their abode? Wouldst thou win their esteem or compassion with rites, austerities, meditations a thousand times repeated? Nor weariness nor zeal will move them: yet if thou call upon their name, they shall assist in operations which seek to receive inspired thought or mystical understanding, or to develop capacity for such.

57   *Lords of the Heavens of Crystal.*
△   These are encompassed in a shining place ever-changing, with tints of the rainbow and with sounds of strange voices singing: very calm is their aspect. Their heed is for works seeking to explore and to comprehend music, natural rhythm, harmonies: also for all works dependent upon the occult use of colour.

58   *Princes of Dominion, the Mighty Princes of the Lesser Seal.*
△   Great is their power in all works which seek to produce reform: great is their power to release influences of change upon the earth.

59   *Smiters of the hands of scorpions from the necks of the Living.*
△   Pale are they, and their garments are as ashes: yet are their eyes of diamond, and their hands as burnished blades. They fly swiftly without wings, and no place is sealed to them: they murmur, and the caverns beneath Barcaea have heard them. The White Work is theirs to aid, and also any work towards gaining new skill or power.

60   *The Crimson-robed Princes of the Wasteland.*
△   Upon the black rocks of the land of desolation have the Princes
cast their mantles, and they brood wordless: arouse them not for
light cause. Where works are performed for victory in thought
and word, as in matters of law, they will aid: great power and
high truth they will bring also to the consecration of a Sword.

61   *Those who pour upon the Earth Waters of Vision from Cups of*
△   *Celadon.*
Vast eyes are theirs, orbs of granite and of bland turquoise: some
among them bear pallid cups of gracious form, others bear sweet-
sounding harps. Grey is their vesture, girded with banded scarves of
blue and russet and crimson. They will aid in works of skrying, and
of converse with Elementals: in all works which require services
to be performed by true Elementals, these of the Waters of Vision
if sought will aid thine authority.

62   *The Sickles that Chaunt of the Day of Reaping.*
△   Their bodies are of silver mingled with gold, and in form as the leaves
of tall reeds: greatly exulting is their song, but the words of it are concealed. They will give most strong assistance to works which would
bring about the formulation of well-grounded plans, and the estab-
lishment thereof: also to works performed to gain visions of truth.

63   *Prophets of the Strong Tower, the Criers of Victory.*
△   These will give aid in works concerned to establish or to maintain
peace, inward or outward: also works to turn aside the weapons
of an assailant, or to avoid mischance.

64   *Daughters of the First, Strength of the Halls of Marble.*
△   These are seated at height and height: tremendous murmurings
circle about them: in their hands are emblems of dominion. He
who calls upon their aid shall gain it for rites of invisibility: likewise for works mathematical (such as the calculations of astrology)
or other purposes of an abstract nature.

65   *The Comforters whose Eyes are Basilisks of Ruby.*
▽   Dark are their taloned heels, dark from time's winepress and the
vats of death. Turn thy gaze only upon their talons, for most
dreadful is their countenance: look not upon it as in silence they
come, but utter thy will if thy work be of their kind: mighty is
their aid. These be for all works of Art Magick which depend for
operation upon the material remains or the psyche of the dead
(except such works as are comprised in 53 above).

66   *The Stewards of Fury, the Jasper-headed Princes of Rage.*

67-87 *The Powers of the Vials of Wrath.*
     (In operibus de sigillo AEMETH.)

88   *The Hoarse Voices, the Thorn-clad Sisters of Vengeance.*
▽    These run barefoot over the land and upon the waters. With their
     hands they twist the spear and beneath their feet they trample
     the caltrop. They flee, and smite not: yet through them is the
     slayer slain. They give aid for works undertaken to win success
     in commerce, for ceremonial works of divination in all forms, for
     operations toward recovery of stolen property.

89   *The Beryl-clad Ministers of Peace.*
▽    All veiled are these in a starry shining, bluish and greenish: and
     with them moves a shrill and joyous music of flutes. In troops do
     they go upward and downward, as moving in free air and not in
     bonds of earth. Works which concern them are those to further
     the interests of fraternal association, to give peace of mind, and
     for the circulation of earthly benefits.

90   *Bringers of Lights to the Feast.*
▽    These seem as a great host of small golden birds, but of count-
     enance human: most rapid of flight, and their voice is as the
     chiming of bells. Before thy rite, pour unto them the water of a
     swift-flowing stream, if the purpose of the operation be to work a
     good of which thou shalt not be known as the author.

91   *Singers at the Hidden Loom in the Citadel of Truth.*
▽    These are mantled in sad colours and upon their heads are garlands
     of rue, yet do they go upon the backs of lions. They will assist if
     thou dost call upon them at the institution of the Great Work:
     also for works of compassion, and for rites seeking protection
     during the night watches.

     *In the list of works included in the table above, naturally not
     every shade of possible application is expressed. Only hints could be
     given, and these are in many instances necessarily vague:— a greater
     explicitness would err by too closely limiting either the range or the
     level of application.*

If the magician be resolved to employ the Liber Scientiae in a rite, he will choose, as appropriate, *one only* of the 91 Aerial subdivisions. Invocation of the chosen forces of the Liber Scientiae is to be made at a critical point in the magical work which it is intended to implement (whether Enochian or other): earlier rather than later in the course of the rite, but not before the main lines thereof are developed and a channel has been established for the force invoked. If care be not taken as to this, the new force may rush in, ungoverned and ungovernable, to the ruin of the work. At the same time it is needful that the invocation should be made before the climax of the rite, so that the force brought into operation may unite with that proper to the rite itself. It is said, again, that in certain instances, the conditions being perfect, this invocation could produce an intended result with no other rite performed: but in such instances the conditions themselves might be understood as constituting the necessary magical framework.

It is therefore essential that the magician should first resolve upon his intended method of working, and should establish all the particulars of the ritual proper with its appurtenances, correspondences and action before considering the ancillary portion thereof which will derive from the Liber. When he then comes to plan that ancillary portion, the Element of the working,* be it $\triangledown$, $\triangle_{,}$, $\triangle$ or $\triangledown$, will already be established and will NOT depend upon the elemental sign attached to the Aerial subdivision of his choice, which may or may not coincide with the Element (or elemental affinity) of the working. As an example:— the evocation to visible appearance may be proposed, of a Spirit of Mars. The attribution of the working being ♂, the elemental affinity of the working is $\triangle$. It is possible that the Aerial subdivision chosen to assist the work may be number 46. The elemental sign of that subdivision is △: still, the elemental affinity of the working remains △. We shall return to this point presently.

A distinction is here drawn. In the case of an elemental working, reference can correctly and simply be made to "the Element of the working:" ▽, △, △ or ▽ as the case may be. In the case of a planetary working, where the Element associated with the working is established by affinity (△ for ♂, ▽ for ☿ and so on) this Element is properly referred to as the *elemental affinity* of the working. However, having acknowledged this distinction, we feel we have done our duty by it. Henceforward, in the present paper, for the sake of convenience, the Element of an elemental rite and the elemental affinity of a planetary rite will alike be referred to as "the Element of the working."

### *Order of Invocation of Forces of the Liber Scientiae*

The operator faces, across the Bomos, the quarter of the Element of the working; the relevant Enochian Tablet is displayed on the Bomos, letters uppermost.

The Second Angelic Key is vibrated, and is directly followed by vibration of the Key of the Thirty Ayres. The name of the Ayre to be uttered in this last Key will depend upon the Aerial subdivision chosen for the invocation: for example, if the subdivision chosen is 46, then upon consulting the columns of the Liber Scientiae the student will find that this is the first subdivision of the Sixteenth Ayre, the title of which is LEA. The opening words of the Key of the Thirty Ayres will therefore in this case be MADRIAX DS PRAF LEA . . . , O you hevens which dwell in the *Sixteenth Ayre* . . . Or as another example, if the subdivision chosen is 60, this is found to be the third subdivision of the Twentieth Ayre, the title of which is CHR.

Now is vibrated the appropriate name from column III of the Liber Scientiae. Pursuing our previous examples, in the case of subdivision 46 this name is CUCNRPT: in the case

of subdivision 60 it is TOTOCAN. At the same time that the
name is vibrated, the Sigil of that name is traced above the
surface of the Tablet and in a plane parallel to it, of a size not
exceeding the bounds of the Tablet. The names in column III
of the Liber are in fact Briatic, thus Archangelic: they are
drawn from the Enochian Elemental Tablets in accordance
with the *characteres symmetrici,* "divinely given harmonious
figures" or Sigils.* The initial letter of each of these names
appears upon its Tablet as a capital.

The Sigil which is to be traced with the name from
column III is of course the relevant one of the *characteres
symmetrici.* In our diagrams *(De Rebus Enochianis 1,* texts
b, c, d, e) we have numbered the *characteres* according to "the
unbroken succession of 91 parts". Thus, the Sigil for the
name CUCNRPT is numbered 46: the Sigil for TOTOCAN is
numbered 60. The diagram upon which the Sigil is to be found
can readily be identified by the elemental sign attached to
the subdivision.

---

It is at this stage of the procedure that the difference, if
such exists, between the Element of the working and the
elemental sign of the subdivision will come to the fore: the
Enochian Tablet upon the Bomos is that of the Element of
the working, while the Sigil to be traced above it relates to
the Element of the subdivision. If these are both of the same
Element, there is no difficulty. If however the Element of the
subdivision differs from that of the working, an invocation
must now be made of one of the four Great Elemental Kings.
The force resulting from this invocation of a King will not
directly affect the patterns and powers of the main working,
since it will be completely absorbed in refocusing the invoked
forces of the Liber, and in harmonising these with the Element

* See below, Note B.

of the working.

The method of achieving this can be illustrated by resuming one of our previous examples. In the evocation to visible appearance of a Spirit of ♂, the Element of the working is △, but the chosen Aerial subdivision is 46 which has the elemental sign of △. Immediately after vibration of the Briatic name of column III, CUCNRPT, with the simultaneous tracing of its Sigil, the Enochian Tablet of the working is turned over so that its Characters are uppermost. A circle is traced round the Tablet. The Sigil previously used is now traced again above the Tablet, this time however without vibration of the Briatic name. This done, invocation is made of the Elemental King of Fire *(the Element of the working),* as set forth in part III of this paper, the left hand in this instance not being placed upon the central Character of the Tablet, but upon that smaller Character T which is related to △ *(the Element of the Aerial subdivision).* Because of this difference in procedure, the words "and behold the [First, Second, or other] Seal whereon my hand is set" are omitted when the words of invocation are vibrated. Invocation of the King being concluded, the Tablet remains with the Characters uppermost until invocation of the forces of the Liber Scientiae has been concluded: should the Tablet not thereafter be required for use with letters uppermost, it remains with the Characters uppermost until the conclusion of the main working.

To take a different example. In the consecration of a Talisman of ☉, the Element of the working is △, but the chosen Aerial subdivision is 31 which has the elemental sign of ▽. Immediately after vibration of the Briatic name of column III, MOLPAND, with the simultaneous tracing of its Sigil, the Tablet of the working (△) is turned over so that its Characters are uppermost. A circle is traced round the Tablet. The Sigil is traced again above the Tablet, without vibration of the name. This done, invocation is made of the Elemental King of Air *(the Element of the working),* the left hand in this instance being placed upon that smaller Character $\frac{b|6}{4|b}$ which is related to $\triangledown$ (*the Element of the Aerial subdivision*).

---

Now, following vibration of the name from column III, with the simultaneous tracing of its Sigil (or following invocation of the Great Elemental King if this was necessary), the appropriate name from column VIII of the Liber Scientiae is vibrated: this is the name of the Yetziratic Angel King. In the case of subdivision 46 this name is ZIRACAH, in the case of subdivision 60 it is ALPUDUS, and so on. The Liber Scientiae gives twelve names of Ruling Angel Kings, and it will be observed that each of the subdivisions of the Liber is represented at the Yetziratic level by one or other of these twelve names.

The final part of the order of invocation relates to the Yetziratic Ministers of the chosen subdivision. The number of Spirits of each subdivision is given in column VI of the Liber. This number, and the title of the Ministers as in the A.S. table, are incorporated into the utterance (with any needful grammatical adjustment), together with the name of the Ayre, as the following examples illustrate.

(Subdivision 46)

O you Spirits of the 24th Part of a Moment, Timeless Movers, you whose number is nine thousand nine hundred and twenty: thus in the name LEA do I move you.

(Subdivision 60)

O you Crimson-robed Princes of the Wasteland, you whose number is three thousand six hundred and thirty four: thus in the name CHR do I move you.

(Subdivision 63)

O Prophets of the Strong Tower, you Criers of Victory, you whose number is five thousand six hundred and fifty-eight: thus in the name ASP do I move you.

(Subdivision 39)

O Daughters of Death, Guardians of the Secrets Eight Nine Eight Seven, you whose number is four thousand two hundred and thirteen: thus in the name ZIM do I move you.

(Subdivision 37)

O you keepers of the Mystery wherein are the Swords six hundred thousand of length, you whose number is eight thousand one hundred and eleven: thus in the name ZIM do I move you.

*Summary Analysis of the Foregoing*

> Vibration of the Second Key
> |
> Key of the Thirty Ayres, with title of appropriate Ayre (col. V)
> |
> Vibration of Briatic name (col. III)
> and tracing of its Sigil
>
> { Here may be included the invocation of a Great Elemental King (if Element of working differs from Element of subdivision)
>
> Vibration of Yetziratic name (col. VIII)
> |
> Address to Yetziratic Ministers

*Notes:*

A)    None of the three subdivisions of the Tenth Ayre, 28, 29, 30, is used in connection with the order of invocation given above. The use of the Briatic names of these subdivisions in column III, in connection with the First Angelic Key, has been indicated.

B)    When, in invocation of the forces of the Liber Scientiae, subdivision 65 is employed, the Briatic name PAOAOAN (col. III) is not used. The Sigil which belongs to subdivision 65 shows the Briatic name LAXDIZI, and this is the name rightfully to be vibrated when subdivision 65 is employed in invocation of the forces of the Liber. The name PAOAOAN is entirely reserved to vibration with the Second Angelic Key in the use of that Key independently of the Key of the Thirty Ayres.

*N.B. All Enochian words and Angelic Keys given in De Rebus Enochianis appear in Appendix C according to the A.S. system of pronunciation.*

# INDEX OF WORKS

*This index is intended to provide the student with a means of easy reference to the various works indicated in the A.S. documentation on the aerial subdivisions of Liber Scientiae (pages 232 through 244). Each entry is followed by the number of the aerial subdivision to which it relates.*

# PART V

# CONSECRATIONS

*XXIV*

*THE HOLY PENTACLES**

1. *The Topaz Lamen* is the especial Lamen of the Adeptus Minor, worn by him for Inner Order group-workings, and for private works relating *directly* to his personal mystical life. In basic form, a Greek Cross, with a topaz set at the centre, suspended invariably from a collar of white silk. The cross may be 4½ cm. to 7½ cm. in height, and may be of gold, silver-gilt, jewellers' bronze, or gilded wood; the topaz should preferably be a genuine stone.

2. *The Pentacle of the Quintessence* is the general Lamen of the Adeptus Minor, worn by him for works which do not require the high authority of the Topaz and which do not directly relate to the mystical development of the wearer.† In form, the Pentacle of the Quintessence is a disc not exceeding 8 cm. in diameter. The field of the Pentacle on both sides is white. The obverse bears the Symbol of the Quintessence in black, surrounded by a narrow circular border of scarlet. The reverse of this Pentacle will be blank unless a sigil is shown thereon: in neither case is there a circular border. The Pentacle of the

*The symbol
of
the Quintessence*

* Pentacle, from the French *pendre au col*.

† The individual magician may well devise and create his own general Lamen for use in place of the Pentacle of the Quintessence. This should represent his work and authority as he sees it.

249

Quintessence is suspended from a collar of the colour appropriate to the working, or may be suspended from a chain about the neck. In the latter case, an over-vestment (cloak, stole, tabard, etc., as preferred) may be added as a colour charge, though this would be unnecessary if the basic robe itself were of the colour indicated for the working.

3. *The Enochian Pentacles*. For essentially Enochian workings, that is, workings whose main attributions and framework are Enochian, the following Pentacles are employed. In form they are discs not exceeding 8 cm. in diameter.

For Air, the Character of the Air Tablet is depicted on the natural ground-colour of the disc, the Tau Cross in dove-grey, the four surmounting beams or flames in white. The Pentacle has a border of red. It is suspended from a yellow collar; or from a chain, in which case the colour-charge of yellow is otherwise worn.

For Water, the Character of the Water Tablet is depicted on the natural ground-colour of the disc, wholly in blue-grey. The Pentacle has a border of green. It is suspended from a blue collar; or from a chain, in which case the colour-charge of blue is otherwise worn.

For Earth, the Character of the Earth Tablet is depicted on the natural ground-colour of the disk, in dove-grey. The Pentacle has a black border. It is suspended from a green collar; or from a chain, in which case the colour-charge of green is otherwise worn.

For Fire, the Character of the Fire Tablet is depicted on the natural ground-colour of the disc, in blue-grey. The Pentacle has a border of white. It is suspended from a red collar; or from a chain, in which case the colour-charge of red is otherwise worn.

The reverse of each of these Pentacles is blank, unless the Pentacle is intended for use in a rite of evocation to visible appearance, in which case the appropriate sigil is depicted thereon. In all cases, the Pentacle is lacquered on both sides.

4. *The Lamen of the Work or the Great Pentacle* is the especial distinguishing symbol in the Outer of the authority of the Magus, the Celebrant in the Outer. None other may wear this Lamen on any occasion  soever, and the Magus himself wears it only when conducting official Order rites in the Outer. In form the Lamen of the Work is a disc not exceeding 8 cm. in diameter. On both sides, the field of the disc is black: on the obverse it bears the design of a green square interlaced with a yellow lozenge, containing an equal-armed cross of white, voided, which in turn contains a smaller equal-armed cross of scarlet. The whole of this design  is surrounded by a narrow circular border of violet. On the reverese, the Lamen bears the Symbol of the Quintessence, in scarlet, surrounded by a narrow circular border of white.

The Great Pentacle is, in certain circumstances, allowed to be embroidered upon the robe of the Magus; specific modifications to the design are for this purpose provided by the A.S.

5. *The Pentacle of the New Life* is the Lamen of the Chief of the Aurum Solis exclusively. In form it is a disc not exceeding 8 cm. in diameter. The field of the Pentacle on both sides is black. The design of the obverse is as the Banner of the New Life. On the reverese, the Pentacle bears the symbol of the Quintessence.

6. *The Lamen of the Sodalites* is the Lamen of the members of the College of the Aurum Solis (other than the Chief). In form it is a disc not exceeding 8 cm. in diameter. The field of the Pentacle on both sides is black. The obverse bears a cross potent in white, enclosed by a narrow circular border of white. On the reverse, the Pentacle bears the Symbol of the Quintessence.

*NOTE*

*Concerning The Preparation Of An Anointing Oil For Use In Aurum Solis Rites*

The student should prepare, for use in his magical workings, a planetary anointing oil of his own devising. Such an oil, while unique to himself, will be magically balanced and suitable for any working in which he may wish to use it.

The method of determining the proportions for any blend based on planetary correspondences, is to use either the medieval planetary numbers or the Qabalistic numbers of the Spheres, thus:—

| Planet | Medieval Number | Qabalistic Number |
|--------|-----------------|-------------------|
| Saturn | 8 | 3 |
| Jupiter | 4 | 4 |
| Mars | 9 | 5 |
| Sun | 1 | 6 |
| Venus | 6 | 7 |
| Mercury | 5 | 8 |
| Moon | 2 | 9 |

That is to say, if employing the medieval system the student will have *eight* parts of a Saturnian substance with *four* parts of a Jupiterian substance and *nine* parts of a Martian substance, and so on; but employing the Qabalistic system there will be *three* parts Saturnian, four parts Jupiterian, *five* parts Martian, and so on. Oils suitable for inclusion are sugggested below; the student should use only one for each planet. He may if he wishes substitute other aromatic oils of suitable attribution, but Olive Oil should never be omitted.

*Saturn:* Cassia, Violet, Myrrh. *Jupiter:* Olive. *Mars:* Nicotiana, Spearmint. *Sun:* Olibanum, Cinnamon. *Venus:* Bergamot, Rose, Verbena, Sandalwood. *Mercury:* Lavender, Anise, Fennel. *Moon:* Jasmine, Almond, Camphor.

The chosen oils should be blended within the period of a waxing moon, and during any seasonal Tide except *Tempus eversionis*. Having made ready beforehand in the Chamber of Art all that is needed, the student should begin the work at sunrise with the Morning Adoration. He should then perform the Setting of the Wards of Power, and should proceed forthwith to the preparation of his anointing oil.

## XXV

## THE HIGH CONSECRATION OF THE TESSERA

*Tides:—*
> Tempus sementis, New Moon, Akasha.

*Magician:—*
> Basic robe, etc. Pentacle of Quintessence. Colour-charge white (cf. *The Holy Pentacles.*)

*Bomos:—*
> Spectrum yellow drape.

*Equipment on Bomos:—*
> 1. The Tessera.
> 2. The Lamp.
> 3. Lustral vessel and Water.*
> 4. Phial of Anointing Oil.
> 5. Bell.
> 6. Lighting taper.
> (A small finger-linen)

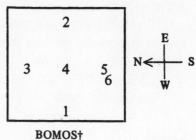

BOMOS†

*Strike once upon the bell.*

*Perform the Hebrew Setting of the Wards of Power, beginning from East of Bomos; if working Sub Rosa Nigra, use the Setting of the Wards of Adamant.*

---

\* Lustral water may be freshly gathered sea-water, or sweet water to which a small quantity of sea-salt has been added.

† It is to be generally understood that whenever the Bomos is present in a working and no position assigned to it, it stands in the centre of the place of working.

*Go to West of Bomos, face East. Make and maintain Ave;\* intone the Latin Invocation of the Eternal:—*

| | |
|---|---|
| **AVE ORTUS OMNIUM,** | Hail, Beginning of all things, |
| **TU IPSE SINE ORTU;** | Thou thyself without beginning; |
| **AVE FINIS OMNIUM,** | Hail, End of all things, |
| **TU IPSE SINE FINE;** | Thou thyself without end; |
| **AVE VITA OMNIUM,** | Hail, Life of all things, |
| **TU IPSE ULTRA OMNES MUNDOS.** | Thou thyself beyond all worlds! |

*Dismiss the Ave.*

*Vibrate the First Enochian Key, and follow this with:—*

Thus do I invoke you, you Great Archangels LEXARPH, COMANAN, TABITOM, whose garments of light are beautified with admiration, and who dwell within the radiance of the Eternal.

*Strike 1-2-1-2 upon the bell, and intone the Ogdoadic Catena:—*

Salutation and again salutation to the High Guardians of the Glorious Star, who were, and are, and are to come. Salutation and again salutation in the splendour of the Star which unites us.

O you High Guardians, Hidden Adepti, Dwellers in Eternity: you have given signs and you have shown wonders, and you have revealed yourselves unto your children.

EN GIRO TORTE SOL CICLOS ET ROTOR IGNE.

Such are the Words, such is the Greeting!

*Strike once upon the bell before continuing with the Catena.*

In a voice of mystery do we call upon you, High Guardians, we who are the continuators of your Work: O Luminous Ones, behold and hear us. Not without our own questing do we ask to know, nor without our own endeavour to attain: but that the sowing shall be crowned in the harvest. For oneness of purpose do we call unto you, for that joy of resolve which is the wine of the will, transforming all that was strange to it. For living light and for luminous life do we call unto you, O Hidden High Ones! So Light and Life shall be drawn at last to the radiance of one Star, and that Star shall mount to the unshadowed height.

---

\* See *The Setting of the Wards of Adamant.*

*Strike once upon the bell, then vibrate the Greek from the Hymnodia Krypte of Hermes Trismegistus, Logos XIII, 18:—*

| | |
|---|---|
| ΑΙ ΔΥΝΑΜΕΙΣ ΑΙ ΕΝ ΕΜΟΙ | O powers within me, |
| ΎΜΝΕΙΤΕ ΤΟ ΕΝ ΚΑΙ ΤΟ ΠΑΝ | hymn the One and the All: |
| ΣΥΝΑΙΣΑΤΕ ΤΩΙ ΘΕΛΗΜΑΤΙ ΜΟΥ | chant in harmony with my will, |
| ΠΑΣΑΙ ΑΙ ΕΝ ΕΜΟΙ ΔΥΝΑΜΕΙΣ | all ye Powers within me! |
| ΓΝΩΣΙΣ ʽΑΓΙΑ | Holy Gnosis, |
| ΦΩΤΙΣΘΕΙΣ ΑΠΟ ΣΟΥ | illuminated by thee, |
| ΔΙΑ ΣΟΥ ΤΟ ΝΟΗΤΟΝ ΦΩΣ ΎΜΝΩΝ | through thee I hymn the light of thought, |
| ΧΑΙΡΩ ΕΝ ΧΑΙΡΑΙ ΝΟΥ | I rejoice in the joy of the mind. |
| ΠΑΣΑΙ ΔΥΝΑΜΕΙΣ ΎΜΝΕΙΤΕ ΣΥΝ ΕΜΟΙ | All ye Powers, chant with me! |

*Go to the East: perform Orthrochoros.\* Conclude in East, return to West of Bomos. Facing East, make the Ave.*

*Strike once upon the bell.*

*Extending both palms above the Tessera, declaim:—*

Light and Life shall be drawn at last to the radiance of one Star, and that Star shall mount to the unshadowed height.

FIAT.          FIAT.          FIAT.

*Take the Tessera with the left hand, and place it upon the palm of the right hand. Dip the forefinger of the left hand into the lustral water, then trace clockwise upon the surface of the Tessera the white square, beginning with the top left corner. Keeping the Tessera in this position, raise the left hand above it, and intone:—*

Hear now, O Tessera, concerning the Body!

Certain as the morning, established as the fertile plains, She awaits time without time. She contemplates that which comes to pass, in beauty and stillness as of mountain summits that gaze into heaven's height. As the calm brightness of a lake, taking to itself the hue of day

---

\* See *Principles of Ceremonial.*

and of night, so without changing is She transfigured: as the depth of the ocean, as the tranquil swell of the waters, so rests the Soul of Earth in the presence of inspiration divine!

*Transfer the Tessera to the palm of the left hand. With the taper in the right hand, take flame from the lamp. With the lighted taper, trace clockwise, slightly above the surface of the Tessera, the red lozenge, beginning from the topmost point. This done, extinguish the taper and replace it on the Bomos. Maintaining the position of the Tessera on the left palm, raise the right hand above it, and intone:—*

Hear now, O Tessera, concerning the Breath!

Behold, as lightning's fire descends to earth or red flame leaps from earth to the celestial vault, so does He speed. As the rushing of wind, as the high song that calls above the valleys, as its wild song that cries among the branches, so does He exult. As the whirling dance of the storm, so the Victorious Spirit moves all things as He wills: even thus is the triumph of Divinity, over, and through, and entwined with all!

*With both hands, hold the Tessera horizontally at about the level of the solar plexus:—*

And as She is the Form in all things, so He is in all things the Breath of Life. Hail, entwined emblem of that unity, and symbol of the Work! 'The One whose coming forth is as the Phoenix and whose rising is like unto the Morning Star' shall be thy name.

*The Tessera is replaced on the Bomos. Place the right hand on the Tessera, the left hand on the Pentacle of the Quintessence:—*

Hear, O Tessera, concerning the King of Intellectual Fire. Hear concerning the Giver of Light, the Master who holds the Key of the fountain which sustains life; and who makes to flow from on high, into the terrestrial world, the powers of life and of increase.

He dwells above the aether: his throne is the centre, and his ensign is an effulgent circle, yea, the heart of the world! With sustaining power he fills all things, and evokes within man the light of the mind.

| (Hebrew) | (Sub Rosa Nigra) |
|---|---|
| Wherefore, O Tessera, in the Name YHVH ELOAH V'DAATH I conjure thee, that thou gather unto thyself the solar radiance. And further, O Tessera, by NAChASh coiled about the Tau Cross I conjure thee, even in the Name YHShVH, that thou send forth lifegiving beams. | Wherefore, O Tessera, in the Name ONOPHIS I conjure thee, that thou gather unto thyself the solar radiance. And further, O Tessera, by KNOUPHIS encircling the Equal Cross I conjure thee, even by the AGATHODAIMON, that thou send forth life-giving beams. |

*The right hand is now raised, to touch with its palm the left hand upon the Pentacle of the Quintessence. As soon as this movement is completed, both hands are lowered simultaneously to grasp the Tessera.*

*The Tessera is raised high in both hands, face uppermost: it is held thus, while the following is intoned:—*

And now, O you Hidden Adepti, Dwellers in Eternity, whose powerful protection encompasses the Glorious Star of Regeneration: to you we raise this Holy Tessera: behold, the Sign upon it is your own, and to your dominion do we make offering of it. Receive, O Mighty Ones, this Holy Tessera at our hands. Thus shall it not only be to us a symbol of the Great Work, but also shall it be our true bond with you, in the high Company of that Star which has been revered though the ages.

*The Tessera is replaced on the Bomos.*

*The lustral vessel being held in the left hand, the second finger of the right hand is dipped, and the lustral water is touched to the topmost point of the emblem upon the Tessera. The finger is then dipped again, and the next point in deosil succession is touched. The finger is again dipped in the lustral water: and so on, the process of dipping the finger and touching it to a point of the figure being performed eight times in all, so that all the points are touched in deosil order. (In this action, the interlaced figure is treated as a unity, and in consequence the points touched are alternately red and white.) At the lustration of each point, one word is uttered aloud, as follows:—*

| | |
|---|---|
| *Topmost red point:* | EN |
| *Top right white point:* | GIRO |
| *Right-hand red point:* | TORTE |
| *Lower right white point:* | SOL |
| *Lowest red point:* | CICLOS |
| *Lower left white point:* | ET |
| *Left-hand red point:* | ROTOR |
| *Top left white point:* | IGNE |

(N.B.  The "circle" is not joined in this instance.)

*The lustral vessel is replaced. With the taper in the right hand, take flame from the lamp, and trace a circle deosil around the Tessera as it lies upon the Bomos. Within that circle, slightly above and parallel to the surface of the Tessera, the octagram is traced with the flame of the taper, thus:—*

*and with the tracing of each successive line of the figure, a word of the Formula* EN GIRO TORTE SOL CICLOS ET ROTOR IGNE *is vibrated. Thus, while tracing the first vertical, vibrate* EN; *while tracing the first oblique line vibrate* GIRO; *while tracing the first horizontal line vibrate* TORTE; *and so on. The tracing of this figure, with the vibrating of the words, should be executed smoothly so as to form a continuous whole.*

*The taper is extinguished and replaced on the Bomos.*
*NOW PROJECT UPON THE TESSERA BY THE ORANTE FORMULA.*

*Strike 8-8-8 upon the bell.*

* See Paper VIII.

*The phial of Anointing Oil being held in the left hand, oil is taken upon the ball of the right thumb. The Phial is replaced, and with the left hand the Tessera is held but not lifted. A small equal-armed cross is now marked upon the centre of the Tessera with the right thumb, the first stroke from left to right, the second being drawn towards the operator.*

*Hold the left hand slightly above the surface of the Tessera, and place the right hand on the Pentacle of the Quintessence:—*

Into life renewed are the givers of life interwoven!

O Mystic Force outpouring, dark or bright, eight-rayed splendour of the Spiritual Sun! In thy radiance do we share, in thy most secret Centre are we hidden: that the Gold of the Sun may be glorified, and that the wonders of the Treasure House may be ever renewed.

*The left hand is raised to touch with its palm the right hand on the Pentacle of the Quintessence. As soon as this movement is completed, both hands are lowered simultaneously to grasp the Tessera; The Tessera is raised high vertically in both hands:—*

I proclaim the Mystical Tessera: 'The One whose coming forth is as the Phoenix and whose rising is like unto the Morning Star'!

I proclaim the Elder and Veritable Symbol of the Great Work!

I proclaim a true bond with the Hidden Adepti, the Dwellers in Eternity!

*The Tessera is replaced on the Bomos.*

*Strike once upon the bell.*

*If working Sub Rosa Nigra, intone Casmen III, "The Holy One shall arise" etc., as follows; for Hebrew working, intone the Resh stanza of the Song of Praises as given after Casmen III.*

The Holy One shall arise
And his voice shall cry in the dawn,
Yea, his mighty voice shall cry in the dawn.
He shall go forth in his name Knouphis
And his crown of light shall enkindle the worlds.

A thousand Aeons shall adore him,
And men shall seek death.
The earth shall tremble,
The voice of the Holy One shall sound in the tempest.
    The Gnostic shall stand in contemplation.
He shall lift up his hands in adoration.
Above him shall be the Diadem of Light,
And these shall be the words of the Gnostic:—
"Terror and vastness are about me
But the broad wings of the Serpent enfold me.
The fleeing darkness is before me,
But I keep in concealment the glory which is mine
And the time is not yet when I shall unveil my face;
Yet I stand in majesty and power and bliss unending."
These shall be the words of the Gnostic in adoration of the Holy One.

*(The Resh stanza of the Song of Praises:—)*
Rise in thy splendour, O King! — glorious brow,
                       gaze on thy governance
Gladdening all who behold! Soaring as song,
                       rule and illuminate:
Crysoleth gleaming thy crown, rise and inspire,
                       Lion-gold, Falcon-flight,
           Joyous, ambrosial!

*Strike once upon the bell. Proceed to East. Perform Dyseochoros,\* finishing in East. Return to West of Bomos. Face East, and make the Ave. After dismissing the Ave, intone the first section of the Ogdoadic Catena:—*
Salutation and again salutation to the High Guardians of the Glorious Star, who were, and are, and are to come. Salutation and again salutation in the splendour of the Star which unites us.
O you High Guardians, Hidden Adepti, Dwellers in Eternity: you have given signs and you have shown wonders, and you have revealed yourselves unto your children.
EN GIRO TORTE SOL CICLOS ET ROTOR IGNE.
Such are the Words, such is the Greeting!
*Strike 3-5-3 upon the bell.*

---

\* See *Principles of Ceremonial.*

*Notes:*

**A)** The Tessera consists of a square of wood (any wood of neutral colour is suitable) approximately 4" along each side and 3/8" thick. On its obverse it bears the design of the interlaced squares: the square whose sides are parallel to those of theTessera itself being in white, the other square (sometimes referred to as the lozenge) being red. On its reverse, in black, is the Sign of the Quintessence.* The whole is varnished with a clear shellac.

**B)** Between workings, the consecrated Tessera is to be kept wrapped in silk: in use, the Mystical Tessera is placed unwrapped upon the altar of the working, or is otherwise positioned suitably in rites which do not make use of an altar.

**C)** In the text of the Rite of Consecration of the Tessera, the magician speaks sometimes in the plural number—*In a voice of mystery do we call upon you, High Guardians, we who are the continuators of your Work*— and sometimes in the singular—*Thus do I invoke you, you Great Archangels . . .*

The text itself is invariable: that is to say, the magician who consecrates a Tessera by this rite on behalf of the Order, utters the words exactly as we give them, and so does the magical student consecrating a Tessera solely for his own use. The explanation of the variation between *I* and *we* in that text is therefore in no way related to the actual number of persons present. In fact, there are certain passages in which the magician must speak as an individual, though he consecrate on behalf of any number of brethren: thus for instance *Wherefore, O Tessera . . . I conjure thee,* and *I proclaim the Mystical Tessera*—acts which, in spirit as well as physically, can only be performed by the individual—but *To you we raise this Holy Tessera,* and *In thy radiance do we share,* because here are acts which are in the context communal by nature, and even the solitary magical student is not so entirely alone in his ritual as he

* See *The Holy Pentacles.*

may sometimes appear to be. The Consecration of the Tessera brings out this point very clearly: *Thus shall it not only be to us a symbol of the Great Work, but also shall it be our true bond with you, in the high Company of that Star which has been revered through the ages.* With that Company of the Western Tradition does the true student of the Mysteries speak and act in unity, although never losing his responsibility as an individual.

D)    The combination of Tides* cited above—Tempus sementis, New Moon, Akasha—is the optimum for this consecration. However, *Moon new to approaching full, Akasha,* is permissible if strictly necessary during any seasonal tide but Tempus eversionis. None save the Adeptus Plenus may consecrate a Tessera during Tempus eversionis.

* See Book III, Chapter VIII.

## XXVI

## SUB ROSA NIGRA
### THE CONSECRATION OF THE GREAT WAND OR SPEAR

*Tides:—*
First quarter Moon, Akasha.
*Magician:—*
Basic robe, etc. Pentacle of Quintessence. Colour-charge white.
*Bomos:—*
White drape.
*Equipment on Bomos:—*

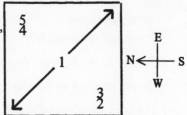

1. Great Wand (head to N.W., butt to S.E.)
2. Thymiaterion.
3. Incense boat.
4. Phial of Oil.
5. The Mystical Tessera.
(A small finger-linen)

Flanking the Bomos, and quite close to it, are two tall candlesticks, or white lamps upon pedestals, one to the North of the Bomos and one to the South. In moving round the Bomos during the working, the operator will pass outside these lights.

*Perform the Setting of the Wards of Adamant, beginning from East of Bomos.*

*Go to West of Bomos, face East. Declaim Casmen II:—*

Hear the Oracles concerning Melanotheos.

He is pursuer of all who seek him not:

They awaken, they turn to find him who has bestirred them;

But he has withdrawn. Beyond the deep of night he has withdrawn.

To the imaging of the mind's lone seeking

The Unmanifest seems as the myriad flame-particles which shadow
forth his being.

One only is there, one in all her forms, to whom without cease
he draws nigh.
She whom he seeks is found, and sought, and found in all worlds to
Time's ending.
Therefore as a quest is Existence transmitted to all;
Therefore is Love the pulse of all being, and the lance of Light is
the source of life.
In silence and darkness he moves
But that which he has wrought shines in flame, dances in water,
And to all who know him through that which he has wrought, the
Father of All is manifold:
The thronging Star-Lords, Daimones,
The glittering dew of heaven imaging the seed-horde of godhead—
The myriad of the star-host in the body of the Goddess of Infinite
Space.
She gives oneness to that multitude, for to her he is one,
And the Gnostic for whom she is Wisdom knows him as one, Melanotheos.
Io, Melanotheos!
Daimones Poliastres, Io!

*Strike with the right hand upon the left 1-1.*

*Strew incense upon the coals of the thymiaterion.*

*Pass deosil to south-east corner of the Bomos, and face north-west across it. Take up the Great Wand, grasping the shaft at about its centre with right hand, and hold it horizontally, symmetrically across your genitals. Proceed thus, deosil, to north-west corner of the Bomos, and face south-east across it.*

*Keeping the right hand at the same position upon the Great Wand, raise the Great Wand so that is is held vertically, the right hand now being held about 12" before you at the level of the heart-centre: the left hand is raised so that its palm supports the butt of the Great Wand in this position.*

*Holding this position throughout, intone each Greek*

*vowel upon its given note, following it with its corresponding utterance upon the same note:—\**

 I   We hymn thee, invisible mystical Spear, living

Spring of the seed of existence;

 E   Then let there descend from thy terrible splendour

a gentle reflection in blessing

 H   While praises are raised to thee, ancient yet ageless,

great Nature's all-radiant creator.

 Ω   Thou older than Nogah or Kokab, thou Sower of

golden the foam of the Zodiac,

 O   Thou Strong One, we honor thy sovereign Wand,

we acknowledge the rod of thy dominance,

 Υ   Saluting thee, viewless one, Numen renewing the

youth of the universe, Kyrie!

 A   Thy masks are the stallion and ram, while the stars

in their vastnesses answer thee, Father!

 We hymn thee, Resplendence, thou great and most

holy one, glory of unity, Father!

\* The notes given represent the harmonic minor key of C. The operator is free to use any harmonic minor key that he finds convenient, provided that the same sequence of intervals be employed.

The initial Greek vowels, and each accented syllable of the utterances, should be stressed and prolonged somewhat in intoning.

No Greek vowel precedes the eighth utterance. When this is reached, continue directly with the utterance itself upon its given note.

Still maintaining the hands with the Great Wand in the same position, proceed deosil to south-east corner of Bomos and face north-west across it. Raise left hand to grasp the Great Wand just below the right hand, which now relinquishes its hold. The Great Wand remains vertical, but is now lowered conveniently for the next phase of the operation:—

Intone the following Greek vowels to their given notes,* and as each is intoned, trace above the top of the Great Wand with the right hand the sigil of the corresponding name which is shown in brackets.†

I          (ΙΕΗΩΟΥΑ  -  ☉)

E          (ΕΗΩΟΥΑΙ  -  ☿)

H          (ΗΩΟΥΑΙΕ  -  ♀)

Ω          (ΩΟΥΑΙΕΗ  -  ♄ planetary)

O          (ΟΥΑΙΕΗΩ  -  ♂)

Υ          (ΥΑΙΕΗΩΟ  -  ♃)

A          (ΑΙΕΗΩΟΥ  -  ☽)

ΙΕΗΩΟΥΑ  (ΙΕΗΩΟΥΑ  -  ♄ supernal)

* Or to the corresponding notes in the preferred key.

† The bracketed name is not to be vibrated but is for the construction of the sigil only; the planetary indication given with the bracketed name in each case refers both to the presigillum required and to the kamea from which the sigillic line is to be obtained. The sigil name and the sound which is to be intoned are identical only in the final instance, the name being uttered in full in its radical form.

*With the right hand now grasp the Great Wand at about the centre of the shaft, that is, just above the left hand. The left hand relinquishes its hold. The Great Wand is now raised vertically so that the right hand is at the level of the heart-centre. The left hand is raised so that its palm supports the butt of the Great Wand.*

*Proceed thus, deosil, to West of Bomos, and face East.*

*Lower the left hand, strike once with the butt of the Great Wand upon the centre of the Bomos; then lay tne Wand with its head towards the North, its butt towards the South, upon the western side of the Bomos.*

*The Phial of Oil being held in the left hand, oil is taken upon the ball of the right thumb. The Phial is replaced. The Great Wand being steadied with the left hand, the head of the Great Wand is anointed twice.*

*With the right hand, take the Great Wand just below the centre of the shaft, and hold it across your chest so that the head points obliquely upwards towards your left shoulder. Proceed thus, deosil, to south-west corner of Bomos, and face north-east across it.*

*Raise the Great Wand, extending your right arm so as to point with the Great Wand in a straight line towards the north-east, but upwards at an angle of about 45°. After a moment, flex the elbow so as to bring the Great Wand back to its previous position, pointing obliquely upwards towards your left shoulder. Proceed thus, deosil, to West of Bomos, and face East.*

*Raise the Great Wand on high and proclaim:—*

Thus have I consecrated the Great Wand: ἘΡΣΑΔΟΤΗΣ ΟΥΡΑΝΙΟΣ is its name.

*The Great Wand is replaced on the Bomos in its original position, head to north-west, butt to south-east.*

*Strike with the right hand upon the left 1-1.*

*Intone Hymne à l'Etre Suprême:—*\*

Father of Worlds, supreme Intelligence
Whose bounties on unheeding man are poured,
To thankfulness thou art revealed, and thence
    By thankfulness adored.

The hills, the winds, the seas, thy temple are:
Nor past nor present marks thy endless reign:
The worlds thou fillest from star to furthest star
    Cannot thy power contain.

Thou art the source of all, of all the cause:
All things are bathed in thy divinity:
Out of thy worship rise all rightful laws,
    And from laws, Liberty.

Liberty, scourge most dire to those who scorn
Thy glorious justice in their pride perverse,
Out of that same great thought of thine was born
    Which framed the universe.

Thy champion, mighty God! is Liberty,
Who shows to earthly hearts thy visage true
In nature: thus thine altars unto thee
    She consecrates anew.

O thou who makest, like a spark, at will
The great sun to flame forth in day above,
Do more: our hearts with living wisdom fill,
    Kindle them with thy love.

Make thou our souls strong against tyranny,
Against ambition vain, and pride of place:
Against those worse-than-tyrants, flattery,
    Sloth, and corruption base.

---

\* Composed by Desorgues in 1794 e.v., for Robespierre's Festival. A.S. translation.
For original text see Note F below.

Mend thou our errors, make us true and just,
Reign in the great Beyond eternally:
Hold fast all nature to thy rule august —
Leave man his liberty!

*Strike with the right hand upon the left 3-5-3.*

*Notes:*

A)   Between workings, the Great Wand should be kept wrapped in silk.

B)   The Great Wand or Spear consists of a shaft of ash-wood surmounted by a suitably proportioned spearhead. The shaft should be cylindrical, plain, and polished; the spearhead should be of gilded metal. The overall length of shaft and head should be 24".

C)   As incense for this particular working, the student is recommended to use a Jupiterian compound with an undertone of Saturnian aromatics: cedarwood and nutmeg should predominate, oil of violet being suggested as one of the trace ingredients.

D)   It is most desirable that the student should commit to memory, so as to be able to reproduce them vocally in the working, the musical tones given in the text. However, a companion may assist in the place of working, by sounding the musical tones upon an instrument, or by playing a previously-made recording of these tones.

E)   The name of the Great Wand signifies Heavenly Dew-Giver.

F)      Père de l'univers, suprême intelligence,
        Bienfaiteur ignoré des aveugles mortels,
        Tu révélas ton être à la reconnaissance,
            Qui seule éleva tes autels.

        Ton temple est sur les monts, dans les airs, sur les ondes:
        Tu n'as point de passé, tu n'as point d'avenir:
        Et sans les occuper, tu remplis tous les mondes
            Qui ne peuvent te contenir.

        Tout émane de toi, grande et première cause:
        Tout s'épure aux rayons de ta divinité:
        Sur ton culte immortel la morale repose,
            Et sur les mœurs, la liberté.

        Pour venger leur outrage et ta gloire offensée
        L'auguste liberté, ce fléau des pervers,
        Sortit au même instant de ta grande pensée
            Avec le plan de l'univers.

Dieu puissant! elle seule a vengé ton injure,
De ton culte elle-même instruisant les mortels,
Leva le voile épais qui couvrait la nature,
    Et vint absoudre tes autels.

O toi! qui du néant ainsi qu'une étincelle
Fis jaillir dans les airs l'astre éclatant du jour:
Fais plus... verse en nos cœurs ta sagesse immortelle,
    Embrâse-nous de ton amour.

De la haine des rois anime la Patrie,
Chasse les vains désirs, l'injuste orgeuil des rangs,
Le luxe corrupteur, la basse flatterie,
    Plus fatale que les tyrans.

Dissipe nos erreurs, rend-nous bons, rend-nous justes,
Règne, règne au-delà du tout illimité:
Enchaine la nature à tes décrets augustes,
    Laisse à l'homme sa liberté.

## XXVII

### THE CONSECRATION OF THE GREAT WAND OR SPEAR
#### (Hebrew Working)

*Tides:*
> First quarter Moon, Akasha.

*Magician:—*
> Basic robe, etc. Pentacle of Quintessence. Colour-charge white.

*Bomos:—*
> White drape.

*Equipment on Bomos:—*
> 1. Great Wand (head to N.W., butt to S.E.)
> 2. Thymiaterion.
> 3. Incense boat.
> 4. Phial of Oil.
> 5. Mystical Tessera.
> (A small finger-linen)

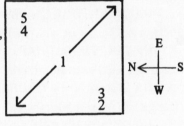

Flanking the Bomos, and quite close to it, are two tall candlesticks, or white lamps upon pedestals, one to the North of the Bomos and one to the South. In moving round the Bomos during the working, the operator will pass outside these lights.

*Perform the Hebrew Setting of the Wards of Power, beginning from East of Bomos.*

> *Go to West of Bomos, face East. Declaim:—*
> Youth everlasting art thou, timeless as light
> > going forth silently,
>
> Prince of the ripening grain, hand that creates,
> > changes and fecundates,
>
> Touching the stars that they blaze, touching the vast
> > whorls of the nebulae,
>
> Siring forth galaxies!

271

*Proceed immediately to intonation of the Hebrew of the Qabalistic Litany:—\**

**HO-ADERETh V'HO-EMUNOH, L'ChAI 'AULOMIM.**
Illustriousness and Faithfulness are with the Life of Worlds.

**HA-BINAH V'HA-B'ROKOH, L'ChAI 'AULOMIM.**
Understanding and Blessing are with the Life of Worlds.

**HA-GAAVOH V'HA-GEDULAH, L'ChAI 'AULOMIM.**
Loftiness and Magnificence are with the Life of Worlds.

**HA-DA'ATh V'HA-DIBUR, L'ChAI 'AULOMIM.**
Knowledge and the Word are with the Life of Worlds.

**HA-HOD V'HE-HODOR, L'ChAI 'AULOMIM.**
Splendour and Majesty are with the Life of Worlds.

**HA-VUA'AD V'HA-VUOThIQUTh, L'ChAI 'AULOMIM.**
Promise and Fulfilment are with the Life of Worlds.

**HA-ZAUK V'HA-Z'HAR, L'ChAI 'AULOMIM.**
Brightness and Mindfulness are with the Life of Worlds.

**HA-ChAYIL V'HA-ChAUSEN, L'ChAI 'AULOMIM.**
Strength and Virtue are with the Life of Worlds.

**HA-TEKES V'HA-T'HAR, L'ChAI 'AULOMIM.**
Exactitude and Purity are with the Life of Worlds.

**HA-YIChUD V'HA-YIROH, L'ChAI 'AULOMIM.**
Oneness and Awe are with the Life of Worlds.

**HA-KEThER V'HA-KOVAUD, L'ChAI 'AULOMIM.**
Crown and Glory are with the Life of Worlds.

**HA-LEQACh V'HA-LIBUV, L'ChAI 'AULOMIM.**
Understanding and Wisdom are with the Life of Worlds.

**HA-M'LUKOH V'HA-MEMShOLOH, L'ChAI 'AULOMIM.**
Kingdom and Governance are with the Life of Worlds.

**HA-NAUI V'HA-NETzACh, L'ChAI AULOMIM.**
Effulgence and Victory are with the Life of Worlds.

**HA-SIGUI V'HA-SEGEV, L'ChAI 'AULOMIM.**
Lordship and Transcendence are with the Life of Worlds.

---

\* A.S. title and translation. The original text is from a Qabalistic document from the pen of Ishmael ben Elisha. The transliteration given above is set out to facilitate vocalization: the traditional spelling of familiar Qabalistic words has been retained. A strict transliteration is given in Note F to the present ritual.

**HO-'OZ V'HO-'ONOH, L'ChAI 'AULOMIM.**

Strength and Meekness are with the Life of Worlds.

**HA-P'DUTh V'HA-P'ER, L'ChAI 'AULOMIM.**

Redemption and Exaltation are with the Life of Worlds.

**HA-Tz'VIY V'HA-TzEDEQ, L'ChAI 'AULOMIM.**

Adornment and Righteousness are with the Life of Worlds.

**HA-Q'RIYAH V'HA-Q'DUShOH, L'ChAI 'AULOMIM.**

Invocation and Holiness are with the Life of Worlds.

**HO-RAUN V'HO-RAUMÉMUTh, L'ChAI 'AULOMIM.**

Rejoicing and Sublimity are with the Life of Worlds.

**HA-ShIYR V'HA-ShEVECh, L'ChAI 'AULOMIM.**

Song and Laudation are with the Life of Worlds.

**HA-T'HILOH V'HA-TIPhARETh, L'ChAI 'AULOMIM.**

Praise and Beauty are with the Life of Worlds.

*Strike with the right hand upon the left 1-1.*
*Strew incense upon the coals of the thymiaterion.*
*Raise the hands to the heavens and intone:—*
Holiest ADONAY, who ridest the heavens in thy name YAH . . .
*(here place the right hand across the centre of the Great Wand, the left hand upon the Pentacle of the Quintessence),* . . .
deign to accept this Wand as a fitting instrument of the Art Magical, and do thou bless it, that blessèd it shall be.

*Withdraw hands. Pass deosil to south-east corner of the Bomos, and face north-west across it. Take up the Great Wand, grasping the shaft at about its centre with right hand, and hold it horizontally, symmetrically across your genitals. Proceed thus, deosil, to north-west corner of the Bomos, and face south-east across it.*

*Keeping the right hand at the same position upon the Great Wand, raise the Great Wand so that it is held vertically, the right hand now being held about 12" before you at the level of the heart-centre: the left hand is raised so that its palm supports the butt of the Great Wand in this position.*

*Holding this position throughout, intone the verses of*

*the Sevenfold Affirmation:—\**

Great is he and mighty in the infinite heavens,
Manifest in Light is he, in Light covered wholly.
His Geburah, his Gedulah, strength his and greatness:
Might is his, and his dominion, All-Potent, Living!
Therefore most exalted he, whose kingdom over all things is extended.

Builded in the heavens are his high habitations,
Steeps of Splendour whence he sendeth rain on the mountains!
Even they within the deeps, the Fallen, he knoweth:
Knower of all deeds is he and Lord of the Record.
Therefore most exalted he, who foundeth in the deeps his habitations.

Designate is he the chief of multitudes holy,
Glorious before them all, and all-overcoming;
His the portal of the shrine, within which his path lies,
He acclaimed of holiness the Triumph, the Beauty!
Therefore most exalted he, whose pathway lies within the shrine
                                                    supernal!

Reckoning of days and years unceasing he maketh;
He to all existence giveth times, giveth seasons,
Sending glory forth amid the High Lords assembled,
Giving mind of knowledge clear to hearts that love wisdom.
Therefore most exalted he, beneath whose burning gaze the rocks are
                                                    parted.

Powerfully doth he forge and fashion all beings;
His the strength that makes them strong; his might magnifies them.
Great and terrible is he, and true in each scruple:
To and fro beneath the sun like sparks run his Watchers.
Therefore most exalted he austere, who forms and governs every
                                                    creature.

---

\* A.S. title. The text is adapted from portions of the tenth century AMRV
LALHIM by Kalonymos. The stanzas of the Sevenfold Affirmation follow the
Qabalistic order of the planets from Luna to Saturn.

Kingly is his throne established, founded in justice,
Righteousness, magnificence, and wisdom of judgment.
Earth and sea are in his hand, the world and the heavens;
All he doth sustain, and all in equity ruleth.
Therefore most exalted he, who nurtureth the souls that long for justice.

Therefore through the worlds is he acclaimed: he is mighty!
Therefore is he praised, who has the patience of ages;
Anger passes, times go by, his truth is unchanging:
Those who come in trust to him, to new life he bringeth.
Therefore most exalted he, and through the worlds of Life his name is
glorious!

*Still maintaining the hands with the Great Wand in the same postion, proceed deosil to south-east corner of Bomos and face north-west across it. Raise left hand to grasp the Great Wand just below the right hand, which now relinquishes its hold. The Great Wand remains vertical, but is now lowered conveniently for the next phase of the operation:—*

*Intone the following Hebrew lines to their given notes:\* during the intonation of the first line, trace above the top of the Great Wand with the right hand the sigil of YHVH, employing the presigillum  of the Supernal Saturn. After the first line, the right hand is placed upon the Pentacle of the Quintessence.*

\* The notes given represent the harmonic minor key of C. The operator is free to use any harmonic minor key that he finds convenient, provided that the same sequence of intervals be employed.

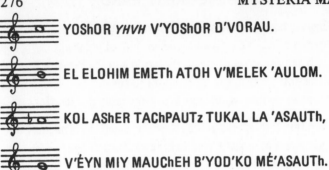

YOShOR *YHVH* V'YOShOR D'VORAU.

EL ELOHIM EMETh ATOH V'MELEK 'AULOM.

KOL AShER TAChPAUTz TUKAL LA 'ASAUTh,

V'ÉYN MIY MAUChEH B'YOD'KO MÉ'ASAUTh.

L'KO YHVH HA-BINAH V'HA-GEDULAH V'HA-GEBURAH
V'HA-TIPhARETh   V'HA-NETzACh   V'HA-HOD   V'HA-YESOD.

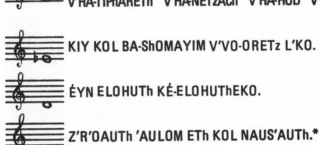

KIY KOL BA-ShOMAYIM V'VO-ORETz L'KO.

ÉYN ELOHUTh KÉ-ELOHUThEKO.

Z'R'OAUTh 'AULOM ETh KOL NAUS'AUTh.*

With the right hand, now grasp the Great Wand at about
the centre of the shaft, that is, just above the left hand. The
left hand relinquishes its hold. The Great Wand is now raised
vertically so that the right hand is at the level of the heart-
centre. The left hand is raised so that its palm supports the
butt of the Great Wand.

Proceed thus, deosil, to West of Bomos, and face East.

Lower the left hand, strike once with the butt of the
Great Wand upon the centre of the Bomos; then lay the
Wand with its head towards the North, its butt towards the
South, upon the western side of the Bomos.

The Phial of Oil being held in the left hand, oil is taken

---

* The transliteration given above is set out to facilitate vocalization: the traditional spelling of Qabalistic words and formulae has been retained. A translation
is given in Note G to the present ritual.

*upon the ball of the right thumb. The Phial is replaced. The Great Wand being steadied with the left hand, the head of the Great Wand is anointed twice.*

*With the right hand, take the Great Wand just below the centre of the shaft, and hold it across your chest so that the head points obliquely upwards towards your left shoulder. Proceed thus, deosil, to south-west corner of Bomos, and face north-east across it.*

*Raise the Great Wand, extending your right arm so as to point with the Great Wand in a straight line towards the north-east, but upwards at an angle of about 45°. After a moment, flex the elbow so as to bring the Great Wand back to its previous position, pointing obliquely upwards towards your left shoulder. Proceed thus, deosil, to West of Bomos, and face East.*

*Raise the Great Wand on high and proclaim:—*

**Thus have I consecrated the Great Wand: SUSCITATOR FULGENS is its name.**

*The Great Wand is replaced on the Bomos in its original position, head to north-west, butt to south-east.*

*Strike with the right hand upon the left 1-1.*

*Intone Hymne à l'Etre Suprême, as given at the conclusion of the Sub Rosa Nigra Consecration of the Great Wand.*

*Strike with the right hand upon the left 3-5-3.*

*Notes:*

    *Notes A through D are as given in the Notes to the Sub Rosa Nigra Consecration of the Great Wand.*

E)    The name of the Great Wand signifies Shining Awakener.

F)    HADRTh VHAMVNH LChI OVLMIM. HBINH VHBRKH etc. HGAVH VHGDLH etc. HDOTh VHDBVR etc. HHVD VHHDR etc. HVOD VHVThIQVTh etc. HZK VHZHR etc. HChIL VHChSN etc. HTKS VHThR etc. HIChVD VHIRAH etc. HKThR VHKBVD etc. HLQCh VHLBVB etc. HMLVKH VHMMShLH etc. HNVI VHNTzCh etc. HS(h)GVI VHS(h)GB etc. HOZ VHONVH etc. HPDVTh VHPAR etc. HTzBI VHTzDQ etc. HQRIAH VHQDShH etc. HRN VHRVMMVTh etc. HShIR VHShBCh etc. HThHLH VHThPARTh LChI OVLMIM.

**G)**   Upright is YHVH and forthright is his utterance.
       O God, God of Truth art thou and King to eternity.
       All that is thy pleasure is within thy power,
       and none is there who can restrain the deed of thy hand.
       To thee, YHVH, belong understanding, magnificence and might,
                                   beauty, victory, splendour, foundation;
       for all that is in the heavens and upon the earth belongs to thee.
       No godhead is as thy divinity,
       and the Everlasting Arms are the support of all.

## XXVIII

## THE CONSECRATION OF THE SWORD

*Tides:—*
    Moon approaching full, **Agni.**
*Magician:—*
    Basic robe, etc. Pentacle of Quintessence. Colour-charge white.
*Bomos:—*
    Spectrum red drape.
*Equipment on Bomos:—*

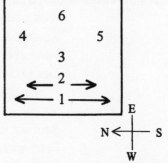

1. Sword (hilt to South, point to North.)
2. Great Wand (head to North.)
3. Lamp.
4. Phial of Oil.
5. Bell.
6. The Mystical Tessera.
(A small finger-linen)

Conveniently close to south-west of Bomos, but allowing of easy passage between itself and the Bomos, is the thurible-stand with thurible and incense boat.

At the quarters, just within the intended area of working, are large candlesticks, or pedestals each of which supports a lamp. If candlesticks are placed at the quarters the Lamp upon the Bomos should be uncoloured: if lamps are placed at the quarters, these and the Lamp upon the Bomos should all be red. In the Setting of the Wards, care should be taken to include the lights within the astral circle.

*Strike once upon the bell.*

*Perform the Setting of the Wards of Power, Greek or Hebrew form as suitable, beginning from East of Bomos. After the Setting, turn deosil to face West, and take the Great Wand from the Bomos: then turn deosil to face East.*

279

*With the Wand, trace in the air before you the presigillum of Mars; then trace about it the invoking heptagram of Mars, vibrating as you trace this* ELOHIM GEBOR *for Hebrew working, or* SABAO *for Sub Rosa Nigra working. After this stirring of the Light, turn deosil and replace the Wand on the Bomos, then proceed to the West of the Bomos and face East across it.*

*Strike 1-1-1-1-1 upon the bell. Make and maintain Ave. Intone:—*

The Gates are open. Those who cry IO TRIUMPHE! greet both Yesterday and Tomorrow.

*Dismiss the Ave.*

*Strike 2-1-2 upon the bell. Place the palm of the right hand upon the hilt of the Sword, and the palm of the left hand upon the blade towards the point. Intone:—*

> Wake to my words,
> Warrior-weapon!
> Forth of earth's flames
> Like to the lightning
> Searing the sight
> Menacing, molten,
> Born was thy body.
> Force wrought thy form,
> Strife gave thee strength:
> Clash of thy kindred
> Fires with the freezing
> Wash of the waters!
> Harsh was that hold,
> Stern was that schooling,
> Noble thy nurture.
> Out of the ordeal
> Coming with courage,
> Knowing the knotted
> Strength of thy sinews
> Toughened and true—

Glorious, gleaming,
Laughing and lissome,
Gladly the golden
Sun thou salutedst:
Kin to his clearest
Beams was thy blade!

*Pass deosil to East of Bomos, face West across it. Extend both hands so that the palms are approximately 8" above the Sword, the left hand being above the hilt, the right above the blade towards the point. Intone:—*

The Lame One sired and fashioned the Sword, for the fierce War-god he fashioned the Sword. The Lame One, its maker, he who fell from heaven's height to the deeps of ocean, he fashioned the Sword and gave it of his nature. To the Sword, the serpent-child, he gave of his mystery. This was the deed of the Lame One.

Then was the Sword favoured of the fierce War-god. He took the Sword, he took it and raised it in exultation. He cleft the air with it and its glitterings smote the earth. The light of the sun flashed to fire in the blade of the Sword, and the Sword was of him. Thus he made the Sword his own, and in his domain was its power supreme. This was the deed of the War-god.

And the Priests raised their shields and shook them, they shook them with a sound as of thunder; and they danced to the loud-wailing flutes. This was the deed of the Priests.

Then warriorlike did the Sword champion all men, yea all men who with true heart sought its strength to assist them. This was the deed of the Sword.

*Return deosil to West of Bomos, and face East. Place incense in the thurible, then cense the Sword, swinging the thurible twice towards the hilt, twice towards the point, and once across the centre of the blade. Replace the thurible.*

*Taking the Sword with the right hand, support the blade near the point with the left forearm, so that the blade lies horizontally before you, quite close to but not touching your body. In a clearly audible whisper, address to the Sword the following:—*

O Sword, hear the words of the Priest of Vulcan, which he spake before the God and before the altars:—

"Far hence do I decree that all those should depart who have taken evil into their hands, or who have but in their heart been moved towards it."

O Sword, keep these words of the Priest of Vulcan.

*Return the Sword to the Bomos.*

*Assuming the Wand Posture, energise self by means of the Second Formula of the Clavis Rei Primae. The Formula having been completed, pause for a few moments before proceeding.*

*The arms are raised at the sides to form a Tau, the palms being upturned. This position is maintained while the invocation is begun as follows:—*

| *(Hebrew)* | *(Sub Rosa Nigra)* |
|---|---|
| ELOHIM GEBOR! Indomitable majesty of the Godhead austere! | SABAO! Indomitable majesty of the Godhead austere! |

*The arms are now crossed upon the breast, right over left, and then simultaneously extended to the Sword. The palm of the right hand is placed upon the hilt, the palm of the left hand upon the blade towards the point. After these movements, which should be performed smoothly and swiftly so as to occasion only minimal pause after "austere," the invocation continues:—*

Vouchsafe to breathe into this Sword the effulgence of thy triumphant holiness, that it may know valiance, and that it may be a strong and inexorable instrument of the Art Magical, a true and unfailing Regent of Defence, a doer of thy Justice and a manifestor of thy Rectitude.

*Removing the hands from the Sword, take the Great Wand and trace with it above the name on the blade the sigil of that name (see Note B below). While the sigil is being traced, solemnly vibrate the name itself—ELOHIM GEBOR or, for Sub Rosa Nigra working, SABAO . Replace the Wand.*

*The palm of the right hand is now laid again upon the hilt, the palm of the left hand upon the blade towards the point:—*

|   (Hebrew)   |   (Sub Rosa Nigra)   |

KAMAEL! thou great and terrible Archangel of Geburah, | DORYXENOS! thou great and terrible Archon of Geburah, whensoever this Sword shall be wielded in true service of the Light Ineffable, thine be the hand upon its hilt, O Mighty One.

*Removing the hands from the Sword, take the Great Wand and trace with it* above the hilt *the sigil of the Briatic name employed, meanwhile again vibrating that name. Replace the Wand.*

*The Phial of Oil being held in the left hand, oil is taken upon the ball of the right thumb. The Phial is replaced. The blade of the Sword is now anointed once, near the hilt.*

*Strike once upon the bell.*

*Intone:—*

Thus have the Mavorian virtues entered into this Sword, and the name of the Sword is IUBAR!

*Take the Sword from the Bomos with the right hand. Rest the blade near its point upon the left forearm as previously described, and carry it thus deosil to the East of the Bomos. Face West across the Bomos.*

*The right arm is fully extended, holding the Sword horizontally at shoulder height, pointing across the Bomos to the West. This position is maintained for but a few moments.* *

---

* Although this pointing of the Sword horizontally from East to West is but a momentary action in the rite, its symbolism is of great occult interest. During the rite—before consecration has been effected—the blade is oriented from South to North, denoting that as a natural bar of steel it follows the South-North magnetic current, and also that its origin is in Fire (South) while its work is in Earth (North). Immediately after consecration, the pointing of the Sword from East to West affirms that the place of the consecrated weapon is in Light and its work is primarily in Darkness; thus also this moment presents a mystical interpretation of the medieval alchemical dictum, that *alchemical iron is non-magnetic.*

*The Sword is now raised aloft, so as to be held in that*
*position steadily throughout recital of the following:—*

And this is the Song of Iubar!

Hail to the heavens,
Source of my shining!
Honour to Earth,
Mother of Metals,
Mother of Men!
Blessing or bane
Finding, I further:
Hear, O ye hostile
Spirits and scornful,
Mutable, mocking,
Craven and cruel!
Will ye or waver ye,
Mine is the mandate:
Bow to my bidding!
Creatures of chaos,
Sons of destruction,
Ply not for peace—
Worthless your word!
Movers of malice,
Reapers of ruin,
Dare not of doom
Reckless my wrath!
Certain my stroke—
Lo, as the levin
Blasting the bole!
Truth is my treasure,
Justice my jewel—
Strength of the Strongest—
Wield me, ye Wise.
Forward in freedom,
Lovers of Light!
Claim ye the cause,

Name ye the need:
Mine is all Magick,
Mine is all Mystery:
Searcher of Secrets,
Friend of the fearless—
Victor invincible,
Sunbeam of Steel!

*Lower the Sword. Turn deosil to face East.*

*With the Sword, trace in the air before you the presigillum of Mars; then trace about it the banishing heptagram of Mars, vibrating as you trace this* ELOHIM GEBOR *or* SABAO *as appropriate.*

*Return to West of Bomos and face East. Place the Sword on the Bomos as before.*

*Strike 3-5-3 upon the bell.*

*Notes:*

A)    Between workings, the consecrated Sword is kept sheathed, and wrapped in silk.

B)    The Sword to be consecrated should be cross-hilted with a double-edged straight blade. The Sword should never have been employed in physical combat, but the edges should be sharpened.

The handle of the Sword may be painted red, but preferably should be covered with red leather bound with gilt wire. The crossbar should be gilded, or may be burnished brass; the same applies to the pommel, but this latter can alternatively be of mounted crystal.*

The inscription upon the blade (ΣΑΒΑΩ, or גבור אלהים ,
or the Martian name from the magician's elected series of Magical Formulae) should be painted, or engraved and filled, with red. The height of the letters should be approximately one-third the width of the blade, the centre of the name should be located as nearly as possible one-third the length of the blade from the hilt. The lettering should face the beholder when the hilt of the Sword is to his right and the point to his left.

C)    The name of the Sword is *Iubar:* which is to say, Sunbeam.

---

* But if the handle and hilt have such beauty and character that the magician does not wish to tamper with them, let him leave them as they are.

*XXIX*

## THE HIGH CONSECRATION OF THE GRAIL
### *(The Primary Formula of Four Crowned by Three)*

*Tides:–*
> Full Moon, Akasha.

*Magician:–*
> Basic robe, etc. Pentacle of Quintessence. Colour-charge white.

*Bomos:–*
> Indigo drape.

*Equipment on Bomos:–*
1. Grail.
2. Rose of Concealment.*
3. Lustral vessel and Water, sprig of cypress.
4. Anointing Oil.
5. Bell.
6. Lighting taper.
7. The Mystical Tessera.
(A small finger-linen)

Conveniently close to south-west of Bomos, but allowing of easy passage between itself and the Bomos, is the thurible-stand with thurible and incense boat.

Just within the intended area of working are three large candlesticks, or three lamps upon pedestals; these are positioned at the East, south-east and south-west. If lamps are used, these should be indigo (smoked glass is acceptable.)

*Strike once upon the bell.*

*Perform the Hebrew Setting of the Wards of Power, beginning from East of Bomos; if working Sub Rosa Nigra, use the Setting of the Wards of Adamant.*

---

\* See Note C to the present ritual.

*Go to West of Bomos, face East. If working Sub Rosa
Nigra intone Casmen I, "Thus shall the praises" etc., as follows;
for Hebrew working, intone the Tau and Mem stanzas of the
Song of Praises as given after Casmen I.*

Thus shall the praises sound of Leukothea; ever thus while praise
shall be:—

The crystal-flashing splendour of her love pervades all things,
nourishing and renewing.

Of her bounty she gives secret dew into an earthen cup: those who
love her drink deeply of it, and she casts around them the brightness
of her regard.

Where is the Great Serpent, where is he, her Lord? She has overcome him, she has shattered his fangs: from her womb is he born anew,
a toothless babe.

Yet is she Ally of the Strong, a mighty helper to the Sons and
Daughters of Gnosis.

Before the white-fire face of the Moon she chants in shadow,
and the Moon's self stoops to hear the song of allurement.

Before the white-fire face of the Moon she chants; and a lone
devotee, ensorcelled, staff broken and magick set at naught, casts
himself, powerless, into the dark gulf of her being. Thus without
choice he waits, until the vision of splendour and flame arise, and
wisdom be his, or madness.

Upon her palm the single flame quivers, seeming air-nurtured.
Hand upon hand. Sign most awesome.

The beryl-stone in her circlet becomes a pool filled with waters
of compassion and clear vision; whoso gazes therein shall mount a
winged steed.

The crystal-flashing splendour of her love pervades all things,
nourishing and renewing.

*(The Tau and Mem Stanzas of the Song of Praises:—)*

Thine is the Sign of the End, being fulfilled
                                   Sum of existences:
Thine is the ultimate Door opened on Night's
                                   unuttered mystery:
Thine, the first hesitant step into the dark
                                   of those but latterly

Born to the Labyrinth!
Mother of waters profound, dark are thy halls,
bitter thy fragrances:
Voices of love and of awe call thee: arise,
leave thou thy sorrowing!
Robe thee in web of thy waves, Mother of Life,
robe thee in radiance,
Sing of thy Mysteries!

*Strike 2-4-2 upon the bell, and intone the Ogdoadic Catena:—*

Salutation and again salutation to the High Guardians of the Glorious Star, who were, and are, and are to come. Salutation and again salutation in the splendour of the Star which unites us.

O you High Guardians, Hidden Adepti, Dwellers in Eternity: you have given signs and you have shown wonders, and you have revealed yourselves unto your children.

EN GIRO TORTE SOL CICLOS ET ROTOR IGNE.

Such are the Words, such is the Greeting!

*Strike once upon the bell before continuing Catena.*


In a voice of mystery do we call upon you, High Guardians, we who are the continuators of your Work: O Luminous Ones, behold and hear us. Not without our own questing do we ask to know, nor without our own endeavour to attain: but that the sowing shall be crowned in the harvest. For oneness of purpose do we call unto you, for that joy of resolve which is the wine of the will, transforming all that was strange to it. For living light and for luminous life do we call unto you, O Hidden Ones! So Light and Life shall be drawn at last to the radiance of one Star, and that Star shall mount to the unshadowed height.

*Strike 1-1-1 upon the bell. Pause for a few moments, then intone:—*

|             (Hebrew)             |             (Sub Rosa Nigra)          |
| O thou glorious and dread Lady, AIMA, | O thou glorious and dread Lady, TURANA, |

whose Throne is established for ever in the secret place of holiness, thou dost separate and thou dost restore to peace.

O thou wondrous Eternal in whom is every way of Truth, thou hast spun the thread of my life on a hidden Wheel and thou knowest the secret of my being.

*Pause for a few moments, then grasp the bowl of the Grail with fingers and thumbs of both hands simultaneously, but do not lift the Grail. Intone:—*

The King's Daughter is all glorious within;
Her robe is golden and bordered with variety.

*Raise both hands to touch briefly and symmetrically the Pentacle of the Quintessence upon the breast.*

*Using the cypress-sprig, sprinkle the Grail thrice.*

*Place incense in the thurible, then cense the Grail with three forward swings. Replace the thurible.*

*Strike once upon the bell.*

*Proceed deosil to South of Bomos, face North across it.*

*Perform the Calyx.*

*Then take up the Grail, clasping the bowl thereof with fingers and thumbs of both hands simultaneously, and bring it close to you, to hold it at the level of your heart-centre. Maintaining the Grail in this position, intone:—*

I am a goblet brimmed with strong, with living wine,
Cool shadowed purple winged with invincible fire.
Up from its surface move ever dimly forms lovely or grim to discern:
    A fume of dreams
To the skies mounting in shapes of the skyey lords.
There the great serpent turns slowly in undulant coils,
While bright under rein of rose-limbed heroes the cloud-steeds rear
And veil or tress ambrosial gleams, and orb of breast, as womanshape
                                  ascends.

    Wide to the heights have I spread my heart
And the heights have beheld their likeness, have drawn it forth,
No mirrored tincture, no semblance inert, but my dreams—
Exult, ye heavens, even as my heart!—
You have won my dreams, as I have caught your fire.

*Replace the Grail. Proceed deosil to North of Bomos and face South across it.*

*Perform the Calyx.*

*Take up the Grail to hold it as before, and intone:—*

I am a sapphire bowl, dark and immense, that holds
   In ancient ward the glorious horde of the stars,
   Multitudinous ferment seething, a scintillant nectar,
   A vortex frenzied, unresting, wherein to its depths
   Around, sequent, or counter, run the sparks enweaving.
It teems, foaming, the sweet and terrible tide
Whose least gleam is dayspring to aeons of life;
And I environ it, I gaze through it ever—
     I, dark and hidden Mother—
With fervid cosmic splendour veiling brow of dwale.
I encompass, I guard the luminous treasures of destiny
And in my gift is the viewless strength beyond destiny:
I am Night, and Dread, and the Void. My lovers have called me death.

*Replace the Grail. Proceed deosil to East of Bomos and face West across it.*

*Perform the Calyx.*

*Take up the Grail to hold it as before, and intone:—*

I am the mystic Grail, Virgin of Light and Mother of Ecstasy.
   I am virgin silver as Anadyomene new-risen,
   As the apple-blossoms that made the maiden waist of Blodeuedd,
     As the moon's first slender bow:
As the light of the moon's first crescent, cold upon snows at Imbolc.
I am the armed maiden forth spoken from mouth of the Father;
The strong Daughter am I, the King's Daughter, helmed and mantled
                            in silver—
Ah, but fiery-golden my robe, and my love is as gold in the crucible
                            molten!
I who am Daughter of the Voice, mine is the deeper mystery:
Mother am I of the Logoi and Mother of Life Undying.
Myrrha am I, and Marah am I, and Mem the Great Ocean.
     Within me mingle Time and Eternity:
I am the Mother of All Living, and I am the Womb of Rebirth.

*Replace the Grail. Proceed deosil in a complete circumam-*
*bulation of the Bomos, then upon returning to East continue*
*deosil without pausing to West of Bomos (1½ circumambul-*
*ations). Face East across Bomos.*

*Strike 1-1-1 upon the bell, and intone:—*

O thou Mother of Love and of Knowledge, thou by whose deed all
forms exist, let descend upon me a fold of thy veil, that in that sacred
darkness no forms may separate me from thee.

*With eyes closed, head bowed and arms crossed right over*
*left upon the breast, make a fitting pause.*

*Having dismissed this posture, take up the taper in the right*
*hand and proceed to the candle or lamp at the eastern limit*
*of the place of working. Light the taper from the flame, then*
*turn deosil and proceed with it directly to the candle or lamp*
*at the south-western limit of the place of working. Touch the*
*flame of the taper to that of the south-western light, then*
*turn deosil and proceed directly to the candle or lamp at the*
*north-western limit. Touch the flame of the taper to that of*
*the north-western light, then turn deosil and proceed directly*
*to the eastern candle or lamp. Touch the flame of the taper*
*to that of the eastern light, then turn deosil and proceed*
*directly to the eastern side of the Bomos. Face West across it.*

*Breathe once into the bowl of the Grail, then with the*
*flame of the taper trace a complete circle about it (the flame*
*not entering the bowl of the Grail). Intone:—*

O  thou Womb, thou Womb! — thou Space before Creation, thou
Pause before Manifestation.

*Transfer the lighted taper to the left hand. Using the cypress-*
*sprig, sprinkle thrice into the bowl of the Grail. Having replaced*
*the cypress-sprig, transfer the lighted taper to the right hand.*
*Again approach it to the Grail; on this occasion, dip the flame*
*into the bowl of the Grail, once and briefly, not touching the*
*metal. Intone:—*

O thou Womb, thou Womb!—thou Ocean whence cometh Life.

*Extinguish the taper. Proceed deosil to West of Bomos,*

*replace taper, and place incense in the thurible.*

*With the thurible, move deosil to East of Bomos and face West across it. Cense the Grail with three forward swings, then with a single complete circle about it.*

*Return deosil to West of Bomos and replace thurible.*

*Take lustral vessel in left hand, cypress-sprig in right. Dip the sprig into the lustral water, touch it to the foot of the Grail on the side nearest to you, turn about deosil and cast the water from the sprig to the West. Carrying the lustral vessel and the sprig, move deosil to North of Bomos and face South across it; repeat the previous actions, casting the water to the North. Move deosil to East of Bomos and face West across it; repeat the actions, casting the water to the East. Move deosil to South of Bomos and face North across it; repeat the actions, casting the water to the South. Move deosil to West of Bomos and replace lustral vessel and sprig.*

*Strike 7 upon the bell.*

*Perform the Calyx.*

*This completed, rest the left hand upon the Pentacle of the Quintessence. With the right hand, trace above the Grail the sigil of the name* AIMA( אימא) *for Hebrew working, or that of the name* TURANA *for Sub Rosa Nigra working,* * *vibrating the name meanwhile.*

*Raise the right hand to cover for a moment the left hand upon the Pentacle; then withdraw both hands, proceed deosil to East of Bomos and face West across it.*

*Perform the Calyx.*

*Take up the Grail, clasping the bowl thereof with fingers and thumbs of both hands simultaneously, and bring it close to you, to hold it at the level of your heart-centre. Maintaining the Grail in this position, intone:—*

O Powers within me, hymn the One and the All: chant in harmony with my will, all ye Powers within me! Holy Gnosis, illuminated by thee, through thee I hymn the light of thought, I rejoice in the joy of

---

* The correspondence being to Supernal Saturn in either case.

the mind. All ye Powers, chant with me!

*Replace the Grail. Proceed deosil to West of Bomos and face East.*

*Place the right hand on the Pentacle of the Quintessence, the left hand on the Tessera; now raise the left hand to cover for a moment the right hand upon the Pentacle, then extend both hands simultaneously to lift the Grail. Bring it towards you and centre it above the Tessera, its foot a few inches above the surface thereof.*

*Holding the Grail in this position, vibrate:—*

EN GIRO TORTE SOL CICLOS ET ROTOR IGNE.

*Replace the Grail.*

*The Phial of Anointing Oil being held in the left hand, oil is taken upon the ball of the right thumb. The Phial is replaced. Holding the Grail by its stem with the left hand, raise it to a convenient height and, taking care not to tilt the Grail, anoint it once underneath its foot. Replace the Grail.*

*Strike 8 upon the bell.*

*Raise the Grail on high in both hands, and proclaim:—*

Thus have I consecrated the Grail: 'Mystery of the Firstborn' is its name.

*The Grail is replaced on the Bomos, and is covered with the Rose of Concealment.*

*Strike once upon the bell, then make the Ave. After dismissing the Ave pause for a few moments, then intone the first section of the Ogdoadic Catena:—*

Salutation and again salutation to the High Guardians of the Glorious Star, who were, and are, and are to come. Salutation and again salutation in the splendour of the Star which unites us.

O you High Guardians, Hidden Adepti, Dwellers in Eternity: you have given signs and you have shown wonders, and you have revealed yourselves unto your children.

EN GIRO TORTE SOL CICLOS ET ROTOR IGNE.

Such are the Words, such is the Greeting!

*Strike 3-5-3 upon the bell.*

*Notes:*

A)   The Grail is a hemispherical cup with stem and foot, all of silver, or silver-plated, the cup being internally gilded. The ideal height for the Grail is 5 inches. The exterior should be richly figured; a small knop in the stem is permissible, but the large knop typical of ecclesiastical chalices is to be avoided.

B)   Between workings, the consecrated Grail is to be kept upright and covered with the Rose of Concealment, in a small box or cabinet fully lined with white silk. When the Grail is taken from its receptacle for ceremonial use, it remains covered with the Rose of Concealment; this is only removed for theurgic action which specifically involves the Grail.

C)   The Rose of Concealment is a square of white silk, of double thickness, large enough to cover the Grail completely as it stands upon the Bomos. The border of this square is to be embroidered with black and silver; in the centre of the square is to be a stylised, five-petalled Black Rose, of size equal to the circumference of the Grail, and edged with gold. The central disc of the Rose is to be filled by a square lattice design of black lines, showing five lines horizontally and five vertically. When not upon the Grail, the Rose of Concealment should always be folded neatly, to form a small square with the Rose itself uppermost.

*The Disc or Pentacle*

## XXX

## THE CONSECRATION OF THE DISC

*Tides:—*
  New to first quarter Moon, Prithivi.
*Magician:—*
  Basic robe, etc. Pentacle of Quintessence. Colour-charge green.
*Bomos:—*
  Black drape.

The Bomos is situated in the North of the place of working; the North-South axis of the Bomos should lie upon the North-South axis of the place of working. Two tall candlesticks (alternatively, two white lamps on pedestals) are set upon the floor, to the North of the Bomos, just within the intended astral circle, and in line with the East and West sides of the Bomos respectively; the Bomos should be so placed that these candlesticks are at about 18" distant from its northern side.

*Equipment on Bomos:—*
  1. The Disc.*
  2. The Mystical Tessera.
  3. The Phial of Oil.
  (A small finger-linen)

On the Bomos, upon the North-South axis, and fairly close to its southern edge, is placed the Disc. Upon an imaginary line from the centre of the Disc to the right-hand candlestick, and about midway between the Disc and the northern edge of the Bomos, is placed the Tessera; at a corresponding position in relation to the Disc and the left-hand candlestick, is placed the Phial of Anointing Oil.

*See Note D following *Consecration of Elemental Wand.*

297

*Perform the Setting of the Wards of Power, Greek or Hebrew form as suitable, beginning from centre of place of working.*

*After the Setting, remain at the centre, facing East. Intone the Orison of Tiberianus:—\**

O PANKRATES, whom heaven's age of ages doth revere: thou ever one beneath unnumbered potencies, to whom none may impute either number or time; if any name be worthy of thee, now be in words addressed!

O thou AGNOTOS, to whom is holy joy when trembles the great universe, and wandering stars pause in their swift courses! O thou ENOS, thou POLLOS! Thou ALPHA and OMEGA, and OMPHALOS of the World!—yet also shalt thou outlast the world, for thou, thyself unending, shalt give end to the flowing seasons. From Eternity hast thou looked down upon the unheeding destinies of the material universe revolving in inevitable orbit, and upon lives caught into the whirl of time. These thou wilt bring back, to be returned to the higher sphere: just as to the world, exhausted by giving birth, that which has been lost returns in the reflux of the seasons.

Perhaps as a sunbeam of flowing flame thou art, and as swift likeness of dazzling limbs (if towards thee the sense may rightly yearn, seeking that sacred beauty by which thou dost encompass the stars and dost at once embrace the wide spanning aether) so that thou flashing forth light of thine own self beholdest all things thereby, and urgest onward our sun and our day.

Thou art the root of all gods that be, thou art cause of all things and of their energies, thou art the whole of nature, thou art the god ENOS and MYRIOS, thou art filled with the entire power of generation. Of thee is long since born the deity which is this universe, this shining home of gods and men, star-strewn in youthful bloom; of which universe, I pray, grant to one who is willing a knowledge of the reason and manner and mystery of its making. Give me O PATROS that I may be able to know those venerable causes: by what ordinance of substances

---

\* A.S. translation from the Latin of Tiberianus, 4th century e.v. The divine attributes are rendered in Greek.

aforetime thou didst pile up the masses of the world, and of what lightness thou, KYDISTOS, didst weave the soul which partners matter though unlike to it; and what is that energy which manifests through supple bodies as life.

*Vibrate the First Enochian Key, and follow this with:—*

Thus do I invoke you, you Great Archangels LEXARPH, COMANAN, TABITOM, whose garments of light are beautified with admiration, and who dwell within the radiance of the Eternal.

*Turn deosil at centre to face North. With the right hand trace the invoking pentagram of Spirit, vibrating, as you do so,* AGLA *for Hebrew working, or* ISCHYROS *for Greek working. Again with the right hand, trace the invoking pentagram of Earth, vibrating, as you do so,* ADONAI *for Hebrew working, or* KYRIOS *for Greek working.*

*Pause for a few moments, then proceed directly to the Bomos and face North across it.*

*With the clenched hand, knock once upon the Bomos.*

*Rest the right hand lightly upon the Mystical Tessera, then touch with the same hand the Pentacle of the Quintessence upon the breast. Bring up the left hand to cover for a moment the right hand upon the Pentacle, then extend both hands simultaneously to take up the Disc from the Bomos. Raise the Disc horizontally to the level of the heart-centre, and intone:—*

|  (Hebrew) | |  (Greek) |
|---|---|---|
| Most powerful ADONAI, | \| | Most powerful KYRIOS, |

from thy Sacred Dwelling behold this Disc, which by the work of my own hand, with the steadfastness of the Bull, with the aspiration of the Horned Goat and with the carefulness of the Virgin, I have prepared for the governance of the forces of Earth in the workings of Art Magick. Take it as thy footstool, that the world may feel thy presence.

*The Disc is replaced on the Bomos, but the hands remain in contact with it:—*

Even thus, O most powerful    |    Even thus, O most powerful
     ADONAI,    |         KYRIOS,

in the Noble Alchemy of the Great Work, in my offering of that which has been prepared does my soul offer itself; not indeed that it may be destroyed or that it may fail of its purpose, for in service to Divinity is true purpose found and fulfilled. This is my desire as I carry forward this rite: that as I have offered the Disc of my hand, so may the Disc of my deeds be made ready for that service.

*Both hands are now raised to a loosely vertical position, the palms facing forward. Maintaining this position, declaim:—*

In gladness the leaves tell each to each their mysteries, and the tossing of boughs sounds forth a chorus of rejoicing. The roots of the trees are set deep in the earth, and the stars companion their lifted crests. Sweet are their fruits, and sweet their dewy shade. As brothers the fires of heaven they hail, and as sisters the gentle waters.

In gladness the leaves of the forest of life are stirring continually; and the world invisible is thronged with the upward reaching of delicate eager branches of Being. Living columns arise from primordial darkness, to where the lamps of eternity crown their summits. Glad world of life, we invoke benediction upon thee: and upon us may thy peace rest also, for thy God and ours is one.

*Both hands are lowered, the left now being placed upon the Pentacle of the Quintessence, and the right being laid upon the Disc. Intone:—*

I, the essential nature of Earth, beyond rocky crag and in sheltered valley I guard the hidden things of future time. I guard them, and I give them of myself.

Deep in the fertile soil, or wide in the wilderness, I gather and direct the errant powers; all that befalls in my domain I see, and I heed. The sown field and the barrow-mound: are not these alike the slow alembics of my mystery?

That which descends I welcome, and that which ascends I aid; in the act of each is my purpose wondrously achieved. The shadowy cavern, or the stone circle upon the plain: they who seek me through either shall pass beyond me, and thus shall they find me.

*The right hand is now raised to touch the left hand as it lies upon the Pentacle of the Quintessence. The hands are next lowered simultaneously, to be placed upon the surface of the Disc. Address the Disc:—*

Upon thee, O Disc, be the blessing of him whose law
    directs the holy ones,
The blessing of him who reigns without beginning
    and without end:
Upon thee as a most clear shining be the blessing
    of the Highest.

*Raise the hands slightly above the Disc, and maintain them in this position whilst intoning the following:—*

| (Hebrew) | (Greek) |
|---|---|
| O thou holy Archangel AUPHIRIEL, Regent and Messenger of the most powerful ADONAI, | O thou holy Archon AMYNTOR, Regent and Messenger of the most powerful KYRIOS, |

in the name of the same your God, vouchsafe to dower this Disc with the ever-faithful stability of Earth, that it may be wholly harmonious to those Astral Realms in which it is to have authority.

| O thou who art mighty in the Domain of Tzophaun, | O thou who art mighty in the Domain of Arktos, |
|---|---|

where the aether-girdled womb pours forth its variety in the silent darkness, confer upon this Disc the constancy and fruitfulness of Elemental Earth, that in the works in which it participates, like may ever produce like, due effect may ever follow due cause; and the blessedness of abundance and increase may be shown forth in all.

*Withdraw the hands.*

*With the right hand, trace above the Disc the sigil first of the Atziluthic name employed in the above invocation, and then of the Briatic name, in each case vibrating the name as you trace its sigil. (For this purpose, use the Presigillum of the Element Earth, the sigillic line having been obtained from the Kamea of Malkuth.)*

PROJECT UPON THE DISC BY MEANS OF THE ORANTE FORMULA.

*With the clenched hand, knock once upon the Bomos.*

*The Phial of Anointing Oil being held in the left hand, oil is taken upon the ball of the right thumb. The Phial is replaced. The Disc is now taken in the left hand, and is anointed upon the thickness of the circumference, beyond the tip of each of the four long rays.*

*The Disc is now replaced upon the Bomos.*

*The left hand is extended above the surface of the Disc, the right hand is rested upon the Pentacle of the Quintessence, and the following is intoned:—*

Dwell among the Stars, O Disc, but be thou established in Earth.

*The left hand is raised to touch the right hand upon the Pentacle, then both hands are extended simultaneously to take up the Disc. The Disc is now held vertically in both hands at the level of the heart-centre, the designed face being towards the Pentacle.*

*Standing thus, look to the North for a few moments.*

*Carrying the Disc in the same position at the level of the heart-centre, turn about, deosil, to face South. Crossing the centre, advance at an even pace in a straight line to the southern limit of the circle of working; there turn about deosil without pausing, return to the centre, and maintaining the same pace make a smooth turn deosil at the centre through 90° to face East. Without pause, advance to the eastern limit of the circle of working; there turn about deosil, still without pausing, and advance across the centre to the western limit of the circle, where, keeping the same pace, make another smooth turn deosil to face East, and advance to the centre. Maintaining the same steady motion, turn deosil at the centre through 270° to face North; then stop.*

*Raise the Disc high in both hands, and proclaim:—*

Behold the Disc, behold the Priestess of the Temple of Earth!

*Still holding the Disc aloft, make a complete turn deosil at the centre. Facing North again, lower the Disc.*

*With the Disc held in the right hand only, trace the*

*banishing pentagram of Spirit, vibrating* AGLA *or* ISCHYROS
*as appropriate, while doing so. Next trace with the Disc the*
*banishing pentagram of Earth, vibrating* ADONAI *or* KYRIOS
*while doing so.*

*Pause for a few moments, then transfer the Disc to the*
*left hand and turn deosil to face East.*

*Make the Ave to the East.*

*Having dismissed the Ave, turn deosil to face North. With*
*both hands hold the Disc at the level of the heart-centre, and*
*carry it thus directly to the Bomos.*

*Replace the Disc upon the Bomos.*

*With the clenched hand, knock 3-5-3 upon the Bomos.*

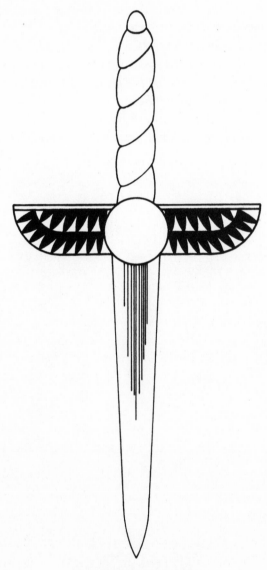

*The Burin or Dagger*

## XXXI

## THE CONSECRATION OF THE BURIN

*Tides:—*
  Full Moon, Vayu.
*Magician:—*
  Basic robe, etc. Pentacle of Quintessence. Colour-charge yellow.
*Bomos:—*
  Black drape.

The Bomos is situated in the East of the place of working; the East-West axis of the Bomos should lie upon the East-West axis of the place of working. Two tall candlesticks (alternatively, two white lamps on pedestals) are set upon the floor, to the East of the Bomos, just within the intended astral circle, and in line with the North and South sides of the Bomos respectively; the Bomos should be so placed that these candlesticks are at about 18" distant from its eastern side.

*Equipment on Bomos:—*
  1. The Burin.*
  2. The Mystical Tessera.
  3. Phial of Oil.
  (A small finger-linen)

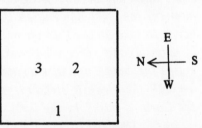

On the Bomos, with its length upon the East-West axis, is placed the Burin: its point towards the East and its handle fairly close to the western edge. Upon an imaginary line from the knop at the intersection of handle and wings of the Burin, to the right-hand candlestick, and about midway between the knop and the eastern edge of the Bomos, is placed the Tessera; at a corresponding position in relation to the knop of the Burin and the left-hand candlestick, is placed the Phial of Anointing Oil.

---

* See Note E following *Consecration of Elemental Wand.*

305

*Perform the Setting of the Wards of Power, Greek or Hebrew form as suitable, beginning from centre of place of working.*

*After the Setting, remain at the centre, facing East. Intone the Orison of Tiberianus (as given in the Disc Consecration Ritual).*

*Vibrate the First Enochian Key, and follow this with:—*

Thus do I invoke you, you Great Archangels LEXARPH, COMANAN, TABITOM, whose garments of light are beautified with admiration, and who dwell within the radiance of the Eternal.

*Remain facing East. With the right hand trace the invoking pentagram of Spirit, vibrating, as you do so,* AHIH *for Hebrew working, or* ATHANATOS *for Greek working. Again with the right hand, trace the invoking pentagram of Air, vibrating, as you do so,* YHVH *for Hebrew working, or* SELAE GENETES *for Greek working.*

*Pause for a few moments, then go straight to the Bomos and face East across it.*

*With the clenched hand, knock once upon the Bomos.*

*Rest the right hand lightly upon the Mystical Tessera, then touch with the same hand the Pentacle of the Quintessence upon the breast. Bring up the left hand to cover for a moment the right hand upon the Pentacle, then extend both hands to take up the Burin from the Bomos. Keeping the Burin horizontal and directed towards the East, the right hand grasps the handle and lifts it; the left palm meanwhile is placed beneath the blade to steady it, so that in one slow movement the Burin is raised to the level of the heart-centre. Intone:—*

| (Hebrew) | | (Greek) |
|---|---|---|
| Most resplendent | | Most resplendent |
| YHVH, | | SELAE GENETES, |

from thy Airy Throne behold this Burin, which by the work of my own hand, with the zeal of the Waterbearer, with the sensitivity of the Balance and with the readiness of the Twins, I have prepared for the governance of the forces of Air in the workings of Art Magick. Let it inscribe thy name, that the world may trace thy ways.

*The Burin is replaced as before on the Bomos. The hands
are placed upon it so as to cover the wings, the thumbs resting
upon the knop and the fingers pointing forward:—*

| Even thus, O resplendent | Even thus, O resplendent |
| YHVH, | SELAE GENETES, |

in the Noble Alchemy of the Great Work, in my offering of that which
has been prepared does my soul offer itself; not indeed that it may be
destroyed or that it may fail of its purpose, for in service to Divinity is
true purpose found and fulfilled. This is my desire as I carry forward
this rite: that as I have offered the Burin of my hand, so may the Burin
of my faculties be made ready for that service.

*Both hands are now raised to a loosely vertical position,
the palms facing forward. Maintaining this position, declaim:—*

Your God speaks thus:

How shall ye see me? How conceive of me? Behold then: I am a
wheeling disc whereon stand twelve royal citadels, six bright with lamps,
and other six dim. Six are of life, and are filled with the winds of life;
six are of death, and thence do the winds sweep many shapes as the
leaves are carried by the winds of winter: yet the bright and the dark, all
are of me, and within the citadels of shadow dwell securely all earthly
beings which are mine. Night falls, and they sleep; day shall return, and
they shall awaken restored.

These twelve citadels I have set in your care, as stations of power
from which shall be governed each age in its turn. Thus working, with
my power shall ye work: thus working shall ye work my will. So speaks
your God.

Rise up then in his Name of Mercy! rise up in his Name of Power!
—for he has given to us the keys of his citadels, and an understanding of
his works.

*Both hands are lowered, the left now being placed upon
the pentacle of the Quintessence; the right hand is laid upon
the Burin, the palm being centred upon the knop. Intone:—*

Without limitation am I, the winged and shining Selfhood of Air. My ever-splendid breath is the breath of all that lives. In my own movement I delight, and delight is mine again in that which stirs to responsive movement.

If I rest, it is in the equalising of force and tremendous force. I whirl together harsh cold and searing heat, then I hover, poised, in their mingling; or I summon upon conjoining winds moisture and drought, then at their union fold my iridescent pinions in brief tranquility.

Yet swiftly do I, the subtle and tireless Deviser of Change fly forth to new action. They who breathe deeply of my vigour shall attain with me to the inscrutable azure.

*The right hand is now raised to touch the left hand as it lies upon the Pentacle of the Quintessence. The hands are next lowered simultaneously upon the Burin so as to cover the wings, the thumbs resting upon the knop and the fingers pointing forward. Address the Burin:—*

Upon thee, O Burin, be the blessing of him whose law
    directs the holy ones,
The blessing of him who reigns without beginning
    and without end:
Upon thee as a most clear shining be the blessing
    of the Highest.

*Raise the hands slightly above the Burin, separating them a little and maintain them in this position whilst intoning the following:—*

| *(Hebrew)* | *(Greek)* |
|---|---|
| O thou holy Archangel RUACHIEL, Regent and Messenger of the resplendent YHVH, | O thou holy Archon SOTER, Regent and Messenger of the resplendent SELAE GENETES, |

in the name of the same your God, vouchsafe to breathe into this Burin the unassailable power of Air, that it may be wholly harmonious to those Astral Realms in which it is to have authority.

| O thou who art mighty in the Vastness of Mizroch, | O thou who art mighty in the Vastness of Eos, |

where the breathable light comes forth from the purple-veiled Gates of Dawn, confer upon this Burin the purity and the luculence of Elemental Air, that in the works in which it participates, strength unseen shall be vindicated over material violence, freedom shall be found without folly, and flexibility without weakness: that vision and inspiration may be nurtured by all.

*Withdraw the hands.*

*With the right hand, trace above the Burin the sigil first of the Atziluthic name employed in the above invocation, and then of the Briatic name, in each case vibrating the name as you trace its sigil. (For this purpose, use the Presigillum of the Element Air, the sigillic line having been obtained from the Kamea of Malkuth.)*

*PROJECT UPON THE BURIN BY MEANS OF THE ORANTE FORMULA.*

*With the clenched hand, knock once upon the Bomos.*

*The Phial of Anointing Oil being held in the left hand, oil is taken upon the ball of the right thumb. The Phial is replaced. While the Burin is steadied by the left hand upon the hilt, the blade is anointed by drawing the right thumb along the central line of the blade, in a single movement from hilt to tip.*

*The left hand is now raised above the hilt of the Burin, the right hand is rested upon the Pentacle of the Quintessence, and the following is intoned:—*

Dwell upon the Holy Mountain, O Burin, but be thou swift in Air.

*The left hand is raised to touch the right hand upon the Pentacle, then both hands are extended to take up the Burin. The right hand clasps the handle, the left hand clasps the right, and the Burin is raised to be held before you, point uppermost, the hands level with the heart-centre and about 12" before you.*

*Maintaining this position, look to the East for a few*

*moments.*

*Carrying the Burin in the same postion, turn about, deosil, to face West. Crossing the centre, advance at an even pace in a straight line to the western limit of the circle of working; there turn about deosil without pausing, return to the centre, and maintaining the same pace make a smooth turn deosil at the centre through 90° to face South. Without pause, advance to the southern limit of the circle of working; there turn about deosil, still without pausing, and advance across the centre to the northern limit of the circle, where, keeping the same pace, make another smooth turn deosil to face South, and advance to the centre. Maintaining the same steady motion, turn deosil at the centre through 270° to face East; then stop.*

*Raise the Burin high in both hands, and proclaim:—*

Behold the Burin, behold the Priest of the Rites of Air!

*Still holding the Burin aloft, make a complete turn deosil at the centre. Facing East again, lower the Burin.*

*With the Burin held in the right hand only, trace the banishing pentagram of Spirit, vibrating* AHIH *or* ATHANATOS *as appropriate, while doing so. Next trace with the Burin the banishing pentagram of Air, vibrating* YHVH *or* SELAE GENETES *while doing so.*

*Pause for a few moments, then transfer the Burin to the left hand and make the Ave to the East.*

*Having dismissed the Ave, clasp the right hand about the left on the handle of the Burin and, hands at the level of the heart-centre and the point of the Burin uppermost, carry the Burin directly to the Bomos.*

*Replace the Burin upon the Bomos.*

*With the clenched hand, knock 3-5-3 upon the Bomos.*

## XXXII

## THE CONSECRATION OF THE CUP

*Tides:—*
New to first quarter Moon, Apas.
*Magician:—*
Basic robe, etc. Pentacle of Quintessence. Colour-charge blue.
*Bomos:—*
Black drape.

The Bomos is situated in the West of the place of working; the West-East axis of the Bomos should lie upon the West-East axis of the place of working. Two tall candlesticks (alternatively, two white lamps on pedestals) are set upon the floor, to the West of the Bomos, just within the intended astral circle, and in line with the North and South sides of the Bomos respectively; the Bomos should be so placed that these candlesticks are at about 18" distant from its western side.

*Equipment on Bomos:—*
    1. The Elemental Cup.*
    2. The Mystical Tessera.
    3. Phial of Oil.
    (A small finger-linen)

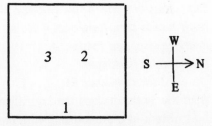

On the Bomos, upon the West-East axis, and fairly close to its eastern edge, is placed the Cup. Upon an imaginary line from the centre of the base of the Cup to the right-hand candlestick, and about midway between the Cup and the western edge of the Bomos, is placed the Tessera; at a corresponding position in relation to the Cup and the left-hand candlestick, is placed the Phial of Anointing Oil.

* See Note F following *Consecration of Elemental Wand.*

311

*Perform the Setting of the Wards of Power, Greek or Hebrew form as suitable, beginning from centre of place of working.*

*After the Setting, remain at the centre, facing East. Intone the Orison of Tiberianus (as given in the Disc Consecration Ritual).*

*Vibrate the First Enochian Key, and follow this with:—*

Thus do I invoke you, you Great Archangels LEXARPH, COMANAN, TABITOM, whose garments of light are beautified with admiration, and who dwell within the radiance of the Eternal.

*Turn deosil at centre to face West. With the right hand trace the invoking pentagram of Spirit, vibrating, as you do so, AGLA for Hebrew working, or ISCHYROS for Greek working. Again with the right hand, trace the invoking pentagram of water, vibrating, as you do so, EL for Hebrew working, or PANKRATES for Greek working.*

*Pause for a few moments, then proceed straight to the Bomos and face West across it.*

*With the clenched hand, knock once upon the Bomos.*

*Rest the right hand lightly upon the Mystical Tessera, then touch with the same hand the Pentacle of the Quintessence upon the breast. Bring up the left hand to cover for a moment the right hand upon the Pentacle, then take up the Cup, clasping the bowl thereof with fingers and thumbs of both hands simultaneously. Raise the cup to the level of the heart-centre, and intone:—*

| *(Hebrew)* | *(Greek)* |
|---|---|
| Most majestic EL, | Most majestic PANKRATES, |

from thy Station beyond the Crystalline Sphere behold this Cup, which by the work of my own hand, with the receptivity of the Fishes, with the adaptiveness of the Crab, and with the resoluteness of the Scorpion, I have prepared for the governance of the forces of Water in the workings of Art Magick. Let it stand before thee, that the world may behold thy splendor.

*The Cup is replaced on the Bomos, but the hands remain*

*in contact with it:—*

| Even thus, O most majestic | Even thus, O most majestic |
| EL, | PANKRATES, |

in the Noble Alchemy of the Great Work, in my offering of that which has been prepared does my soul offer itself; not indeed that it may be destroyed or that it may fail of its purpose, for in service to Divinity is true purpose found and fulfilled. This is my desire as I carry forward this rite: that as I have offered the Cup of my hand, so may the Cup of my aspirations be made ready for that service.

*Both hands are now raised to a loosely vertical position, the palms facing forward. Maintaining this position, declaim:—*

Your God speaks thus:

From the East with the course of the sun have I passed to the South, and on the glowing heights have I stood at gaze. Where are ye, my fruitful thunders?—where, ye storms of the South? Time moves to its ripening and to its plenitude: answer then with your voices of the cataract, clothe yourselves in purple clouds and come forth, my thunders, for this is your destined season. Yours it is to quicken the seed that was planted aforetime, the seed which holds the promise of the new beginning; to you have I given that power, and now is the season of its need, that the new age may come strongly to birth. Come then in your might, come in your beauty! Laugh O ye thunders, and sing, ye voices of rain! Visit the earth, O ye sons of delight, and bring to it abundance! for I am the Lord your God who is, and who lives.

So does he speak to you, Powers of the world of waters, fair friends and strong deliverers. So be ye to us, and with us lift voice in his praise.

*Both hands are lowered, the left now being placed upon the Pentacle of the Quintessence, and the right lightly clasping the bowl of the Cup without lifting it. Intone:—*

I am the Soul of Water, pellucid, inexorable. Most pliant is my aspect; but upon the vast rocks of justice and of destiny have I graven my imprint forever, so unalterable is my regenerative will.

Resolute am I, and subtle. With white mists do I veil myself in concealment, or majestically I crown my surging torrents with the

many-jewelled arc. I penetrate every deepest crevice of existence. I
carry upon my course stone and tree, living things and the seeds of life
to be; man and the works of man are in my hand; yet all increase comes
of my abundance. I receive with joy the benediction of the light, and
pass onward singing.

*The right hand is now raised to touch the left hand as it
lies upon the Pentacle of the Quintessence. The hands are next
lowered simultaneously, so that the bowl of the Cup is clasped
by fingers and thumbs of both hands. (The Cup is not raised.)
Address the Cup:—*

> Upon thee, O Cup, be the blessing of him whose law
>             directs the holy ones,
> The blessing of him who reigns without beginning
>             and without end:
> Upon thee as a most clear shining be the blessing
>             of the Highest.

*Raise the hands simultaneously to a loosely horizontal
position, palms downward, slightly above the bowl of the
Cup, and maintain them in this positon whilst intoning:—*

|                  *(Hebrew)*                  |                  *(Greek)*                  |
|---|---|
| O thou holy Archangel MIEL, | O thou holy Archon ASPHALEIOS, |
| Regent and Messenger of the most | Regent and Messenger of the most |
| majestic EL, | majestic PANKRATES, |

in the name of the same your God, vouchsafe to fill this Cup with the
all-pervading magnetism of Water, that it may be wholly harmonious to
those Astral Realms in which it is to have authority.

| O thou who art mighty in the | O thou who art mighty in the |
|---|---|
| Expanse of Ma'arob, | Expanse of Zophos, |

where living dews distil at the Portals of the Star-Bearer, confer upon
this Cup the loveliness and limpidity of Elemental Water, that in the
works in which it participates, gentleness may ever prevail by perseverance, strength may ever be characterised by gracefulness; and life may
be refreshed and sustained by all.

*Withdraw the hands.*

*With the right hand, trace above the Cup the sigil first of the Atziluthic name employed in the above invocation, and then of the Briatic name, in each case vibrating the name as you trace its sigil. (For this purpose, use the Presigillum of the Element Water, the sigillic line having been obtained from the Kamea of Malkuth.)*

*PROJECT UPON THE CUP BY MEANS OF THE ORANTE FORMULA.*

*With the clenched hand, knock once upon the Bomos.*

*The Phial of Anointing Oil being held in the left hand, oil is taken upon the ball of the right thumb. The phial is replaced. The Cup is now taken up in the left hand, and is anointed once, inside the bowl at its base.*

*The cup is replaced upon the Bomos.*

*The left hand is extended above the Cup, the right hand is rested upon the Pentacle of the Quintessence, and the following is intoned:—*

Dwell in the Firmament, O Cup, but be thou mighty in Water.

*The left hand is raised to touch the right hand upon the Pentacle, then both hands are extended simultaneously to the Cup. The Cup is raised, the right hand grasping the bowl and the left hand supporting the foot. The Cup is now held upright in both hands at the level of the heart-centre. Maintaining this position, look to the West for a few moments.*

*Carrying the Cup in the same position at the level of the heart-centre, turn about, deosil, to face East. Crossing the centre, advance at an even pace in a straight line to the eastern limit of the circle of working: there turn about deosil without pausing, return to the centre, and maintaining the same pace make a smooth turn deosil at the centre through 90° to face North. Without pause, advance to the northern limit of the circle of working: there turn about deosil, still without pausing, and advance across the centre to the southern limit of the circle, where, keeping the same pace, make another smooth turn deosil to face North, and advance to the centre. Maintaining the same steady motion, turn deosil at the centre through 270° to face West; then stop.*

*Maintaining the position of the hands, raise the Cup high and proclaim:—*

Behold the Cup, behold the Priestess of the Vision of Water!

*Still holding the Cup aloft, make a complete turn deosil at the centre. Facing West again, lower the Cup.*

*With the Cup held by its stem and in the right hand only, trace the banishing pentagram of Spirit, vibrating* AGLA *or* ISCHYROS *as appropriate while doing so. Next trace with the Cup the banishing pentagram of Water, vibrating* EL *or* PANKRATES *while doing so.*

*Pause for a few moments, then transfer the Cup to the left hand and turn deosil to face East.*

*Make the Ave to the East.*

*Having dismissed the Ave, turn deosil to face West. With both hands hold the Cup at the level of the heart-centre as before, and carry it thus directly to the Bomos.*

*Replace the Cup upon the Bomos.*

*With the clenched hand, knock 3-5-3 upon the Bomos.*

*The Elemental Cup*

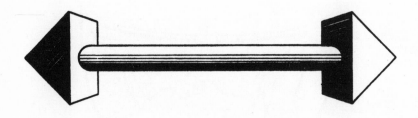

*The Elemental Wand*

*XXXIII*

## *CONSECRATION OF THE WAND*

*Tides:–*
> Full Moon, Agni.

*Magician:–*
> Basic robe, etc., Pentacle of Quintessence. Colour-charge red.

*Bomos:–*
> Black drape.

The Bomos is situated in the South of the place of working; the South-North axis of the Bomos should lie upon the South-North axis of the place of working. Two tall candlesticks (alternatively, two white lamps on pedestals) are set upon the floor, to the South of the Bomos, just within the intended astral circle, and in line with the East and West sides of the Bomos respectively; the Bomos should be so placed that these candlesticks are at about 18" distant from its southern side.

*Equipment on Bomos:–*
  1. The Elemental Wand.*
  2. The Mystical Tessera.
  3. Phial of Oil.
  (A small finger-linen)

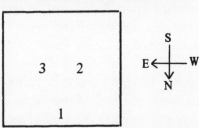

On the Bomos, with its length upon the South-North axis, is placed the Wand: its black pyramid points toward the South, its white pyramid being fairly close to the northern edge of the Bomos. Upon an imaginary line from the midpoint of the Wand to the right-hand candlestick, and about midway between the Wand and the southern edge of the Bomos, is placed the Tessera; at a corresponding position in relation to the midpoint of the Wand and the left-hand candlestick, is placed the Phial.

---

* See Note G following *Consecration of Elemental Wand.*

*Perform the Setting of the Wards of Power, Greek or Hebrew form as suitable, beginning from centre of place of working;*

*After the Setting, remain at the centre, facing East. Intone the Orison of Tiberianus (as given in the Disc Consecration Ritual).*

*Vibrate the First Enochian Key, and follow this with:—*

Thus do I invoke you, you Great Archangels LEXARPH, COMANAN, TABITOM, whose garments of light are beautified with admiration, and who dwell within the radiance of the Eternal.

*Turn deosil at centre to face South. With the right hand trace the invoking pentagram of Spirit, vibrating, as you do so, AHIH for Hebrew working, or ATHANATOS for Greek working. Again with the right hand, trace the invoking pentagram of Fire, vibrating, as you do so, ALHIM for Hebrew working, or THEOS for Greek working.*

*Pause for a few moments, then go directly to the Bomos and face South across it.*

*With the clenched hand, knock once upon the Bomos.*

*Rest the right hand lightly upon the Mystical Tessera, then touch with the same hand the Pentacle of the Quint-essence upon the breast. Bring up the left hand to cover for a moment the right hand upon the Pentacle, then extend both hands to take up the Wand from the Bomos. Keeping the Wand horizontal and directed towards the South, the right hand grasps the shaft and lifts it: the left hand meanwhile is placed beneath the black pyramid, so that in one slow movement the Wand is raised to the level of the heart-centre. Intone:—*

*(Hebrew)*                 *(Greek)*

Most wonderful ELOHIM,     Most wonderful THEOS,
from thy Chariot of the Celestial Fires behold this Wand, which by the work of my own hand, with the creativity of the Ram, with the perceptivity of the Archer, and with the liberality of the Lion, I have prepared for the governance of the forces of Fire in the workings of Art Magick. Let it go forth with the light of thy countenance, that the world

may know thy power.

*The Wand is replaced as before on the Bomos. The finger-tips of the left hand are placed lightly upon the black pyramid and those of the right hand upon the white pyramid; the two hands are thus parallel, the left directly before the right:—*

Even thus, O wonderful ELOHIM,   |   Even thus, O wonderful THEOS, in the Noble Alchemy of the Great Work, in my offering of that which has been prepared does my soul offer itself; not indeed that it may be destroyed or that it may fail of its purpose, for in service to Divinity is true purpose found and fulfilled. This is my desire as I carry forward this rite: that as I have offered the Wand of my hand, so may the Wand of my will be made ready for that service.

*Both hands are now raised to a loosely vertical position, the palms facing forward. Maintaining this position, declaim:—*

Between earth and heaven cluster the fires of the firmament, where nine great Spirits move them. Adorn your heads, O ye righteous, with garlanded flames; gladden your brows as with shining crocus and as with lilies cool to the touch. Like a vine through the world spreads the fire, and the wine of its flames shall be an envenomed draught of torment to the wicked: but its shoots shall be fiery darts for the winnowing of the world. Seven and six and nine and nine again form the number of the winnowers; continually do they visit the earth and surely as the tides of ocean or the turning of the seasons, for unceasing is the sifting of the grain of truth.

Wherefore give heed, ye Fiery Ones, and be moved in power and in presence; for your works shall be as a song of honour, chanted in praise of your God.

*Both hands are lowered, the left now being placed upon the Pentacle of the Quintessence, the fingers of the right hand lightly clasping the shaft of the Wand without lifting it. Intone:—*

I, Incorporeal Flame, in the veins of the universe I run as living blood. My spirit is mighty, my energies animate the spheres.

From the gathering dusk, from the unthinking silence, without warning, leap I lightning-crowned upon the world. My spirit is intrepid:

my deeds enkindle the earth.

From the holiest ground do I, the golden one, the brilliant-robed, soar heavenward. My spirit is joyous, joyous! my laughter challenges the void.

*The right hand is now raised to touch the left hand as it lies upon the Pentacle of the Quintessence. The hands are next lowered simultaneously, so that the fingers of the left hand are placed lightly upon the black pyramid and those of the right hand upon the white pyramid, as previously. Address the Wand:—*

Upon thee, O Wand, be the blessing of him whose law
    directs the holy ones,
The blessing of him who reigns without beginning
    and without end:
Upon thee as a most clear shining be the blessing
    of the Highest.

*Raise the hands to a loosely horizontal position slightly above the Wand, palms down, the left hand remaining in advance of the right and being raised somewhat higher. Maintain the hands in this position whilst intoning:—*

| *(Hebrew)* | *(Greek)* |
|---|---|
| O thou holy Archangel ASHIEL, Regent and Messenger of the wonderful ELOHIM, | O thou holy Archon ALASTOR, Regent and Messenger of the wonderful THEOS, |

in the name of the same your God, vouchsafe to endue this Wand with the victorious radiance of Fire, that it may be wholly harmonious to those Astral Realms in which it is to have authority.

| | |
|---|---|
| O thou who are mighty in the Altitude of Doraum, | O thou who are mighty in the Altitude of Notos, |

where the refulgent flame leaps flashing to the central heaven, confer upon this Wand the glory and the pride of Elemental Fire, that in the works in which it participates, all inessentials which might obscure the judgment shall disappear, the materia of the rites and likewise the participants shall be refined as gold, and true marvels may abound without deceit.

*Withdraw the hands.*

*With the right hand, trace above the Wand the sigil first of the Atziluthic name employed in the above invocation, and then of the Briatic name, in each case vibrating the name as you trace its sigil. (For this purpose, use the Presigillum of the Element Fire, the sigillic line having been obtained from the Kamea of Malkuth.)*

*PROJECT UPON THE WAND BY MEANS OF THE ORANTE FORMULA.*

*With the clenched hand, knock once upon the Bomos.*

*The Phial of Anointing Oil being held in the left hand, oil is taken upon the ball of the right thumb. The Phial is replaced. The Wand is taken up in the left hand and is held vertically just above the Bomos, the black pyramid uppermost. The tip of this pyramid is now anointed by drawing the right thumb once across it, after which the Wand is reversed so that the white pyramid is uppermost. The tip of this pyramid is similarly anointed. The Wand is reversed again and is then replaced upon the Bomos.*

*The left hand is extended above the shaft of the Wand, the right hand is rested upon the Pentacle of the Quintessence, and the following is intoned:—*

Dwell above the Storm, O Wand, but be thou potent in Fire.

*The left hand is raised to touch the right hand upon the Pentacle, then both hands are extended to take up the Wand. The right hand clasps the shaft, the left hand clasps the right, and the Wand is raised to be held vertically before you, black pyramid uppermost, the hands level with the heart-centre and about 12" before you.*

*Maintaining this position, look to the South for a few moments.*

*Carrying the Wand in the same position, turn about, deosil, to face North. Crossing the centre, advance at an even pace in a straight line to the northern limit of the circle of working; there turn about deosil without pausing, return to the centre, and maintaining the same pace make a smooth turn deosil at the centre through 90° to face West. Without pause, advance to the western limit of the circle of working; there turn about deosil, still without pausing, and advance across the centre to the eastern limit of the circle, where, keeping the same pace, make another smooth turn deosil to face West, and advance to the centre. Maintaining the same steady motion, turn deosil at the centre through 270° to face South; then stop.*

*Maintaining the position of the hands, raise the Wand vertically on high and proclaim:—*

**Behold the Wand, behold the Priest of the Voice of Fire!**

*Still holding the Wand aloft, make a complete turn deosil at the centre. Facing South again, lower the Wand.*

*Holding the Wand in the right hand only, reverse it so that the white pyramid is uppermost. With the Wand held thus, trace the banishing pentagram of Spirit, vibrating* **AHIH** *or* **ATHANATOS** *as appropriate while doing so. Next trace with the Wand the banishing pentagram of Fire, vibrating* **ELOHIM** *or* **THEOS** *while doing so.*

*Pause for a few moments, reverse the Wand so that the black pyramid is uppermost, transfer it to the left hand and turn deosil to face East.*

*Make the Ave to the East.*

*Having dismissed the Ave, turn deosil to face South. Hold the Wand vertically with both hands at the level of the heart-centre, and carry it directly to the Bomos.*

*Replace the Wand upon the Bomos.*

*With the clenched hand, knock 3-5-3 upon the bomos.*

*Notes to the Four Elemental Consecration Rites:*

A)    Between workings, each of the Elemental Weapons should be kept wrapped in silk.

B)    Tzophaun ( צָפוּן ), Mizroch ( מִזְרָח ), Ma'arob ( מַעֲרָב ), and Doraum ( דָּרוֹם ) are the Hebrew names of the quarters.

Arktos (ΑΡΚΤΟΣ), Eos (ΗΩΣ), Zophos (ΖΟΦΟΣ) and Notos (ΝΟΤΟΣ) are the Greek names of the quarters.

C)    In each of the above Elemental Rites, the combination of movements in the paced figure, after the act of consecration and until the final return to the quarter, is unsuited to the use of a text to be carried about the place of working. It should, therefore, be practised beforehand, and will be found to present no difficulty.

D)    The Disc is constructed of fine-grained wood (preferably white-wood), and is approximately 13.00 cm. in diameter and 1.25 cm. in thickness. The outermost circle is 1.00 cm. from the circumference of the disc, each of the four segmented bands being 5 mm. across and the spaces between them being 2 mm. across. The central circle is 1.25 cm. in diameter.

The central circle and twelve wavy rays are spectrum yellow or deep cadmium yellow. The four 5 mm. segmented bands, taken in order from the inmost outwards are (1) citrine, (2) olive, (3) russet, (4) black. The background is left as natural.

E)    The Burin is approximately 24.00 cm. in length. The haft and the central knop are white. The wings are painted white on all surfaces, then patterned as in the diagram at the beginning of the *Burin Consecration* rite: the upper edge of the wings remains white: the inner sections of the plumes are black upon a red ground, the outer section has violet plumes upon a white ground.

F)    The Cup is of opaque or translucent blue glass, approximately 12 cm. high. Upon the exterior of the Cup is carried out the design of a sea-dragon. The main coloring of the dragon is black, with details of scales, coils, etc., in white: the crest and fins of the dragon are colored orange, with details in black or white as may be deemed suitable.

G)    For the Elemental Wand, take a piece of copper tube of 1.50 cm. external diameter and 19.60 cm. long, burnished and lacquered.

On a base line of exactly 6.00 cm., construct an isosceles triangle having each of the other two sides 5.70 cm. in length. Cut out in thin card four such triangles, also a square having each side 6.00 cm. long. With adhesive tape, join the sides of the triangles carefully to one another, and each of the base-lines to a side of the square, so as to form a model pyramid. It will be found that although the perpendicular distance from apex to base of each triangle is about 4.80 cm., the height of the three-dimensional model is only about 3.90 cm., owing to the slope of the sides.

Using this card structure as a model, carve, cast or otherwise achieve two such pyramids of solid material. Provide in the center of the base of each pyramid a hole 1.50 cm. in diameter (a close fit for the copper tube) and as exactly as possible 1.30 cm. deep.

Paint one of the pyramids with the sides glossy white and the base black, the other with sides glossy black and the base white.

Fit each pyramid firmly to an end of the prepared copper tube. The ends of the tube should be authentically buried to the depth of 1.30 cm. in the pyramids. This is not merely so that the weapon may be securely assembled, but is a vital condition for its magical efficiency: the center of gravity of the pyramid lies at a point which is measured from the base up the central perpendicular of the pyramid, one-third the length of that perpendicular: in the present instance, 1.30 cm.

This Aurum Solis weapon is wielded with the *black* pyramid uppermost to invoke, the *white* pyramid uppermost to banish.

## XXXIV

## ON THE USE OF THE MAGICAL WEAPONS

### The Great Wand or Spear

The Great Wand is the characteristic weapon of the Western Tradition. Its authority derives from that of the Primal Father: an origin which renders the authority of the Great Wand not only unquestioned but unquestionable, since it is associated with that quality of *fascination* which belongs to its phallic connotations. The Great Wand is mighty in the World of Yetzirah: it awakens and calls forth all those forces which are within the magician's right to command, and its principle use is in invocation of the planetary and zodiacal forces of Yetzirah. Though in special circumstances it is used to command Elemental Forces, it is not used in the invocation of *Elementals* properly so called, the Four Elemental Weapons fulfilling that function. On no account is the Great Wand used to *banish* forces, since this would be in opposition to its function of fascination, its power of enchantment: neither is it to be used for Goetic invocations, in which it might destroy the very conditions in and through which the magician has to work.

### The Sword

The Sword is the great weapon of defence and of magick might: its attribution is to Mars, but more occultly it has besides a secondary association with the fiery aspect of solar force.

Being of steel which is, fundamentally, iron, it is of the

327

great magical metal of more than one western cult, and symbol of the mysteries of the lame Hephaestus.

The powers of the Sword are many. It is the executive symbol of Divine Strength. It is used as an instrument of banishing, its function of invocation being limited to Goetic forces generally, and allowably to the Yetziratic forces of the Sephirah Geburah. It is also introduced into the workings to implement such acts as binding, limiting, forbidding, defence, severance, and cautery.

(A temple of the A.S. has its own set of the Magical Weapons, which are consecrated by an appointed officer in the presence of witnesses. These are wielded, in the name of the Order, by duly appointed officers, and are absolutely *not* for the private use of any individual member. A Sword consecrated for the Order never leaves its temple. The temple Sword is the immediate guardian of that current from the Inner Planes which is the true magical life of the Order.)

*The Grail*

Sufficient has been said of the Grail, both in this book (see *Principles of Ceremonial)* and in Book II, Ch. VIII, to enable the student to appreciate the occasions of its use.

*The Four Elemental Weapons*

By virtue of its consecration an Elemental Weapon is potent not only with regard to *Elementals,* but throughout the whole range of its Element of attribution in Yetzirah, both in banishing and in invoking.

When an Elemental Weapon is used in any rite which is other than elemental but which requires an elemental base, it is restricted to the invocation and subsequent banishing of *Elementals.*

In a purely elemental working, the appropriate Elemental Weapon can be used as suitable within the Yetziratic range of its attribution. However, a special case is to be noted: in an evocation to visible appearance, even though this be of a purely elemental attribution, the use of the Elemental Weapon is restricted solely to the initial invocation of *Elementals*. The Great Wand and the Sword are in such a case used in the ceremony proper, and the Sword is used for the banishings.

Since only those weapons which have real meaning and purpose in a working may be introduced, this, in the case of the Elemental Weapons, will mean that either the one Elemental Weapon which corresponds to the Element of the working can be present, or else all four when the rite is of all four Elements. There is no occasion for having upon the Bomos three of the Elemental Weapons, or two of them. In sub-elemental working, still only the weapon of the principal Element may validly be employed for its sub-elements. (This is especially pointed out, so that the student may not be misled by the chaotic and indiscriminate use of the Elemental Weapons found in other systems.)

# PART VI

# RITUAL FORMULAE

# XXXV

## SPHERE-WORKING

We give the name of Sphere-working to a class of magical operation which has as its objective meditation within the ambience of one or other of the seven planetary spheres. Despite their innate simplicity, Sphere-workings are of considerable importance, being a source of magical experience which provides the greater part of ordinary group activity in Second Hall work.

One of the formulae to which these workings are constructed—the so-called Dionic Formula—is given below. The development of this formula into a working for a chosen sphere will involve a judicious use of the correspondences, not only with regard to suitable arrangement of the place of operation and the fixing of the time of working for harmonious Tides, but also in relation to the actions and sounds of the rite.

### The Dionic Formula

i. The Setting of the Wards of Power is performed (preferably by a participant other than the director of the working.)

ii. The astral matrix is formulated by the group; this may be accomplished in silence, or to accord with the enunciation by the director of an inspiring passage which describes the Astral Temple as a vivid reality.

iii. Clavis Rei Primae 1st Formula, the Rousing of the Citadels, is performed by all members of the group simultaneously (all hands may be linked while this takes place.) Following the Rousing occurs a dialogue to begin establishing the general tone of the Sphere, and/or, where the participants have specific functions in the working, to proclaim these functions.

333

iv.    The director now makes adoration of the God-force
       of the Sphere, and asks, in what form he will, that
       this working may be so infused by the divine influence
       that the group may through the working attain to a
       true perception and understanding of the mysteries
       of the Sphere.

v.     Whatever action has been devised, or is spontaneously
       to occur, for the purpose of establishing the ambience
       of the Sphere in this working, now takes place. Music,
       speech, dance, the enactment of a mythic theme, aral
       circumambulations:— any combination of these, or
       whatsoever means may be judged fitting, is here
       included to create a pageant or celebration appropri-
       ate to the Sphere. The building-up of "atmosphere"
       is for this step of the work the major consideration.

vi.    The group now formulates the Magical Image of the
       Sphere, and when this has been powerfully built up
       the director vibrates the Divine Name of the Sphere.

vii.   After standing for some moments in silence, all
       assume the God-form posture (chairs having been
       placed beforehand) and proceed into meditation with
       eyes closed, allowing impressions to rise into con-
       sciousness and exploring inwardly the living actuality
       of the Sphere of operation. This meditation should
       continue for at least twenty minutes before the
       director gives the signal to withdraw from it.

viii.  The director addresses the God-force of the Sphere
       with adoration and thanksgiving.

ix.    All recite an appropriate Magical Hymn or other text
       in celebration of the Sphere.

x.     Valediction is given by the director.

N.B.   *None of the consecrated implements is employed in
       Sphere-working, save the Tessera, which should be
       upon the Bomos.*

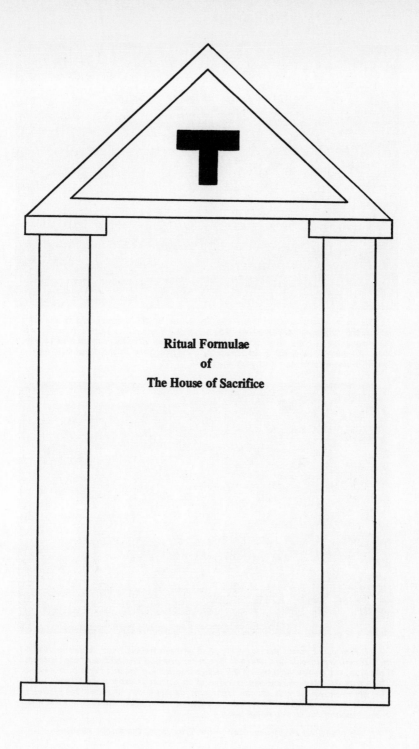

Ritual Formulae
of
The House of Sacrifice

*The most exact account that can be given of this ivory panel is that the carving is Byzantine and was executed between the X and XII centuries. It represents the amazement of the witnesses at finding the Holy Sepulchre open and empty. Most notable for us is the clear House of Sacrifice form of the sepulchre, with a central column forming a Tau with the lintel.*

*This panel forms part of a jewelled and enamelled cross, which originated in XIII century France and which is rich in the mystical symbolism of the Ogdoadic Tradition, the geometric areas of the design confirming the intention of the whole. The cross has five picture-panels relating to different aspects of Regeneration. The panel shown here is on the right arm of the cross: it shows the House of Sacrifice in its traditional form, with the Signum Tau being painted over the lintel in the blood of the slain paschal lamb.*

*Both reproductions are by Courtesy of the Trustees of the British Museum.*

## XXXVI

## RITUAL FORMULAE OF THE HOUSE OF SACRIFICE

A ritual formula is a presentation of the necessary skeletal structure upon which the magician can construct his own working for a particular purpose. The process of constructing a working from a formula may be compared to the building of a house, or the making of a garment, from tried and tested plans, patterns and instructions. Each object so created will be an individual thing, according to the understanding and skill which the operator brings to the undertaking, the availability of materials, the choice of them, judgment and taste regarding additions and adornments, and, in short, the adaptation of a minimal and essential framework to a particular and personal requirement for a specific time and place.

Each of the following examples from the A. S. range of ritual formulae is divided into five sections, corresponding to the parts of the House of Sacrifice (cf. Book II, Chapter IV):—

Sections I and II correspond to the doorposts or pillars, sections III, IV and V to the superstructure. This formulation thus equates to Dyad and Triad of the ancient Qabalistic-Gnostic pattern which is set forth in Book I, Chapter VI.*

The following table shows in simple form the correspondences of the parts of the psyche to the parts of the House of Sacrifice, together with some key-concepts which relate to

---

* The higher medieval mysteries, wherein the sections III and IV of the *Domus Sacrificii* transpose, are not herein to be set forth.

337

the general use of each part of the fivefold pattern in the ritual formulae.

The Fivefold Pattern

Dyad
{
I:    ANIMA (Breath). *Ruach.* The forces of the rite, spiritual considerations, the Intent.

II:   CORPUS (Body). *Nephesh.* Materials, persons, place, material considerations.
}

Triad
{
III:  IUSTITIA (Justice). *Neshamah.* Any aspects of severity, deprivation, offering, renunciation, limitation, conditioning.

IV:   CLEMENTIA (Mercy). *Chiah.* The essential operation of the rite.

V:    CANDOR (Glory). *Yechidah.* Locking, confirmation, proclamation, showing forth of completed work. The Quintessence.
}

Every use, medieval or modern, of the pattern of the House of Sacrifice interprets that pattern in terms peculiar to its own requirements. That is to say, the allocation of material to the various parts of the fivefold pattern is entirely dependent upon the significance of that material in the particular case; so that the relationship of a working or a formula to the primal pattern, while always implicit, is not necessarily explicit. It is not, indeed, necessary that the relationship should be explicit. The pattern of the House of Sacrifice is, in itself, a most potent means of setting in due order material which has by ritual use to be made active either through, or upon, the psyche.

When building a rite upon one of the A.S. formulae, it is the student's responsibility to utilise everything that he considers will promote the atmosphere and the energies of his particular working. He must collate the correspondences at all levels.

At the head of each of our formulae will be found a basic

table of requirements, but the student may in a particular case consider it desirable to introduce additional materials or equipment.

Music of one kind or another can be of great value, whether as an atmospheric background, or to accompany dancing or mime, or as an episode in its own right.

With regard to the speeches, the student has considerable scope and freedom in composing these, provided only that they fulfil the stated requirements of the formula. Where material is given in detail in the formula, that material must be employed as directed; but any other material may be added if suitable, whether found in this series or elsewhere.* Provided the basic structure of the rite be kept as given in the formula, other ritual acts may also be incorporated to bring out the significance of the rite and to further its purpose.

The harmony and purpose of the whole rite is to be borne in mind no less than the details which require attention; the finished product may be complex or simple, but should be an example of Art Magick skilfully wrought as the operator can devise.

Three of the formulae we give are hierarchical, namely, *Evocation to Visible Appearance in the Triangle of Art*, *Evocation to Visible Appearance in the Crystal*, and *Consecration of a Talisman;* three are non-hierarchical, namely, *The Magician, Transubstantiation*, and *The Gnostic*.

The formula of *Transubstantiation* and the formula of *The Gnostic* are exclusively Sub Rosa Nigra, and involve the Constellation of the Worshipped.

The formula of *The Magician* may be worked Hebrew, Sub Rosa Nigra, or according to the student's personal system. This formula is, but for the Setting of the Wards of Power,

---

* We are here simply advising the student to be enterprising in bringing suitable material to his private workings, as an alternative on any occasion to composing his own speeches. We are not giving permission here for any public use which would contravene our own or anyone else's copyright!

entirely microcosmic, so that any material introduced into the rite is required to be subordinated to that fact.

The three hierarchical formulae may be worked Hebrew, Sub Rosa Nigra, or according to the student's personal system. When the working of these formulae is Sub Rosa Nigra, the appropriate A.S. Atziluthic Word of Power is employed with the corresponding names from the Archontic Sequence; in Section 2, *The Spiritual Forces,* subsection a, the invocation of the Light and Life of the Godhead should be made under the presidency of the divine name HA (the Constellation not being otherwise employed in a hierarchical working). Of these three hierarchical formulae, the two formulae of *Evocation to Visible Appearance* can also be employed for full Enochian working. Regard must be had in all cases for the relationship of forces in the particular hierarchy of working.

It would go far beyond the scope of the present work to give variant formulae for all needs that the student is likely to encounter. It is intended therefore that the student should learn not only to construct his own rites from the formulae, but further, taking as examples all the uses of the fivefold pattern which we present in these volumes, to construct his own formulae to that pattern. Not otherwise can the scope of the principles given in *The Magical Philosophy* be utilised, nor can the potential of the available material be otherwise brought into realisation.

## XXXVII

## EVOCATION TO VISIBLE APPEARANCE
## IN THE TRIANGLE OF ART
### For Hierarchical Planetary or Elemental Working

(This formula and its ensuing sister-formula for Evocation to Crystal are suited to the evocation of those elemental or planetary entities which may be governed by theurgic rites. They are not for use in the evocation of goetic elemental or planetary entities, nor in the evocation of any zodiacal entities whether theurgic or goetic. For the zodiacal entities, special formulae exist.)

*The Magick Circle:* —
Within the place of working, concentric circles, approximately 9 feet and 8 feet 8 inches in diameter; between the concentric circles, at each of the four quarters, the God-name of the working in its associated script.

*The Triangle of Art:* —
A right-angled triangle, the sides being of 3, 4, and 5 units, and having an inner triangle with sides parallel to the outer, and approximately four inches from it.

Between the outer and inner triangles are inscribed—on the sides of 3, 4 and 5 units respectively—PRIMEMATON, ANEXHEXETON, and the God-name of the working: this last is to be inscribed in its associated script, the other two in the Roman alphabet.

The Triangle of Art is located within the place of working in the quarter of the Element (or elemental affinity) of the working, and as close to the Magick Circle as will allow of easy passage between it and that Circle.

For any quarter, the position of the Triangle relative to the Magick Circle is as follows: the Triangle's side of 4 units lies nearest to the Magick Circle, the side of 3 units being at the right as the operator stands within the Magick Circle looking at the Triangle.

*Tides:* —
As most potent for the working.

*Magician:* —

Basic robe, etc. Pentacle of Quintessence, or Enochian Pentacle as suitable. (On reverse of Pentacle, in all cases, sigil of Angel or Spirit which is to be evoked.) Colour-charge, as appropriate for the working.

*Bomos:* —

Bomos at centre of Magick Circle, square to cardinal points. Colour of drape, as colour-charge. Equipment placed upon Bomos to be arranged with due balance, and suitably for use by the operator when facing the quarter where the Triangle of Art is established.

*Equipment (essential requirements):* —

Mystical Tessera; Great Wand; Sword; Elemental Weapon as appropriate; Enochian Tablet as appropriate; Crater. (The Crater is a small open vessel of brass or copper, of depth about half its diameter; it is supported on a tripod or other suitable small stand. It is prepared beforehand by placing in it a small quantity of alcohol blended with a couple of drops of Anointing Oil.

*Incense and Lights:* —

As deemed fitting and desirable.

## I

1.   *The Astral Defences.*

Setting of the Wards of Power, beginning and concluding within Magick Circle, East of Bomos facing East.

2.   *The Spiritual Forces.*

a) A reverent invocation of the Illimitable Godhead in Kether.

b) The 1st Enochian Key, without invocation of the three Archangels if the Theban Angelic Formula is to be employed later.

c) Energisation of self by 2nd Formula of Clavis Rei Primae. High Spiritual invocation with personal and microcosmic emphasis: for example *Hymnodia Krypte, XIII, 18.*

d) Orthrochoros.

3.   *The Deific Force of the Working.*

Adoration and invocation of the God-force of the Element or Sphere; to be made within the Magick Circle, facing across the Bomos towards the quarter wherein the Triangle of Art is established.

4.  *Spirits of the Element or of the Elemental Affinity.*

Invocation of Elementals;* here the Elemental Weapon is used.

5.  *Proclamation of the Rite.*

To be made from the eastern limit of the place of working facing West. The following is to be intoned:—

"I proclaim a Rite of Evocation in the Element/Sphere of *(name it).*

"This Evocation shall have relation to Time Present and present use.

"It shall have relation to Mysteries far exceeding itself.

"It shall have relation to a Purpose and Intent whereby the Majesty and Name of the All-Highest shall, and may, and of force must, appear with the apparition of his Wonders, and Marvels yet unheard of."

6.  *The Hierarchy.*

Energisation of self by 2nd Formula of Clavis Rei Primae. A worthy and beautiful invocation of God-force of Element or Sphere, followed by aspiration to be a worthy vehicle for the operation of that Divine Influence in the rite about to be performed. A request to be empowered with the utmost power to stir and to cause the obedience of the Angel or Spirit *N* who is to be evoked. Request for the magical aid of the hierarchical forces of the Element or Sphere (other than the entity to be evoked), with utterance of their names. To be accomplished from the station as at 3.

7.  *The Magician.*

To be uttered from the eastern limit of the place of working facing West, the proclamation by the operator of his magical name and status, and the basis of his magical authority; beginning:—

---

* See Appendix D for Form of Invocation and Dismissal of Elementals.

"The Mysteries of the All-Highest gave a Time, and behold, I am provided for that Time: for I am . . . . . . "

8.  *Declaration of Intent.*

To be made in the presence of the Powers, from the same station as at 7. The intention to evoke a certain spiritual entity to visible appearance, in order to obtain a specific benefit (certain knowledge, for instance) by means of *Negotium* with that entity.

II

9.  *The Triangle of Art.*

a) Station as at 3 in Magick Circle; Sword to be taken in right hand and carried deosil round Bomos to quarter where Triangle is established. Operator to leave Magick Circle at that point. From space between Magick Circle and Triangle of Art, outline of Triangle to be traced with Sword in continuous line, taking the sides in order 3-4-5; with tracing of each side, vibration of the Name ascribed thereto.

b) Operator to enter the Triangle, still facing the quarter. Sword being pointed vertically downward to touch ground within Triangle, visualization of self as wearing robe of colour drawn from the Contingent Scale appropriately to the working. This posture and formulation are to be maintained during the following declamation:—

"Within this Triangle of Art, through and according to the Rite and Formula of Evocation, the Angel (or Spirit) *N* will be caused to manifest."

Formulation to be dismissed, operator re-centring on his magical personality. Operator to turn deosil to face Bomos, to step out of Triangle and into Magick Circle, then to proceed deosil around Bomos to resume station as at 3. Sword replaced.

c) Great Wand to be taken in right hand and carried deosil round Bomos to quarter where Triangle is established.

Operator to leave Magick Circle at that point. From space between Magick Circle and Triangle, sigil to be traced of Angel or Spirit which will be evoked: just above surface of ground within Triangle and in horizontal plane.

d) Single deosil circumambulation about Triangle of Art, one stamp being made with the right foot upon return to the point of departure, then movement to be continued to make single widdershins circumambulation of Magick Circle. This completed, operator to turn sharply widdershins to enter Magick Circle, then to proceed deosil around Bomos to resume station as at 3. Great Wand to be replaced.*

10. *The Magick Circle.*

a) Sword to be taken from Bomos with right hand, the Mystical Tessera with left. Thus equipped, operator to assume station East of Bomos facing East. Outer circle (of Magick Circle) to be touched with Sword at due eastern point, Sword then to be raised aloft in a graceful arc so that its tip moves to a point high above centre of Bomos. Keeping sword-tip as nearly as possible to this point, operator to proceed deosil to South, the sword-hilt moving in a quarter-circle with him. Sword next to be lowered in a graceful arc to touch outer circle at due southern point, then raised aloft in a graceful arc to midpoint above centre of Bomos. Maintaining sword-tip thus, operator to proceed to the West, to lower Sword as before to touch outer circle at due western point, then to raise it gracefully to midpoint above Bomos; to proceed thence to North, to touch outer circle with Sword at due northern point, to raise Sword to midpoint above Bomos, to return deosil to East, and finally to lower Sword in a graceful arc to touch the ground at the due eastern point of outer circle. Operator to resume

* From this point until the action in 25, the operator remains within the Magick Circle.

station as at 3; Sword and Tessera to be returned to Bomos.

b) Energisation of self by 2nd Formula of Clavis Rei Primae.

c)With both hands on the Pentacle at breast, operator to visualize himself as wearing robe of colour drawn from the Contingent Scale appropriately to the working. Threefold vibration of God-name of working, posture and colour-formulation being maintained meanwhile.

11. *Preliminary Adjuration to the Entity to be Evoked.*

Great Wand being taken in right hand, operator to assume station in quarter where Triangle is established, and facing that quarter. Left hand to be laid upon Pentacle at breast, and to remain there while a preliminary adjuration is begun, addressed to the Angel or Spirit which is to be evoked:—

In the name of the God-force of Element or Sphere, the Angel or Spirit to be called upon by name and title, and its sigil to be traced towards the quarter with the Great Wand; the Angel or Spirit being bidden to hear the operator who is about to make evocation of it.

The remainder of the preliminary adjuration to be given from the station as at 3, the left hand remaining on the Pentacle meanwhile:—

Angel or Spirit *N* to be conjured in the Divine Name, that it move and appear when operator shall invoke it.

Angel or Spirit adjured in the Divine Name, to do as operator shall command; to come promptly, and in fair and intelligible form, when summoned; to manifest in the Triangle of Art outside the Magick Circle (operator here to point with Great Wand towards Triangle); and to answer truly, clearly, and unequivocally, when manifest.

Great Wand to be replaced.

### III

12. *Liber Scientiae.*

Station as at 3. Enochian Tablet to be unveiled and placed on its burse; invocation of chosen forces. Great Wand to be used for sigil, and for circle if invocation requires it.

13. *First Conjuration.*

Great Wand being taken in right hand, operator to assume station in quarter where Triangle is established, and facing that quarter.

An authoritative hierarchical conjuration of the Angel or Spirit *N* to visible appearance in the Triangle of Art. The conjuration to be thorough, celebrating the forces and their relationships as the operator may find fitting; and summoning the Angel or Spirit with complete authority in joyful confidence and assurance, but in manner as a friend. Sigils to be employed:— of Divine Force, and of Angel or Spirit to be evoked.

Station to be resumed as at 3, Great Wand replaced.

14. *Prodromos.*

A prose or verse oration, setting forth vividly the essential qualities of the Element or Sphere of operation: this to be chosen or devised for its appeal to the imagination of the operator. It can be extempore. Movements, gestures, or circumambulations about Bomos, to be introduced as suitable. Throughout, operator to visualize himself as wearing robe of colour as before. To conclude in station as at 3.

15. *Second Conjuration.*

Operator to take Great Wand in right hand and to rest left hand upon Pentacle at breast:—

A forceful hierarchical enchantment, rich in imagery and filled with spiritual exaltation, of the Angel or Spirit *N* to visible appearance in the Triangle of Art; in manner as an oracular priest charging a hearer with a destined enterprise. All sigils to be employed.

IV

16. *The Magical Flame of Creation.*

Great Wand still in right hand, and left hand upon Pentacle, operator to formulate his Corona Flammae; then to visualize within the Triangle of Art a swift but controlled vortex of light, of colour drawn from the Iconic Scale as appropriate to the working.* Maintaining posture and visualizations, operator to make an address to the Angel or Spirit *N* (tracing sigil) in noble language, announcing himself as Flammifer, Bringer of Light; as Priest and Instrument of the Highest God; and as one who in his own nature partakes of all worlds. He is to declare, further, that the Angel or Spirit will by materialization be enabled to taste the mingling of Four Elements in this earthly sphere;† that the nature of the Angel or Spirit will be expanded through the evocation, and its abundance of delight in existence magnified; and that through its participation in the Great Work the Angel or Spirit will receive great blessing.

Posture and formulation of vortex of light to be dismissed, Great Wand to be replaced on Bomos. (Formulation of Corona to be retained for the ensuing 2nd Formula C.R.P.)

17. *Third Conjuration.*

Energisation of self by 2nd Formula of Clavis Rei Primae (formulation of Corona Flammae to be reaffirmed after assumption of Wand Posture.)

Operator to take Great Wand in right hand and briefly to touch Pentacle upon breast with left hand:—

---

* Provided the subject of evocation be *other* than an entity  of the Enochian hierarchy, then as an alternative to the vortex of light the image of the subject of evocation may be formulated within the Triangle of Art at this point. This image will of course be in Contingent Scale colours.

† Although the one Element (or Elemental Affinity) of the working predominates, the place of working holds all Four Elements in pure and puissant form: the influences of the guardian Regents invoked in the rite of the Wards.

A hierarchical conjuration of the Angel or Spirit *N* to visible appearance, now, in the triangle of Art. To be an oration of high fascination, rhythmic and sonorous in language and ample in duration; vibrated in a tone of majestic command, and as a deity calling forth a devotee to rites of ecstasy. All sigils to be employed.

*If an entity of the Enochian hierarchy is the subject of evocation, then the above in this section 17 is to be replaced by the following:—*

a) Energisation of self by 2nd Formula of Clavis Rei Primae (Corona to be reaffirmed after Wand Posture.)

b) The Theban Angelic Formula; Great Wand to be employed as appropriate.

c) Operator to take Great Wand in right hand and briefly to touch Pentacle upon breast with left hand:—

A jussive declaration, conjuring the Angel *N* to visible appearance, now, in the Triangle of Art. This to be hierarchical, adequate, but not prolonged. All sigils to be employed.

N.B.  *The Angel or Spirit may have appeared in the Triangle, whether fully or imperfectly, at any time from the completion of section 13. In every case, however, the rite should be continued as far as and including the conclusion of section 17. If necessary, a few minutes may be allowed after the conclusion of section 17 for the manifestation to take place. From that point, the Angel or Spirit having appeared, the operator should proceed to section 19.*

*If however the entity still has not appeared within a few minutes of completion of section 17, then the operator should proceed with section 18 as follows, and thence to section 19.*

18.  *Supplementary Operation.*

a) Great Wand to be replaced on Bomos, operator to assume station West of Bomos facing East. A reverent salutation and address to the Atziluthic and Briatic forces of the working, the operator confidently asking the necessary magical power to accomplish the evocation of the Angel or Spirit *N*.

b) Operator to assume station East of Bomos facing West. Energisation of self by 2nd Formula of Clavis Rei Primae.

c) With both hands on Pentacle, operator to visualize himself as wearing robe of colour drawn from the Contingent Scale appropriately to the working; threefold vibration of God-name of working, posture and colour-formulation being maintained meanwhile.

d) Station as at 3. Operator to breathe solemnly upon the liquid contained in the Crater, then to fire it. When flame has died down, operator to proceed to:—

e) Energisation of self by 2nd Formula of Clavis Rei Primae. Great Wand having been taken in right hand, operator to make a most grave and potent hierarchical conjuration of the Angel or Spirit *N* to visible appearance in the Triangle of Art; in manner as a prince, spiritual and benign, to a subject who wishes to avoid his regard. All sigils to be employed.

19. *The Complete Manifestation of the Angel or Spirit.*

Great Wand to be replaced.

An incantation enjoining, by the Deific Force of the working, the Angel or Spirit *N* to complete manifestation; this to be terse but sublime.

V

20. *The Welcoming and the Oath.*

a) When the manifestation appears stable, operator to face Triangle of Art from East of Bomos. Operator to address the manifestation courteously and formally, requiring it, in the name of the Deific Force of the working, to declare its own name; and, reply having been received, to welcome the Angel or Spirit *N*.

b) Station as at 3. Energisation of self by 2nd Formula

of Clavis Rei Primae. Sword to be taken in right hand
and carried deosil round Bomos to quarter where Triangle
is established. Sword to be extended so that the blade,
with the flat uppermost, reaches into the Triangle, the
operator remaining within the Magick Circle. The entity
then, upon the command of the operator, is to place its
hand in a clearly-defined manner upon the blade and
make oath. The oath proposed for the entity must have
been devised beforehand with extreme care, that it
express what it should with no ambiguity or rash assumption, and that it be wholly in accord (as must be the
Intent of the evocation) with the nature of the entity. It
is to be made in the name of the Deific Force of the
working, and shall require the entity to say truly and to
perform faithfully as the operator shall command. The
operator is to administer the oath, phrase by phrase, with
exactitude, and is to give serious attention to the responses
of the entity, lest any change be made or lest any part
be inaudible.

Station to be resumed as at 3. Sword to be replaced
on Bomos.

21. *Negotium.*

From whatever position within the Magick Circle
seems most appropriate, the Negotium of the rite is now
to be conducted; the operator strongly visualizing his
Corona Flammae throughout.

*Here in the Negotium is no place for high-flown or
elaborately symbolic language, nor for the apt quotation.
The operator here addresses an entity whose being knows
no insensitive husk of matter and whose comprehension
is accustomed to no shell of words. All that the magician
utters now, therefore, must be altogether his own—must
be himself, as simply as utterance can be.*

22. *The Banishing of the Angel or Spirit.*

Station as at 3. Operator to thank the Angel or Spirit *N*

for its aid, and to give it blessing in the name of its God.

Energisation of self by 2nd Formula of Clavis Rei Primae. Operator to take Sword in right hand, and by appropriate form to license the Angel or Spirit to depart, bidding it also to do no harm to any living being or inanimate thing in the manner of its going.

*After the manifestation has in due course withdrawn, operator to replace Sword without undue haste, and to proceed to:—*

23. *Gratulatio.*

Operator to make adoration of the God-force of the Element or Sphere, then to thank the hierarchical forces for their assistance.

24. *Spirits of the Element or of the Elemental Affinity.*

Dismissal of Elementals; here the Sword is used.

(Hereafter, no Element predominates; the Elements are restored to equilibrium, the unbroken astral circle of the Wards continuing to receive the pure influences of the Regents.)

25. *Dysechoros.*

Operator to proceed to eastern limit of place of working, and thence to perform Dysechoros.

26. *Calyx.*

Operator to assume station within Magick Circle, East of Bomos facing East, there to perform the Calyx.

## XXXVIII

## EVOCATION TO VISIBLE APPEARANCE IN THE CRYSTAL
### For Hierarchical Planetary or Elemental Working

(This operation is not to be confused with scrying, which is other in nature and in method.)

*Crystal and Ring of Enclosure:—*

The Crystal should be a sphere of about 3½ inches in diameter. It should be set upon a small and low stand (a wooden ring about one inch across and ¼ inch thick is ideal) placed exactly centrally within the Ring of Enclosure: the whole to stand upon a pedestal of convenient height in the quarter of the Element (or elemental affinity) of the working. No scrying-cloth is present.

The Ring of Enclosure is of wood or card, having a smooth and whole surface whereon are inscribed concentric circles. The inner circle is of exactly the same diameter as the Crystal, the outer is inscribed ¾ of an inch beyond the inner. Just within the inner circle is inscribed the sigil of the Angel or Spirit to be evoked; the sigil should be clear and distinct but not over-large, so that the stand for the Crystal shall not impinge upon it. Between the inner and outer circles, and just outside the sigil, is inscribed in its own script the God-name of the working.

Upon the pedestal, the Ring of Enclosure is so placed that sigil and God-name face the Bomos.

*Tides:—*

As most potent for the working.

*Magician:—*

Basic robe, etc. Pentacle of Quintessence, or Enochian Pentacle as suitable. (On reverse of Pentacle, in all cases, sigil of Angel or Spirit which is to be evoked.) Colour-charge, as appropriate for the working.

*Bomos:—*

Bomos at centre of place of working, square to cardinal points. Colour of drape, as colour-charge. Equipment placed upon Bomos to be arranged with due balance, and suitably for use by the operator when facing the quarter where the Crystal is established.

*Equipment (essential requirements):—*
Mystical Tessera; Great Wand; Sword; Elemental Weapon as appropriate; Enochian Tablet as appropriate; Crater.

*Incense and Lights:—*
As deemed fitting and desirable.

# I

*This section, 1 through 8, is as in the preceding formula, save that in 1 and 3 the words "within Magick Circle" do not apply, and that in 3 the reference to* the Triangle of Art *is to be replaced by* "the Crystal Stone."

# II

9. *The Crystal Stone and the Ring of Enclosure.*

a) Station as at 3; Sword to be taken in right hand and carried to quarter where Crystal Stone is established. Operator facing quarter of working, outer circle of Ring of Enclosure to be traced deosil with Sword; with tracing of outer circle, vibration of Name ascribed to Ring of Enclosure.

b) Operator to transfer Sword to left hand. Sword being pointed vertically downward to touch ground, operator to place right hand upon Crystal Stone. Visualization of self as wearing robe of colour drawn from the Contingent Scale appropriately to the working. This posture and formulation are to be maintained during the following declamation:—

"Within this Crystal Stone, through and according to the Rite and Formula of Evocation, the Angel (or Spirit) *N* will be caused to manifest."

Formulation and posture to be dismissed, operator re-centring of his magical personality. Operator to turn deosil and to proceed to Bomos, resuming station as at 3. Sword replaced.

c) Great Wand to be taken in right hand and carried to quarter where Crystal Stone is established. Operator facing quarter of working, sigil to be traced of Angel or

Spirit which will be evoked: just above Crystal Stone, and in horizontal plane.

d) Single deosil circumambulation about the Crystal Stone, one stamp being made with the right foot upon return to the point of departure, then movement to be continued widdershins to resume station as at 3. Great Wand to be replaced.

10. *The Microcosm.*

a) Energisation of self by 2nd Formula of Clavis Rei Primae.

b) With both hands on the Pentacle at breast, operator to visualize himelf as wearing robe of colour drawn from the Contigent Scale appropriately to the working. Threefold vibration of God-name of working, posture and colour-formulation being maintained meanwhile.

11. *Preliminary Adjuration to the Entity to be Evoked.*

Great Wand being taken in right hand, operator to proceed deosil round Bomos and to take up station at opposite side of it, facing the quarter where the Crystal Stone is established. Left hand to be laid upon Pentacle at breast, and to remain there while a preliminary adjuration is begun, as in the preceding formula.

The remainder of the preliminary adjuration to be given from the station as at 3, the left hand remaining on the Pentacle meanwhile:—

Angel or Spirit *N* to be conjured in the Divine Name, that it move and appear when operator shall invoke it.

Angel or Spirit adjured in the Divine Name, to do as Operator shall command; to come promptly, and in fair and intelligible form, when summoned; to manifest in the Crystal Stone (operator here to point with Great Wand towards Crystal Stone); and to answer truly, clearly, and unequivocally when manifest.

Great Wand to be replaced.

## III

12. *Liber Scientiae.*

   As in the preceding formula.

13. *First Conjuration.*

   Great Wand being taken in right hand, operator to proceed deosil round Bomos and to take up station at opposite side of it, facing the quarter where the Crystal Stone is established.

   An authoritative hierarchical conjuration of the Angel or Spirit *N* to visible appearance in the Crystal Stone; the conjuration otherwise to be as in the preceding formula.

   Station to be resumed as at 3, Great Wand replaced.

14. *Prodromos.*

   As in the preceding formula.

15. *Second Conjuration.*

   Operator to take Great Wand in right hand and to rest left hand upon Pentacle at breast:—

   A forceful hierarchical enchantment of the Angel or Spirit *N* to visible appearance in the Crystal Stone; otherwise to be as in the preceding formula.

## IV

16. *The Magical Flame of Creation.*

   As given in the preceding formula, save that the vortex of light (or image, if suitable) is to be visualized in the Crystal Stone, and that the clause is to be omitted which states that the Angel or Spirit will by materialization be enabled to taste the mingling of Four Elements in this earthly sphere.

17. *Third Conjuration.*

   In all particulars as in the preceding formula, save that each reference to the Triangle of Art is to be replaced by "the Crystal Stone."

18. *Supplementary Operation.*

In all particulars as in the preceding formula, save that the reference to the Triangle of Art is to be replaced by "the Crystal Stone."

19. *The Complete Manifestation of the Angel or Spirit.*

As in the preceding formula.

V

20. *The Welcoming and the Oath.*

a) As in the preceding formula, save that the reference to the Triangle of Art is to be replaced by "the Crystal Stone."

b) Station as at 3. Energisation of self by 2nd Formula of Clavis Rei Primae. Sword to be taken in right hand and carried deosil round Bomos to quarter where Crystal Stone is established. Sword to be extended so that its point, with the flat uppermost, rests upon the sigil inscribed within the Ring of Enclosure: care being taken that the Sword shall not touch the Crystal Stone itself. Operator to administer the oath, phrase by phrase, with exactitude, and to give serious attention to the responses of the entity, lest any change be made or lest any part be inaudible. The oath proposed for the entity must have been devised beforehand with extreme care, that it express what it should with no ambiguity or rash assuption, and that it be wholly in accord (as must be the Intent of the evocation) with the nature of the entity. It is to be made in the name of the Deific Force of the working, and shall require the entity to say truly and to perform faithfully as the operator shall command.

Station to be resumed as at 3. Sword to be replaced on Bomos.

21. *Negotium.*

In all particulars as in the preceding formula, save that the reference to the Magick Circle is to be replced by "the place of working." Also see Note below.

*The remainder of this section, 22 through 26, is as in the preceeding formula, save that in 26 the words* "within Magick Circle" *do not apply.*

### Note

Evocation to Crystal is in some circumstances to be preferred to Evocation to Visible Appearance in the Triangle of Art. It may for various reasons be inconvenient or quite impossible to mark out (or to lay out) the Magick Circle and the Triangle of Art in a distinct and safe manner in the place of working; or, again, information may be desired from the entity, which can better be conveyed by visual means than verbally. It is noteworthy that in Evocation to Triangle the Negotium will take place altogether or almost altogether verbally, the evoked entity being visibly present throughout to declare, to reply, to explain; whereas in Evocation to Crystal, although the evoked entity and the operator should be distinctly audible each to each, yet on both sides a natural inclination will be found, to reduce verbal utterance in the Negotium to that which is strictly necessary. The entity will often give replies in the form of visionary images in the crystal, and is likely to vanish from sight while these are present. This form of communication is suitable when, for instance, a person, a locality, or a route has to be identified, when a visual image is at once more useful than any verbal description.

On the other hand, it must be admitted that the opportunity for exact verbal exchange being less in Evocation to Crystal, the opportunity for deception or misunderstanding is greater. Wherever this possibility is of any consequence, therefore, Evocation to Triangle is to be preferred. In the present volume no formula is given for evocation of goetic entities; however, we would instance the fact that the Aurum Solis provides for the evocation of such entities to the Triangle, but not to the Crystal.

## XXXIX

## *THE MAGICIAN*

(This psychosophical formula of integration is sometimes called "The Mututinal Establishing of Harmony," since it is regarded as being most effective when worked at the day's beginning.)

*Tides:—*
> As most potent for the working.

*Magician:—*
> Basic robe, etc. Topaz Lamen.

*Bomos:—*
> Bomos slightly to East of centre, so that the operator when standing at centre is directly before it. White drape.

*Equipment (essential requirements):—*
> Mystical Tessera upon the Bomos.

*Incense and Lights:—*
> As deemed fitting and desirable.

### I

1.  *The Astral Defences.*

    Setting of the Wards of Power, beginning and concluding at the centre of the place of working.

2.  *The Higher Self.*

    a) Operator to place left hand upon Tessera, right hand upon Topaz Lamen, and to maintain this posture while the following is uttered:—

    "Hastening the chariot of my heart's desire
    My Goddess-guided powers have carried me
    To find that inner road, that glorious road
    Known to the wise. Hast thou not burned, my soul? —

359

Yea, chariot-wheels almost to flame aglow—
Seeking my longed-for goal, the home of Truth?
From the Gates of Night I have come to the sill of Day,
I have passed the Brazen Door. She has grasped my hand—
        The Goddess, my Queen—
And has bidden me still seek truth on the inward road
Of Knowledge, while Opinion roams the world."*

b) Operator to raise his arms, palms uppermost, in the form of a Tau, and to formulate his Corona Flammae.

Keeping this posture and formulation, operator to contemplate in silence that which the Corona symbolises:—the Self of himself, that particular nucleus or bud in the Divine Mind, from which his psyche has emanated. Great reverence and wonder belong to this mystery.

Posture to be dismissed. (Formulation of Corona to be retained for the ensuing 2nd Formula of the Clavis Rei Primae.)

c) Energisation of self by 2nd Formula of Clavis Rei Primae (formulation of Corona to be reaffirmed after assumption of Wand Posture.)

d) Operator to celebrate in words of joyous awe, discipleship and dependence, his Triune Neshamah, his Spirit; the Beautiful, the Good and the True at the centre of his being. The Triune Neshamah to be celebrated first in its own right, then in relation to the Ruach. Operator then to express the aspiration that through Knowledge he may attain to the True, that through Love he may attain to the Good, and that through Bliss he may attain to the Beautiful.

## II

3.   *The Lower Self.*

a) Operator to turn about deosil to face West, and to perform the Calyx.

    b) From the viewpoint of the Ruach, operator to declare his firm but benevolent authority over his Nephesh and his physical body; in eloquent words he is further to rejoice in his relationship with them, since this relationship gives a mode of expression to the Ruach and a mode of spiritual fulfilment to the Nephesh and the physical body.

4.   *The Prince of Equity.*

    Operator to close his eyes, and to raise his arms, palms uppermost, in the form of a Tau. In this posture he is to imagine himself growing vast in stature, then to formulate his Corona Flammae.

    Posture and formulations being maintained, operator to direct goodwill and blessing to his Nephesh and his physical body.

    Operator to dismiss posture and to allow vastness formulation to be gradually replaced by normal awareness of his physical proportions. The eyes to be opened. (Formulation of Corona to be retained for the ensuing 2nd Formula of the Clavis Rei Primae.)

III

5.   *The Oblate.*

    a) Operator to turn about deosil to face East.

    Energisation of self by 2nd Formula of Clavis Rei Primae (formulation of Corona to be reaffirmed after assumption of Wand Posture.)

    b) Operator to salute his Triune Neshamah with love and with trust, giving it thanks, insofar as he is able, for all the circumstances relating directly or indirectly to his present incarnation. Those circumstances which he considers unpleasing should be included as well as the others; since all are, or have been, alike necessary to the developing pattern on the loom, and to accept all alike is a mark of complete dependence as well as of inner balance.

    With sincere utterance the operator is to open his

heart to the influences of his Higher Self.

### IV

6.  *The Rousing*

Operator to proceed deosil to the eastern limit of the place of working, and to face West.

Rousing of the Citadels (1st Formula of Clavis Rei Primae) to be performed.

7.  *Simulacrum.*

In his visual imagination, operator to eject Nephesh-substance from the region of his upper abdomen, directing it towards the western limit of the place of working and formulating a simulacrum of himself, facing towards him.

8.  *Exhortation.*

Operator to address the simulacrum with gentle authority and concern, as to a young one; exhorting it, in the name of his Higher Self, to give full assistance in the Great Work. (Any needful particulars should be added. This point in the rite allows a valuable opportunity for the operator to convey any admonition which may be required; but all should be spoken sincerely with love.)

9.  *Beatus.*

Operator to thank his Nephesh for its participation in this rite; and to give it blessing in the name of his Higher Self.

10.  *Orante Formula.*

The simulacrum and the connecting "cord" being kept clearly in visualization, operator to project upon the simularcrum by means of the Orante Formula.

### V

11.  *Simulacrum.*

Operator to re-absorb the simulacrum.

12.  *The Rousing.*

Rousing of the Citadels to be performed.

13.  *The Magician.*

Operator to affirm verbally as his own the resolutions lately enjoined upon the simulacrum.

14.  *Gratulatio.*

Having returned to the centre of the place of working, and facing East, operator to perform the Calyx.

# XL

## SUB ROSA NIGRA
## TRANSUBSTANTIATION

*Tides:—*

As most potent for the working.

*Magician:—*

Basic robe, etc. Topaz Lamen.

*Bomos:—*

Bomos slightly to East of centre, so that the operator when standing at centre is directly before it.

Traditionally, the drape for this Magical Solar Mass is chosen from the following:— white, yellow, gold, red and gold, blue and gold, white and gold. The operator makes his choice to express either a particular interpretation of the rite itself, or the keynote of any programme of work in hand.

Equipment placed upon Bomos to be arranged with due balance, each piece suitably for use from eastern or western side as required.

*Equipment (essential requirements):—*

Mystical Tessera; Patella and Goblet (these vessels of any preferred material and design, to hold bread and wine respectively); Great Wand; Sword (not to be placed upon Bomos); Veil of white linen.

A small table, bare or covered with a white drape, is placed at the western limit of the place of working. The Goblet and Patella are set here initially, the Goblet containing red wine, the Patella containing bread. These two vessels should be placed side by side upon the table, the Goblet towards the North, thus to the right when the table is approched from the centre. N.B. The Grail is not to be used for this working.

*Incense and Lights:—*

As deemed fitting and desirable.

## (THE DYADIC RITE)

### I

1.  *The Astral Defences.*

    Setting of the Wards of Adamant, beginning and concluding at centre of place of working.

2.  *Constellation.*

    Station at East of Bomos facing East. Energisation of self by 2nd Formula Clavis Rei Primae.

    A three part invocation of "the Worshipped." The first part, maintaining the same station, to be of HA; as it were the sacred and elevated utterance of a priest of the ancient mysteries. The second part, at North of Bomos facing East, to be of the Lady Leukothea; as it were the sublime and noble utterance of a virgin prophetess. The third part, at South of Bomos facing East, to be of the Lord Melanotheos; as it were the vigorous and heroic utterance of a warrior chieftain.

3.  *The Spirit.*

    Station at West of Bomos facing East. Energisation of self by 2nd Formula of Clavis Rei Primae.

    Adoration and invocation of the Agathodaimon, by the "Crown of Twelve Rays" as follows, or by any preferred form.

    "Ancient and potent Protector, Agathodaimon, hail: we adore thee and thee we invoke.

    Glorious Serpent-God, encircling the Equal Cross, Knouphis—
    —Agathodaimon, hail: we adore thee and thee we invoke.

    Abundant goodness bestowing, Agathodaimon, hail: we adore thee and thee we invoke.

    Terrible invincible God, Knouphis-Agathodaimon, hail: we adore thee and thee we invoke.

    Holy Shepherd of thy People, Agathodaimon, hail: we adore thee and thee we invoke.

    O thou Winged Splendour with broad pinions of emerald and gold, Knouphis-Agathodaimon, hail: we adore thee and thee we invoke.

Divine Priest of the Sun, thou white and scintillant, Agathodaimon, hail: we adore thee and thee we invoke.

Aid of the Seeker for Truth, Knouphis-Agathodaimon, hail: we adore thee and thee we invoke.

Immortal Guide of the Wise, Agathodaimon, hail: we adore thee and thee we invoke.

Mighty Champion of the Way, Knouphis-Agathodaimon, hail,: we adore thee and thee we invoke.

Orient Spirit of Light, Agathodaimon, hail: we adore thee and thee we invoke.

Now and ever blessed, crowned with the Crown of Twelve Rays, Knouphis-Agathodaimon, hail: we exalt thee!"

4.   *The Telling of Joy.*

From the eastern limit of the place of working facing West, the following is to be uttered:—

"This is the joy of the Priest-initiates of the Glorious Star: the Sacrament of the Sun and the Ecstasy of the Snake. This is the joy of the Lords of Topaz: the Indwelling Fire and the Irradiation of the Temple. This is the joy of the God: the conjoined Ecstasy of Adorer and Adored in the Rite of Agathodaimon.

And these things shall be."

## II

5.   *Stella Gloriosa.*

a) From West of Bomos facing East across it, operator to intone the Ogdoadic Catena.

b) Left hand to be placed on Lamen, right hand to be rested on the Mystical Tessera; right hand then to be raised to rest upon left as it lies upon the Lamen; hands to be kept in this position while operator moves to East of Bomos, and faces West. Posture then to be dismissed.

6.   *Gnosco.*

Here are affirmed Spiritual principles, as desired.

7.   *The Enfolder.*

Operator to turn about to face East, and to begin intoning Casmen III (as given in the Tessera Consecration

Rite); after the words "The voice of the Holy One shall sound in the tempest", he is to turn to face West.

Then, having uttered "The Gnostic shall stand in contemplation", he is to assume the Wand Posture; having uttered "He shall lift up his hands in adoration", he is to raise both his arms; having uttered "Above him shall be the Diadem of Light", he is to formulate the Ophiomorphic God-form of the Agathodaimon as rising from coils behind him (the head of the Serpent being in a horizontal position just above his own head and surrounded by the twelve rays, the wings of the Serpent coming forward and being folded across the operator's body). Maintaining this formulation and posture, the operator is to continue and conclude Casmen III.

Posture to be dismissed, operator to withdraw from formulation, re-centring on his magical personality.

8.    *The Elements.*

Operator to move to West of Bomos, and to face West.

The vessels containing the elements of Bread and Wine are now to be brought from West of place of working directly to West of Bomos. Operator, holding the vessels in his hands (Goblet in his right), to face East across Bomos; then to assume the Anthropomorphic God-form of the Agathodaimon. Maintaining this formulation, operator to turn deosil through 270°, and without pause to proceed deosil in one complete circumambulation about the Bomos. Again facing East across it, he is to place the vessels side by side upon the Bomos, somewhat East of its centre.

Operator to withdraw from the formulation, re-centring on his magical personality.

*(THE TRIADIC RITE)*

III

9.    *Dedication.*

Operator to place his hands upon Goblet and Patella,

and to make a simple and explicit oration, declaring the elements of Bread and Wine to be a destined focal point in time and space for the Divine Power in Presence of the Agathodaimon.

10. *Dedication.*

Operator to raise his arms to form the *Psi* and to vibrate the 2nd Enochian Key, following this with invocation of the Great Archangel PAOAOAN. Operator to fold his arms across his breast, left over right, and to remain a few moments in silent contemplation.

11. *The Lady.*

a) Station East of Bomos facing West.

Operator to raise slightly from Bomos the Goblet and Patella (Goblet in his left hand), and to celebrate, in what form he will, the natural dignity of the Creatures of Bread and Wine, sacred to Leukothea (in her earth-aspect) in their own right. Vessels to be replaced.

b) Operator to take the Sword and, standing at eastern side of Bomos, to trace with the Sword a threefold widdershins circle encompassing both vessels upon Bomos. Sword to be replaced.

Operator to raise his hands, palm downward, slightly above the vessels; then, in the holy and dread name of Aiana, and with celebration of her (but without addressing her), he is solemnly to declare that he sets these Creatures of Bread and Wine apart from the uses of earthly nourishment and refreshment. Hands to be withdrawn.

c) Remaining at eastern side of Bomos, operator to assume the anthropomorphic God-form of the Agatho-daimon: in this formulation he is to turn deosil through 270°, and without pause to proceed deosil about Bomos to its western side, there to face East across it. Maintaining the formulation, operator to take up the vessels containing the elements (Goblet in his right hand), to turn deosil through 270°, to proceed deosil around the Bomos to its eastern side, there to make a turn deosil to face the East.

Still in the formulation, operator to raise both vessels simultaneously to the level of his brow-centre. Continuing to hold vessels thus, he is to withdraw from the Agathodaimon formulation, re-centring on his magical personality. Then, in the sweet and powerful name of Aglaia, and with celebration of her (but without addressing her), the operator is solemnly to affirm that these Creatures of Bread and Wine, having been duly set apart, and now having been by the Agathodaimon raised up in service to the Light, are worthy to fulfil their destined spiritual purpose.

Vessels to be lowered. Operator to turn about deosil to face West, and place vessels again upon Bomos. (Goblet and Patella will now have exchanged places from their previous positions upon the Bomos.)

d) Casmen I (as given in the Grail Consecration Rite) to be intoned.

12. *The Lord.*

a) Operator to take Great Wand in right hand, and to make one deosil circumambulation of the Bomos. Again facing West, with the Great Wand operator to trace an equal-armed cross: the first line from South to North above the two vessels, the second descending vertically between them. Great Wand to be replaced.

Operator to raise his hands, palm downward, slightly above the vessels, then in the name of Melanotheos, and with celebration of him (but without addressing him), solemnly to bless the Creatures of Bread and Wine. Hands to be withdrawn.

b) Casmen II (as given in the Great Wand Consecration Rite) to be intoned.

IV

13. *The Circled Cross.*

Energisation of self by 2nd Formula Clavis Rei Primae.

Operator to take Great Wand in right hand and to proceed deosil round Bomos to face East across it. The elements are now to be charged, thus: with Great Wand, operator to trace a circled cross horizontally above the vessels containing the elements, and, while tracing each line, to vibrate the appropriate Divine Name:—

A straight line from North to South. **LEUKOTHEA.**

A straight line from East to West, of equal length to the first. **MELANOTHEOS.**

A circle, deosil, enclosing the cross, beginning and ending East. **AGATHODAIMON.**

Great Wand to be replaced.

14. *The High Invocation.*

Operator to make exalted celebration, rich in allusion and potent in utterance, of the mystic HA, asking the divine aid for the perfect accomplishment of this operation of the Light, this mystery of the Agathodaimon.

15. *The Solemn Affirmation.*

Station East of Bomos facing West. Operator to assume Anthropomorphic God-form of the Agathodaimon.

Maintaining the formulation, operator to raise Patella in both hands and to vibrate the Latin Words of Affirmation:—

| | |
|---|---|
| **EGO AGATHODAEMON** | I, Agathodaimon, |
| **HUNC DONUM PARATUM TOLLENS** | raising this prepared gift, |
| **SANCIO HUNC PANEM** | decree this Bread |
| **CORPUS MEUM VERUM ESSE.** | to be my very Body. |

Patella to be replaced. Operator to take up Goblet in both hands, and, still in the formulation, to vibrate the Latin Words of Affirmation:—

| | |
|---|---|
| **EGO AGATHODAEMON** | I, Agathodaimon, |
| **HUNC DONUM PARATUM TOLLENS** | raising this prepared gift |
| **SANCIO HUNC VINUM** | decree this Wine |
| **SANGUEN MEUM VERUM ESSE.*** | to be my very Blood. |

---

* Both consecrated elements equally carry, magically, the virtue of the total nature of the Agathodaimon, but there is an esoteric distinction between the two in emphasis:—

*Body,* emphasising the personal nature of the God as receptacle of its corresponding Archetype.

*Blood,* emphasising the Archetypal force indwelling the God.

This is the mystical polarity of the consecrated elements in a two-element Eucharist.

Goblet to be replaced. Operator to withdraw from formulation, re-centring on his magical personality.

V

16. *Orante Formula.*

Operator to project upon the consecrated elements, the Bread first, then the Wine, by means of the Orante Formula.

17. *"En Deus Est, Deus Est!"*

Proclamation of the Presence.

18. *"En Deus Est, Deus Est!"*

At this point is to follow some action in honour of the very-present Deity: the manner of this action is to be as preferred. Meditation, silent or spoken adoration, intoned praise, ceremonial devotion, joyful song, music, ecstatic dance: any or all of these things, or any other thing which the jubilant imagination may devise, can rightfully find place here.

19. *Daps Dei.*

Operator to stand East of Bomos, facing West across it.

The consecrated elements are now to be consumed. The following utterances (in Latin or in English), or any others preferred, may be employed, and whatever ceremonial gesture is deemed fitting or felt to be expressive may be introduced:

*Having taken Bread, and immediately before consuming it.*

| | |
|---|---|
| TU O AGATHODAEMON | Thou, O Agathodaimon, |
| TU LUCIS SERPENS MIRABILIS | thou the marvellous Serpent of Light, |
| O TU REFULGENS TU BENIGNE IN ME MANE. | thou refulgent thou benign, dwell within me. |

*Having taken Wine, and immediately before consuming it.*

| | |
|---|---|
| TU O AGATHODAEMON | Thou, O Agathodaimon, |
| TU LUCIS SERPENS MIRABILIS | thou the marvellous Serpent of Light, |
| O TU REFULGENS TU BENIGNE UT FLAMMA ME CORRIPE. | thou refulgent thou benign, sieze upon me as flame. |

20.  *I am He.*

a) After a pause, the empty vessels are to be covered with the white linen.

b) An oration of high exaltation is now to be uttered, in which the operator expresses identification with the Agathodaimon. Herein is to be declared the rejoicing of the God in his own glory, as the ecstatic consciousness may be moved.

21.  *Stella Regenerationis.*

a) After a pause, operator to move to West of Bomos and to face East across it. *First part* of Ogdoadic Catena to be intoned.

b) Left hand to be placed on Topaz Lamen, right hand to be rested on the Mystical Tessera; right hand then to be raised to rest upon left as it lies upon the Lamen. Gesture to be dismissed.

22.  Κογξ ομπαξ

Here may follow any desired valediction.

*Note*

The ancient Qabalistic-Gnostic pattern of the Ogdoadic tradition being concealed in the structure of the Roman Catholic Mass (the Tridentine Rite), the division of parts according to the House of Sacrifice is as follows:—

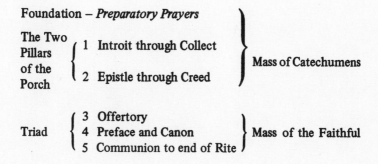

Foundation – *Preparatory Prayers*

The Two Pillars of the Porch
{ 1 Introit through Collect
{ 2 Epistle through Creed
} Mass of Catechumens

Triad
{ 3 Offertory
{ 4 Preface and Canon
{ 5 Communion to end of Rite
} Mass of the Faithful

*ADDENDUM*
## *NACHASH – AGATHODAIMON – CHRISTOS*

In the tradition of Christian Gnosis, the priestly and regenerative figure of Agathodaimon has easily been identified with the mystical Christos; the ophiomorphic aspect of Agathodaimon becoming assimilated to the biblical image of Nachash, the "healing Serpent" raised up by Moses in the wilderness. That episode (Numbers 2:8-9) is an accepted prefiguration of spiritual regeneration. The healing Serpent as a symbol of Christos has scriptural warrant in John 3:14-15, and has further support in Qabalistic thought from the numeration of *NChSh* (Nachash) being identical – 358 – with that of *MShICh* (Messiah).

Thus, if the student wishes to emphasize, in the Sub Rosa Nigra Rite of Transubstantiation, the identification of Agathodaimon with the Christos, this intent will be harmonious to a long historical association. However, to avoid confusion, it is specifically noted here that Aurum Solis has at no time adopted this identification in its practical workings.

## XLI

### CONSECRATION OF A TALISMAN
### LIBER AD AMULETA CONSECRANDA
#### For Hierarchical Planetary Working

(A talisman is a material object, usually of convenient size to be carried upon the person—we are not here considering the wide and equally venerable subject of talismanic objects attached to or buried within walls, or buried in foundations—and intended either to attract to the possessor something seen as good, or to ward off something seen as adverse. In earlier times protective talismans were the more frequent; while modern thought inclines to the adjuvant type, the emphasis thus being upon what we desire rather than upon what we fear. Many talismans have survived from various cultures and ages, some of great antiquity; their materials and designs are most diverse, and so also, as evidenced by relevant texts, have ever been the rites and principles of their activation.)

The formula here given provides a method for the creation of talismans of the planetary spheres; it involves invocation of the theurgic hierarchy down to Intelligence. It is not suited to the creation of elemental talismans.

*The Materium:*

The material of a talisman must, both for mundane and for magical reasons, be durable. The Aurum Solis prefers metal or stone; by tradition, parchment is permissible but we do not advocate it. Stones and metals attributed to the planetary spheres are given in *The Apparel of High Magick;* the available stones remain largely unchanged, but the state of supplies makes it advisable to provide for the use of alternative metals in certain cases. (Quicksilver is in any case impracticable.) The following list of metals is therefore offered:—

3 Lead. Antimony (Arab attribution).
4 Tin. Aluminum.
5 Steel.
6 Gold. Brass.
7 Copper. Phosphor Bronze.
8 Zinc.
9 Silver.

373

The *materium,* as we call the talisman before its consecration, is considered as having two sides: the *obverse,* upon which is to be inscribed only the presigillum of the sphere; and the *reverse,* upon which is to be inscribed the charactery, a sentence or phrase expressing the effect which the intended talisman is to produce. (These are the essential requirements of design for a materium which is to be consecrated according to the present formula.)

The exact statement of the effect should be given most careful consideration. When decided upon it is to be inscribed upon the reverse of the materium, legibly, but in whatever script the operator prefers. (The purport of the charactery will be spoken aloud as part of the Declaration of Intent in the rite of consecration, with any grammatical modification that may be needful.) The lineal figure (polygon, polygram, or both) of the sphere may be added upon the reverse; the charactery may be set out within or around the lineal figure; again, the materium itself may be shaped as a polygon with the appropriate number of sides. No sigils are to be inscribed upon the materium. Save in the case of a parchment materium, the inscription of presigillum and of charactery are to be incised, not merely pigmented on the surface; but the incised lines upon a metal materium may be filled with colour, or enamelling may be employed.

Into the designing and physical preparation of the materium may be brought such traditional matters as astrological considerations, burning of incenses, and so forth; the use of these must depend on the judgment and wish of the individual. Every materium should be newly prepared; *an old talisman must never be re-used.*

*Tides:—*
As most potent for the working.

*Magician:—*
Basic robe, etc. Pentacle of Quintessence. Colour-charge, as appropriate for the working.

*Bomos:—*
Bomos at centre of place of working, square to cardinal points. Colour of drape, as colour-charge. Equipment placed upon Bomos to be arranged with due balance, and suitably for use by operator from all sides necessary in the working.

*Equipment (essential requirements):—*
Mystical Tessera; Materium (initially upon Bomos, presigillum uppermost); Great Wand; Sword (in East of place of working); Elemental Weapon as appropriate; Enochian Tablet as appropriate; Anointing Oil and small finger linen.

*Incense and Lights:—*
   As deemed fitting and desirable.

I

1.   *The Astral Defences.*
        Setting of Wards of Power, beginning and concluding East of Bomos facing East.
2.   *The Spiritual Forces.*
        a) A reverent invocation of the Illimitable Godhead in Kether.
        b) 1st Enochian Key, followed by invocation of the three Archangels.
        c) Energisation of self by 2nd Formula of Clavis. Orthrochoros.
3.   *The Deific Force of the Working.*
        Adoration and invocation of the God-force of Sphere; to be made from West of Bomos facing East across it.
4.   *Spirits of the Elemental Affinity.*
        Invocation of Elementals, to be made facing across the Bomos towards the quarter of the elemental affinity of the working. Here the Elemental Weapon is used.
5.   *Proclamation of the Rite.*
        To be made from the eastern limit of the place of working facing West; the proclamation of a rite of Talismanic Consecration and the Sphere of operation.
6.   *The Hierarchy.*
        Energisation of self by 2nd Formula of Clavis Rei Primae. A worthy and beautiful invocation of God-force of Sphere, followed by aspiration to be a worthy vehicle for the operation of that Divine Influence in the rite about to be performed; a request to be empowered to cause the obedience of the Intelligence $N$ in process of this working; a request for the magical aid of the hierarchical forces of the sphere (not including the Intelligence), with utterance of their names. To be accomplished from West

of Bomos facing East across it.

7.   *The Magician.*

Materium being taken in left hand, operator to move to eastern limit of place of working and, facing west, to make proclamation of his magical name and status and the basis of his magical authority.

8.   *Declaration of Intent.*

To be made in the Presence of the Powers from the same station as at 7. The intention to cause the Intelligence *N* to vitalise the prepared Materium as a Talisman powerful in (or to) whatever purpose; this purpose to be affirmed to be truly represented by the charactery upon the Materium.

## II

9.   *The Materium.*

a) Still holding Materium in left hand, operator to take Sword in right hand and to proceed deosil to western limit of place of working, there to face East. Operator to place Materium upon floor, charactery uppermost, about midway between Bomos and western limit of place of working. Still facing East, operator to make a single downward slashing motion with the Sword, as though severing a taut thread extending from Materium upward in an inclined plane toward the South. Operator to move to North side of Materium and, facing South, to repeat the action, as though severing a taut thread extending from Materium upward in inclined plane toward West. Operator to move to East side of Materium and, facing West (the Bomos being now behind him) to repeat the action as though severing a taut thread extending from Materium upward in an inclined plane toward the North. Operator to move to South side of Materium and, facing North, to repeat the action as though severing a taut thread extending from Materium upward in an inclined plane toward the East. Operator to move again to West side of Materium, and with Sword to trace widdershins circle about Materium.

b) This severing of links having been accomplished, operator to take up Materium in left hand and to proceed deosil to eastern limit of place of working. Sword to be replaced. Operator to proceed directly from that point to East side of Bomos and to replace Materium thereon, presigillum uppermost.

As an alternative, after the tracing of circle about Materium, operator may leave Materium upon floor and may proceed deosil to return Sword to its place; then there may be performed any other preparatory action which is desired concerning the Materium, before the return of Materium to Bomos from the East, presigillum uppermost.

c) Energisation of self by 2nd Formula C.R.P.

d) Turning deosil, operator to make one deosil circumambulation of Bomos. Again facing West across Bomos, operator to place hands right over left upon Pentacle of Quintessence, then to extend both hands simultaneously to the Materium. Operator to raise Materium in both hands and to hold it at arms' length, the presigillum towards him. Maintaining this posture, operator to vibrate God-name of working, the number of times appropriate to Sphere.

Materium replaced on Bomos, presigillum uppermost.

e) With Great Wand operator to trace circle deosil around Materium, then within this circle to trace horizontally the sigil of the Intelligence *N.* Great Wand to be replaced.

10. *Preliminary Adjuration to the Intelligence.*

Operator to move deosil to West of Bomos and to face East across it. Materium to be turned, to rest upon Bomos charactery uppermost.

Great Wand to be held in right hand. In the name of the god-force of the Sphere, the Intelligence to be called upon by name and title, and its sigil to be traced towards the East with the Great Wand; the Intelligence being bidden (operator meanwhile touching Materium with Great Wand) to behold the Materium, and to behold the charactery thereon by which operator's will and purpose is expressed. Great Wand to be raised from Materium.

Left hand now to be placed upon Materium and to remain there to end of Adjuration.

Intelligence to be adjured in the Divine Name that when commanded by the operator it shall stir once for all the substance of the Materium, so that the Materium shall become a Talisman of the Sphere effective according to its charactery and to no other purpose.

Intelligence to be adjured in the Divine Name that it shall not establish itself in the Materium, but that having stirred the substance of the Materium it shall at once withdraw entirely therefrom.

Great Wand to be replaced.

### III

11. *Liber Scientiae.*

Station as at 4 above. Enochian Tablet to be unveiled and placed on its burse; invocation of chosen forces. Elemental Weapon to be used for sigil, and for circle if invocation requires it.

12. *Conjuration.*

Station West of Bomos facing East across it. With Great Wand, operator to trace deosil circle around Materium, once, or number of times appropriate to Sphere.

In manner courteous though with complete authority, as a High Mage to his powerful assistant, operator to make a hierarchical exhortation enjoining the Intelligence *N* to stir powerfully the substance of the Materium. The conjuration to be thorough, celebrating the forces and their relationships as the operator may find fitting. Sigils to be employed:— of Divine Force, and of Intelligence (these to be traced above Materium).

13. *Prodromos.*

A prose or verse oration, setting forth vividly the essential qualities of the Sphere of operation: to be chosen or devised for its appeal to imagination of operator. It can be extempore. Movements, gestures, circumambulations, about the place of working to be introduced as suitable; the action may be built up into a dance if so desired, whether in the course of the oration or after it. Throughout, Materium to be held in right hand.

To conclude at West of Bomos facing East. Materium to be replaced on Bomos, presigillum uppermost.

## IV

14. *Grand Conjuration.*

Energisation of self by 2nd Formula of Clavis Rei Primae. Operator to take Great Wand in right hand and to trace deosil circle around Materium, once, or number of times appropriate to Sphere.

An impelling hierarchical oration, commanding the Intelligence $N$ to stir powerfully the substance of the Materium now; delivered in magnificent and inexorable manner, as of the leader in a high cause urging a noble follower to a vital deed. All sigils to be employed (these to be traced above Materium).

15. *Hegemony of the Magician.*

Operator to raise Great Wand on high and to rest left hand upon Pentacle. In this posture, operator to turn deosil and make one unhurried deosil circumambulation of Bomos. Again facing East across Bomos, operator to touch vitalised Materium with Great Wand. Great Wand to be replaced, right hand to be rested over left upon

Pentacle. Maintaining the hands in this position, operator to move deosil to East of Bomos and to face West across it.

16. *Creature of Talismans*.

Extending both hands simultaneously to the vitalised Materium, operator to turn it so that it lies upon the Bomos charactery uppermost. Both hands being kept in contact with the Materium, operator to address it as Creature of Talismans, conjuring it in the Divine Name that for its one inscribed purpose it shall prevail through the Worlds till its end be accomplished.

Hands to be withdrawn.

V

17. *Orante Formula*.

Operator to project upon vitalised Materium by means of the Orante Formula.

18. *The Talisman*.

a) Station West of Bomos facing East. Talisman to be anointed upon the side bearing the charactery.

b) Proclamation and showing of the Talisman; to be performed where and in what manner operator may desire.

Station West of Bomos facing East. Talisman to be replaced upon Bomos, charactery uppermost.

19. *The Banishing of the Intelligence*.

Operator to thank the Intelligence for its aid, and to give it blessing in the name of its God.

Operator to proceed to East and to take Sword in right hand. With Sword, operator to proceed deosil to western limit of place of working and there, facing East, to banish Intelligence by appropriate form.*

Operator to move deosil to East and to replace Sword.

---

* No, Greatly Honoured Adept; this banishing will *not* discharge the force of our Talisman. The power of the Talisman has been locked by projection, and the Intelligence which stirred the substance of the Materium has not been bound therein.

20. *Gratulatio.*

Station West of Bomos facing East. Operator to make adoration of God-force of Sphere, then to thank hierarchical forces for their assistance.

21. *Spirits of the Elemental Affinity.*

Station as at 4 above. Dismissal of Elementals; here the Elemental Weapon is used.

22. *Dyseochoros.*

Operator to proceed to eastern limit of place of working, and thence to perform Dyseochoros.

23. *Calyx.*

Operator to assume station East of Bomos facing East, there to perform the Calyx.

### Note

A talisman consecrated according to the preceding formula will normally remain potent until its purpose is accomplished, when it will automatically neutralise itself. However, "overloading" a talisman is to be avoided, since this can lead to premature exhaustion of its power. Only common sense can be the guide here. Unless the possessor makes other efforts, he can hardly expect lifelong prosperity to be drawn to him by a half-inch bit of aluminum; nor should one entrust world peace to a coral bead.

In very exceptional cases a talisman may have to be neutralised before expiry. This is not to be lightly undertaken, but circumstances can change, and an objective which was formerly desirable may no longer be so; or experience may show that some serious error has been made in the charactery. If therefore for sufficient cause neutralisation is necessary, the following procedure should be observed:—

i.   Setting of Wards of Power.

ii.  Invocation of Atziluthic force of sphere, with solemn declaration of reason and necessity for neutralisation of talisman. Request for the Divine aid in the work about to be performed.

   iii.   Energisation of self by 2nd Formula of Clavis.
       Defacement of charactery.

   iv.   Energisation of self by 2nd Formula of Clavis.
       Distortion of metal or smashing of stone.

   v.   Energisation of self by 2nd Formula of Clavis.
       With Sword, banishing heptagram; Divine Name vibrated.

(It is recommended that the remains of the talisman be cast into running water at sunrise or sunset.)

## XLII

## SUB ROSA NIGRA
## THE GNOSTIC

(This psychosophical formula of integration provides a potent means of spiritual development, of especial value to the Minor Adept; while even the full Adept may consider it a useful cosmic "toner.")

*Tides:—*
As most potent for the working.
*Magician:—*
Basic robe, etc. Topaz Lamen.
*Bomos:—*
Bomos midway between centre and eastern limit of place of working. White drape, or rose-pink and gold.
Equipment placed upon Bomos to be arranged with due balance, and suitably for use from eastern or western side as required.
*Equipment (essential requirements):—*
Mystical Tessera; Great Wand; Grail (with Rose of Concealment); Coronal (a prepared crown of flowers and/or foliage).
*Incense and Lights:—*
As deemed fitting and desirable.

### I

1.  *The Astral Defences.*

Setting of the Wards of Adamant, beginning and concluding at centre of place of working.

2.  *The Holy One.*

Operator to proceed directly to Bomos and to face East across it. Energisation of self by 2nd Formula of Clavis Rei Primae.

Operator to celebrate the Holy One in glorious terms of praise and love; first making adoration of HA and

speaking aloud his fervent aspiration to the Divine Light
of which HA is the fullness, then making invocation and
adoration of the Agathodaimon, Tipharic Mediator and
Guardian of the Kosmos.

3.    *Oi Tekontes.*

Station East of Bomos facing East. Energisation of
self by 2nd Formula of Clavis Rei Primae.

Adoration and invocation to be made of Lady Leukothea and of Lord Melanotheos, in their own right and
in relationship to one another: in terms of awe and
wonder, of love and filial trust.

4.    *Intention.*

Operator to turn about deosil to face West across
Bomos, and to declare the intention so to participate in
the cosmic drama of the *Mystery of Union* that his
progress towards his own true spiritual integration may
thereby be furthered.

(Alternatively, the spirit of the operation may be
conveyed by a lyrical "telling".)

## II

5.    *Benison.*

Station at centre of place of working, facing East.

Operator to assume the Wand Posture and to raise his
thoughts in silent aspiration to HA, so that drawn by this
contemplation he feels himself growing vast in stature,
and powerful in the omnipotence of HA; operator then
to formulate his Corona Flammae. Maintaining posture
and formulation, operator to proceed with *Accessio
Lucis* as follows:— with the realisation that that which
the Corona represents is a living part of the Divine Mind,
operator to visualize his Corona gradually increasing in
brilliance until he is entirely bathed in radiance from its
dazzling splendor.

Operator to withdraw from formulations, recentring

on his magical personality.

6.    *Anthropos.*

Operator to proceed directly to Bomos and to face East across it. Left hand to be placed on Topaz Lamen, right hand on Tessera; right hand then to be raised to rest upon left, and to remain there while operator makes an elevated and mystical acclamation of himself. This acclamation to be of some length, and to be expressed from the point of view of his single consciousness, calm and stable amid the many levels of his being.

III

7.    *The White One.*

a) Station as above. Calyx to be performed.

b) Celebration of the Great Goddess, the Lady Leukothea, as Mother of All; in manner as her love-inspired and dedicated child, and with such words of passionate praise as weave themselves into triumphal litanies or sing themselves in mystic hymns.

c) Operator to make the Ave, then to turn about deosil and to proceed directly to West of place of working. Facing East, operator to kneel in solemn and silent meditation upon the beauty, power and majesty of the Great Mother. He may in this turn his mind also to whatever in the natural world most impresses him with wonder or delight; for whatever so moves him participates, albeit symbolically, in his perception of her.

d) Operator to arise and to proceed directly to centre of place of working. There, with high rejoicing, operator to address the Lady Leukothea, placing himself and his work within her tutelage, that from the plenitude of her Supernal Glory she may irradiate his being with those powerful and beneficent influences which nurture true attainment, and that the rite may go forward effectually within her ambience.

e) Operator then to proceed directly to Bomos and, facing West across it, to raise his arms to form the *Psi* and to vibrate the 2nd Enochian Key, following this with invocation of the Archangel PAOAOAN. Operator then to fold arms across breast, left over right, and to remain a few moments in silent contemplation.

f) Operator to place upon his own head the prepared coronal; this in honour of the Goddess, whether in silence or declared in speech. (The coronal to be worn throughout the remainder of the working.)

### IV

8.   *The Universal Mysterium.*

a) Station East of Bomos facing West. Energisation of self by 2nd Formula Clavis Rei Primae.

b) Operator to make celebration of the mighty cosmic union of Lord Melanotheos and Lady Leukothea, in terms suitable to a mythic presentment of that sacred and primal mystery.

c) Rose of Concealment to be removed from Grail in silence.

d) Great Wand to be taken in left hand, Grail in right, and both to be raised on high, with utterance or in silence.

Operator then to conjoin Wand and Grail in such manner as to betoken plainly the union of God and Goddess; the action to be accomplished (and followed, should the operator so desire) with whatsoever magical utterance is deemed fitting, taking heed only that the words shall be by their archetypal truth applicable likewise to the union of high forces within the operator. (Dramatic simplicity and the sense of "rightness" are a surer guide here than any subtle elaboration.)

Weapons to be replaced on Bomos.

e) Rose of Concealment to be replaced in silence.

V

9. *The Adored One of the Aeons.*

A glorious eulogy of the Holy One, first celebrating the transcendent HA as sublime originator of the male and female principles, then celebrating Agathodaimon as conceived child of Leukothea and Melanotheos. This eulogy to be delivered from centre of place of working, facing East.

10. *Obumbratio et Lumen Naturae.*

a) Remaining at centre, operator to turn about deosil to face West, and to assume Wand Posture; then to raise his thoughts in  silent aspiration to HA, so that drawn by this contemplation he feels himself growing vast in stature, immensely vast, cosmically vast. He is then to build up the Ophiomorphic God-form of Agathodaimon as arising from a coil behind him, the head of the Serpent being in a horizontal position just above his own head and surrounded by the twelve rays, the wings of the Serpent coming forward and being folded across the operator's body.

b) Operator then to vibrate with all the intensity of his being the Divine Name KNOUPHIS-AGATHODAIMON.

c) Maintaining posture and formulations, operator to become conscious of a gleaming and flashing all around him, at first building up like the Aurora Borealis, then as the flames of a rainbow fire caressing and completely enclosing him, thus replacing his awareness of the God-form. Operator to visualize  this fire gradually increasing in brilliance until he stands scatheless within a pulsating and prismatic frenzy of flame. In a great and calm joy operator to inhale and exhale the radiance of the fire, knowing himself to be thereby magically strengthened and mystically unified in the power of the Holy Guardian of the Kosmos; and to continue in this until the impulse of forces cosmic and microcosmic carries him to ekstasis.

High mystical vision may accompany the ekstasis.

11. *The Kingdom.*

a) When normal consciousness returns, operator to re-centre on his magical personality.

b) Still at centre, operator to turn about deosil to face East, and to perform the fivefold gesture Arista as given in the Setting of the Wards of Adamant.

12. Κογξ ομπαξ

Operator to proceed directly to Bomos, and facing East across it to replace the coronal; thereafter to declaim the *Hymnodia Krypte* of Hermes Trismegistus (in Greek or English) and to conclude the ceremony with any desired valediction.

# APPENDICES

# *APPENDIX* A

## Pronunciation of Enochian

## (Key)

A   *as the first vowel sound in* father
E   *as the vowel sound in* say
I   *as the vowel sound in* meet
O   *as the vowel sound in* hold
U   *as the vowel sound in* food

a   *as the vowel sound in* add
e   *as the vowel sound in* yet
i   *as the vowel sound in* sit
o   *as the vowel sound in* hot
u   *as the vowel sound in* foot

ə *represents the neutral vowel, as the first vowel sound in* parade, *or the second vowel sound in* column.

*Consonants are given their normal values* (G *invariably represents the hard sound of that letter, as in* gold).

χ *represents the guttural, pronounced as the* ch *in German (Woche, suchen).*

*As a general rule, allowing for varied inflexions of the voice in the flow of magical utterance, all the syllables in an Enochian word should be given equal weight. It will be noted that hyphens are frequently inserted in words. These only emphasise the need to give full value to a vowel, or to a syllable, and do not call for a real break in the utterance.*

# APPENDIX A
## PRONUNCIATION OF ENOCHIAN
### (DE VERBIS ANGELICIS)

The pronunciation of every Enochian word occurring in *De Rebus Enochianis* is set out in this Appendix. The method of pronunciation exemplified has been formulated by the Aurum Solis, in order to provide a standard of vocalisation both convenient to the student and effective in magical utterance.

In order to represent this pronunciation, fixed values have been allocated to certain letters and symbols, as shown on the opposite page.

With regard to the vocalisation of the *Forty-Eight Claves Angelicae* specifically, these are normally vibrated in the Magical Voice, but the Aurum Solis allows that they may, equally, be chanted in one or other of the following ways:—

*Cantus instans:* this chant is usually reserved to high ceremonial use. The first line of a Key is chanted on a chosen note, the succeeding lines a tone higher; for the pre-penultimate line the operator returns to the original note, for the penultimate line he drops a tone, and for the final line he returns again to the original note: thus, for example, A—B—A-G—A, or again C—D—C—B$_b$—C.

*Cantus vocans:* this chant is more generally applied than the preceding one. The lines of a Key are chanted on a chosen note, through to the penultimate line which is chanted a tone lower; the final line being chanted on the original note: thus, for example, A—G—A, or, again, C—B$_b$—C.

*Cantus vemens:* this chant is also reserved to high ceremonial use, but specifically for group-working. The entire
Key is chanted on a single note, this being taken from a bell
or gong stroke which is sounded once before each line of the
Key, and once again at the close of the final line.

*(Texts given below in pronunciation form)*

|     |                                         |
| --- | --------------------------------------- |
| i   | Hierarchical Table: Air                 |
| ii  | Hierarchical Table: Water               |
| iii | Hierarchical Table: Earth               |
| iv  | Hierarchical Table: Fire                |
| v   | 48 Claves Angelicae                     |
| vi  | Titles of the Thirty Ayres              |
| vii | Liber Scientiae, Column III             |
| viii| Liber Scientiae, Column VIII            |
| ix  | The four Divine Names of Spirit         |
| x   | Four Archangelic Names (from Column III)|

i

## *AIR HIERARCHY*

### Section I

ORO IBAⱶ A-OZəPI
BATA-IVAⱶ
HABI-ORO, A-A-OZA-IF, HəTaM-ORəDA, AHA-OZəPI,
  HIPO-TəGA. AVə-TOTARə

### Section II

| | |
|---|---|
| *Air of Air:–* | ERoZeLA |
| | RoZeLA, ZeLAR, LARoZ, ARoZeL |
| *Water of Air:–* | E-I-TaPA |
| | I-TaPA, TaPA-I, PA-IT, A-ITaP |
| *Earth of Air:–* | HəTaNə-BeRə |
| | TaNə-BeRə, NəBeRoT, BeRoTaN, RəTaNuB |
| *Fire of Air:–* | HeKS-GəSiD |
| | eKS-GəSiD, GəSiDeKS, SiDeKSiG, DeKSiGəSə |

### Section III

| | |
|---|---|
| *Air of Air:–* | IDO-IGO & ARoD-ZA |
| | (RoZeLA) |
| | KəZeNuS, TOTaT, SI-AS, FaMuNDə |
| *Water of Air:–* | LaLAKəZA & PALAMə |
| | (I-TaPA) |
| | O-I-UBə, PA-OK, RəBeNuⱶ, DI-RI |
| *Earth of Air:–* | A-I-A-O-A-I & O-I-I-ITə |
| | (TaNə-BeRə) |
| | ABeMO, NAKO, OKəNuMə, SəHALə |
| *Fire of Air:–* | A-O-URəRoZ & ALO-A-I |
| | (eKS-GəSiD) |
| | AKəKA, NuPəNuT, OTO-I, PəMOKS |

## ii
## *WATER HIERARCHY*

### Section I

eM∂Piχ ARoSiL GA-I-OL∂
RA-AGI-OSiL
LaSRA-H∂PiM, SA-I-INOV, LA-O-AKSiRoP, SiL-GA-I-OL∂,
   LIGaD-ISA, SONI-ZeNuT

### Section II

| | |
|---|---|
| *Air of Water:–* | E-TA-AD |
| | TA-AD, A-ADeT, AD∂TA, DeTA-A |
| *Water of Water:–* | E-TaDIM |
| | TaDIM, DIMuT, IMuTaD, MuT∂DI |
| *Earth of Water:–* | H∂MAGaL |
| | MAGaL, AG∂LaM, GaLMA, LaMAG |
| *Fire of Water:–* | H∂NuL∂-RoKS∂ |
| | NuL∂-RoKS∂, L∂RoKSiN, RoKSiNuL∂, |
| | eKSiNuL∂R∂ |

### Section III

| | |
|---|---|
| *Air of Water:–* | OB-GOTA & A-AB∂KO |
| | (TA-AD) |
| | TOKO, eN-H∂DeD, PA-AKS∂, SA-IKS∂ |
| *Water of Water:–* | NELA-PiR∂ & OME-BeB |
| | (TaDIM) |
| | MAGaM, LE-OK∂, USiSN∂, R∂VO-I |
| *Earth of Water:–* | MA-LA-DI & OLA-AD |
| | (MAGaL) |
| | PAKO, NuD-ZeN, I-IPO, eKS-RoNuχ |
| *Fire of Water:–* | I-A-A-ASiD & A-TA-PA |
| | (NuL∂-RoKS∂) |
| | eKS-PiKaN, VASA, DAPI, R∂NIL∂ |

### iii

## *EARTH HIERARCHY*

### Section I

MO-Rə DI-AL HəKaTəGA
IKə-ZəHIHAL
LA-IDəROM, AKəZI-NO-Rə, eLZI-NOPO, ALə-HəKaTəGA,
LI-I-ANəSA, A-HəMuL-IKU

### Section II

| | |
|---|---|
| *Air of Earth:–* | ABO-ZA |
| | BO-ZA, OZAB, ZABO, ABOZ |
| *Water of Earth:–* | A-PiHəRA |
| | PiHəRA, HəRAPə, RA-Piχ, AP-HeRə |
| *Earth of Earth:–* | PO-KaNuK |
| | OKə-NuK, KaNəKO, NəKOKə, KOKaN |
| *Fire of Earth:–* | PASiMuT |
| | ASiMuT, SiMTA, MəTASə, TASiM |

### Section III

| | |
|---|---|
| *Air of Earth:–* | ANə-GəPO-I & UNəNAKS |
| | (BO-ZA) |
| | A-I-RA, ORəMuN, RoS-NI, I-ZeNəRə |
| *Water of Earth:–* | A-NA-E-EMə & SONəDeN |
| | (PiHəRA) |
| | OMəGaG, GəBAL, RəLaMU, I-A-HeL |
| *Earth of Earth:–* | A-BALəPiT & ARəBIZə |
| | (OKə-NuK) |
| | OPiNA, DO-OPə, RoKS-A-O, AKS-IRə |
| *Fire of Earth:–* | O-PiMuN-IRə & ILə-PIZə |
| | (ASiMuT) |
| | Mu-SAPə, I-ABA, I-ZeKSiP, SiTIMə |

## iv

### *FIRE HIERARCHY*

#### Section I

O-IPə TE-A-A PiDOKE
EDeL-PiRoNA-A
A-A-ETəPI-O, A-DO-E-O-ETə, ALaN-DəVODə, A-APiDOKE,
    ARI-NuNAP, ANO-DO-INə

#### Section II

| | |
|---|---|
| *Air of Fire:–* | A-DO-PA |
| | DO-PA, O-PAD, PA-DO, A-DOP |
| *Water of Fire:–* | A-A-NA-A |
| | A-NA-A, NA-A-A, A-A-AN, A-A-NA |
| *Earth of Fire:–* | PiPiSAK |
| | PiSAK, SAKaP, A-KaPiS, KaPSA |
| *Fire of Fire:–* | PəZI-ZA |
| | ZI-ZA, I-ZAZ, ZA-ZI, A-ZIZ |

#### Section III

| | |
|---|---|
| *Air of Fire:–* | NO-A-LaMəRə & OLO-AGə |
| | (DO-PA) |
| | O-PiMuN, APəSiTə, SKI-O, VA-SiG |
| *Water of Fire:–* | VA-DA-LI & O-BA-VA |
| | (A-NA-A) |
| | GaMuNə-Mə, E-KOPə, A-MOKSə, BeRAPə |
| *Earth of Fire:–* | VOLaKSiDO & SI-ODA |
| | (PiSAK) |
| | DA-TaT, DI-OMə, O-OPəZə, RoGANə |
| *Fire of Fire:–* | RoZI-ONəRə & NuRoZəFaM |
| | (ZI-ZA) |
| | ADə-RE, SI-SiPə, PA-LI, A-KA-Rə |

v

## 48 CLAVES ANGELICAE

(Key 1)
OLƏ SONuF VORoSiG,
GOHO I-AD BALaT,
LONƏSiʏ KALaZ VO-NuPiHO:
SOBRA ZOLƏ
RO-RƏ I TA NAZePiSAD GRA-A TA MALPiRoG:
DeS HOLaʏ ʏA-A NOTƏHO-A ZIMuZ,
OD KOMƏMAʏ TA NOBLOʏ ZI-EN:
SO-BA TƏHIL GƏNONuP PiRoGE ALƏDI,
DeS URoBeS OBO-LEʏ GRoSAMƏ.
KA-SARoM OHO-RE-LA KABA PIRƏ
DeS ZONƏRENSiG KAB ERoM I-ADƏNAʏ.
PILAʏ FARoZeM ZURƏZA
ADƏNA GONO I-ADƏPIL DeS HOMƏ TOʏ,
SO-BA IPAM,
LU IPAMIS,
DeS LO-HO-LO VEPƏ ZOMuD PO-AMAL,
OD BOGƏPA A-A-I
TA PI-APƏ PI-AMOL OD VO-O-AN.
ZAKARƏ KA OD ZAMƏRAN:
ODO KIKLE ʏA-A:
ZORƏGE:
LAPƏ ZI-RƏDO NOKO MAD,
HO-ATAʏ I-A-IDA.

(Key 2)
ADəGaT VəPA-Aʁ ZONəGOM FA-A-IPə SALDə,
VI-IV aLə,
SO-BAM I-ALPiRoG IZA-ZAZ PI-ADəPiʁ:
KA-SAR-MA ABəRAMəGə TA TALəHO PA-RA-KLEDA,
ʁaTA LORoSiLaʁ TURoBeS
O-OGE BALəTOʁ.
GI-VI KəHIS LU-SiD ORəRI,
OD MIKALəP KəHIS BI-A O-ZONəGON.
LAPə NO-AN TaROFə KO-RoS TA-GE,
Oʁə MA-NIN I-A-I-DON.
TORəZU GOHELə:
ZAKARə KA KəNOʁ-OD:
ZAMəRAN MIKALəZO:
OD OZAZeM U-RE-LaP:
LAPə ZI-Rə I-O-I-AD.

(Key 3)

MIKƏMA  GOHO  PI-ADƏ,

ZI-Rə  KOMə-SE-Lək  A  ZI-ENə  BI-AB  OS  LONə-DOK:

NO-RoZ  KƏHIS  O-TaHIL  GI-GI-PAK:

U-NəDeL  KƏHIS  TA  PU-IM  ikə  MO-SiP-LEk  TE-LO-Kak.

kU-I-IN  TOL-ToRoG  KƏHIS  I  KƏHIS  GE,

EM  OZI-EN  DeSTə  BəRoGDA  OD  TO-RoZUL.

I  LI  E  OLə  BAL-ZARoG

OD  A-A-LA  TaHILaN  OS  NETA-AB,

DeLU-GA  VO-MuSARoG  LON-SA  KAPə-MI-ALI

VO-RoS  KƏLA  HO-MIL  KOKASiB:

FA-FEN  IZ-IZ-OPə

OD  MI-INO-AG  DE  GaNETA-AB

VA-UN  NA  NA-E-ELə,

PANə-PIRə  MAL-PIRoGI

KA-OSiG  PILaD:

NO-AN  U-NA-LAk  BALaT  OD  VO-O-AN.

DO-O-I-AP  MAD,

GOHO-LORə  GOHUS  A-MIRAN.

MIKƏMA  I-E-HUSOZ  KAKAKOM

OD  DO-O-A-IN  NO-ARə  MIKA-OLaZ  A-A-I-OM.

KA-SARMəGə  GOHI-A:

ZAKAR  U-NI-GaLAG  OD  IMU-AMAR,

PUGO  PiLA-PiLI

A-NA-NA-ELə  kA-AN.

(Key 4)
OTəHILə  LASDI  BA-BA-GE
OD  DO-RoPiHA,  GOHOLə,
aGə  KəHIS  GE  AVAVAGO  KO-RoMPə  PiDə
DeSONuF  VI  UDIVə?
KA-SARMI  O-ALI  MAPiM
SOBAM  AG  KO-RoMPO  Kə-RoPiL,
KA-SARMəGə  KRO-ODZI  KəHIS  OD  U-GE-Gə,
DeSTə  KAPI-MA-LI  KəHIS  KAPI-MA-ON:
OD  LONuSiHIN  KəHIS  TA  LO  KəLA.
TORoGU  NO-Rə  ʁU-ASAHI  OD  iFə  KA-OSiGA:
BAGLE  ZI-RENA-I-AD  DeSI  OD  APILA.
DO-O-A-IPə  ʁA-AL,
ZAKAR  OD  ZAMəRAN  OBELI-SONuG,
RESTEL  A-AF  NO-RoMO-LAPə.

(Key 5)
SA-PAʁ  ZIMI-I  DU-IB
OD  NO-AS  TAʁU-ANIS  A-DeROKaʁ,
DO-RoPiHAL  KA-OSiG
OD  FA-ONTaS  PERIPSOL
TABLI-ORə.
KA-SARoM  A-MIPəZI  NA-ZARTaʁ  AF
OD  DeLUGAR  ZI-ZO-Pə  ZəLIDA  KA-OSiGI  TOL  TO-RəGI:
OD  ZeKəHIS  ESI-A-SiKaʁ  eLə  TA-VI-U
OD  I-A-OD  TaHILaD
DeS  HUBARə  PE-O-AL
SOBA  KO-RoMFA  KəHIS  TA  LA  ULaS  OD  iʁə-KOKASiB.
KA  NI-IS  OD  DARoBeS  ʁA-AS:
FETəHARZI  OD  BLI-ORA:
I-A-I-AL  EDəNAS  KIKLES:
BAGLE?  GE-I-AD  I  aLə.

(Key 6)
GAʮ SiDI-U K∂HIS EM∂,
MIKAL∂ZO PIL∂-ZIN:
SOBAM EL HARoG MI-R∂ BA-BA-LON
OD OBeLOK SAMU-ELaG:
DeLUGAR MALPiRoG ARKA-OSiGI
OD AKAM KANAL∂
SOBOL ZAR eF-BLI-ARoD KA-OSiGI
OD K∂HIS ANETAB OD MI-AM
TA VI-U OD eD∂.
DARoSAR SOL PETaʮ BI-EN∂:
BeRITA OD ZAKAM aG∂ MIKAL∂ZO:
SOB-HA-ATaʮ TRI-AN LU-I-AHE
OD-EKRIN∂ MAD ʮA-A ON.


(key 7)
RA-AS ISAL∂MAN PARADIZOD
O-EKRIMI A-A-O I-ALPI-RoGAʮ
ʮU-I-IN E-NA-I BUT∂MON:
OD INO-AS NI PARADI-AL∂
KA-SARM∂G∂ UGE-AR∂ K∂HIRoLAN,
OD ZONAK LUKIF-TI-AN
KO-RoS TA VA-UL∂ ZI-RoN TOLHAMI.
SOBA LO-N∂-DOʮ OD MI-AM
K∂HIS TAD O-DES UMA-DE-A
OD PI-BLI-AR∂,
OT∂HIL∂ RIT OD MI-AM.
KaNOʮU-OL RIT:
ZAKAR∂, ZAM∂RAN:
O-EKRIMI ʮA-DAʮ OD OMIKA-OLaZ A-A-I-OM.
BAGLE PAPiNOR∂ IDeLUGAM LONuS-HI
OD UM-PiLIF UGE-GI BIGaLI-AD.

(Key 8)
BA-ZeMELO ITA PIRIPiSON
OLaN NAZA-U-ABeʁ OKSə:
KA—SARMəGə URANə KəHIS U-GE-Gə
DeS-ABəRAMəGə BALTO-HA
GOHO I-AD:
SOBA MI-AN TaRI-AN TA LOLəKIS
ABA-I-U-ONIN
OD AZI-AGI-ERə RI-ORə.
IRoGILə KəHIS DA DeS PA-A-OKSə
BU-SiD KA-OSiGO,
DeS KəHIS, ODI-PU-RANə TE-LO-Aʁ,
KAKaRoG O ISALəMAN LONuK-HO OD VO-VI-NA KARoBAFə?
NI-ISO, BAGLE A-U-A-U-AGO GOHO-Nə:
NI-ISO, BAGLE MOMA-O SI-A-I-ON
OD MA-BəZA I-AD O I, AS, MOMA-Rə, PO-I-LaP.
NI-IS, ZAMəRAN KI-A-OFI KA-OSiGO
OD BLI-ORoS
OD KO-RoS-I TA ABəRAMIG.

(Key 9)
MIKA-OLI BeRANSiG PiRoGE-Lə
NAPiTA I-ALəPORə
DeS BeRIN EFA-FA-FE iPə VO-NuPiHO OLANI OD OBəZA:
SOBeKA UPA-Aʁ KəHIS TA-TA-Nə OD TaRA-NAN BA-LI-E,
ALARə LUSiDA SOBOLaN
OD KəHIS HOLaʁ KəNOʁU-ODI KI-AL.
U-NAL ALəDON MOMə KA-OSiGO
TA LAS O-LaLO-Rə Ga-NA-I LIMuL-AL:
AMəMA KəHI-IS SOBeKA MADəRID eZə KəHIS:
O-O-ANO-AN KəHIS AVINI DəRI-LaPI KA-OSiGIN,
OD BU-TaMONI PARoM ZUMU-I KaNI-LA:
DAZIS ETəHAMuZ A KəHILDA-O,
OD MI-RoK OZOLə KəHIS PIDI-A-I KOLaLAL.
UL-KININ A SOBAM UKIM.
BAGLE?
I-AD BALəTOʁ KəHI-RoLAN PARə!
NI-ISO, OD IP OFA-FA-FE,
BAGLE A KOKASiB I-KORoS-KA UNIGə BLI-ORə.

(Key 10)
KO-RAKSO
KƏHIS KO-RoMP OD BLANuS LUKALƏ
AZI-A-ZORƏ PA-EB,
SOBA LI-LONON KƏHIS VIRoʟ OP
E-OPiHAN OD RAKLIRƏ
MA-ASI BAGLE KA-OSiGI,
DeS I-ALƏPON DOSIG OD BASiGIM:
OD OKSEKSƏ DAZIS SI-ATƏRIS
OD SAL-BeROKS KINuKS-IRƏ FABO-AN.
UNALƏ KƏHIS KONƏSiT DeS DA-OKS KOKASiG
OL O-ANI-O I-O-RƏ
VOHIM OL GIZI-AKS OD E-ORoS
KOKASiG PiLOSI MOLU-I
DeS PA-GE-IPƏ
LARAG OM DƏROLaN MATORoB KOKASiB EM-NA.
eLƏ PATRALaKS I-OLƏKI MATaB,
NO-MIGƏ MO-NONuS OLO-RA GaNA-I AN-GELARoD.
OHI-O, OHI-O, OHI-O, OHI-O, OHI-O, OHI-O,
NO-IB OHI-O KA-OSiGON!
BAGLE MADƏRID I ZI-ROPƏ KƏHI-SO DƏRI-LaPA.
NI-ISO:
KaRIPƏ IP NIDALI.

(Key 11)
OKSI-A-I-AL HOLƏDO OD ZIROM O KO-RAKSO
DeS ZILƏDARƏ RA-ASI:
OD VABeZIRƏ KAMƏ-LI-AKS OD BA-HALƏ,
NI-ISO:
SALƏMAN TE-LO-Kaʟ KA-SARoMAN HOLaʟ
OD TI TA eZƏ KƏHIS, SOBA KORƏMuF I GA.
NI-ISA BAGLE ABƏRAMƏGƏ NONƏKaP.
ZAKARƏ KA OD ZAMƏRAN:
ODO KIKLE ʟA-A:
ZORƏGE:
LAPƏ ZI-RƏDO NOKO MAD,
HO-ATaʟ I-A-IDA.

(Key 12)
NONƏKI DeSONuF BABAGE OD KƏHIS OB,
HUBA-I-O TIBIBeP,
ALƏLAR A-TaRA-Aɤ OD EFƏ.
DƏRIKSƏ FAFEN MI-AN AR ENA-I O-U-OFƏ,
SOBA DO-O-A-IN A-A-I VONƏPiɤ.
ZAKARƏ GOHUS OD ZAMƏRAN:
ODO KIKLE ɤA-A:
ZORƏGE:
LAPƏ ZI-RƏDO NOKO MAD,
HO-ATaɤ I-A-IDA.

(Key 13)
NAPE-A-I BABAGENƏ
DeS BeRIN UKS O-O-A-ONA LaRINuG VONƏPiɤ DO-ALIM,
E-OLIS O-LaLOG O-RoSi-BA DeS KƏHIS AFƏFA.
MIKƏMA ISiRO MAD OD LONuS-HI-TOKS
DeS I-UMuD A-A-I GROSiB.
ZAKAR OD ZAMƏRAN:
ODO KIKLE ɤA-A:
ZORƏGE:
LAPƏ ZI-RƏDO NOKO MAD,
HO-ATaɤ I-A-IDA.

(Key 14)
NO-RO-MI BAGI-E PASiBeS O-I-AD,
DeS TaRINuT MIRoK OLƏ TƏHIL,
DODeS TOLƏHAM KA-OSiGO HOMIN,
DeS BeRIN ORO-Kaɤ ɤU-AR:
MIKƏMA BI-AL O-I-AD,
A-ISƏRO TOKS DeS-I-UM A-A-I BALƏTIM.
ZAKAR OD ZAMƏRAN:
ODO KIKLE ɤA-A:
ZORƏGE:
LAPƏ ZI-RƏDO NOKO MAD,
HO-ATaɤ I-A-IDA.

(Key 15)
ILaS TABA-AN LI-ALPiRoT
KASARoMAN UPA-AHI KəHIS DARoG
DeS-OKIDO KA-OS9GI O-RoSiKO-Rə:
DeS-OKIDO KA-OSiGI O-RoSiKO-Rə:
DeS OMAKS MONASiKI BA-E-O-U-IB
OD EMETəGIS I-A-I-ADIKS.
OD EMETəGIS I-A-I-ADIKS.
ZAKAR OD ZAMəRAN:
ODO KIKLE ʁA-A:
ZORəGE:
LAPə ZI-RəDO NOKO MAD,
HO-ATaʁ I-A-IDA.

(Key 16)
ILaS VI-U-I-ALPiRoT SALəMAN BALaT,
DeS AKRO-ODZI BU-SiD
OD BLI-ORAKS BALIT:
DeS-IN-SI KA-OSiG LUSiDAN EMOD
DeS-OM OD TəLI-OB:
DəRI-LaPA GEʁ ILaS MAD ZILO-DARoP.
ZAKAR OD ZAMəRAN:
ODO KIKLE ʁA-A:
ZORəGE:
LAPə ZI-RəDO NOKO MAD,
HO-ATaʁ I-A-IDA.

(Key 17)
ILaS DI-ALPiRoT
SOBA UPA-Aʁ KəHIS NANəBA ZIKSiLA-I DO-DeSIʁ
OD BeRINTə FAKSiS HUBARO TASiTAKS ILəSI,
SOBA-I-AD I VONəPO-UNəPiʁ,
ALəDON DAKS IL OD TO-ATARə.
ZAKAR OD ZAMəRAN:
ODO KIKLE ʁA-A:
ZORəGE:
LAPə ZI-RəDO NOKO MAD,
HO-ATaʁ I-A-IDA.

(Key 18)
ILaS MIKA-OLaZ OL-PIRoT
I-ALPəRoG BLI-ORoS
DeS ODO BU-SiDI-Rə O-I-AD
O-U-O-ARoS KA-OSiGO,
KA-SARMəGə LA-I-AD ERAN BeRINTaS KA-FA-FAMə,
DeS I-UMuD AʋiLO ADO-HI
MOZ OD MA-OFiFAS:
BOLaP KOMO-BLI-ORoT PAMəBeT.
ZAKAR OD ZAMəRAN:
ODO KIKLE ʋA-A:
ZORəGE:
LAPə ZI-RəDO NOKO MAD,
HO-ATaʋ I-A-IDA.


(Key of Thirty Ayres)
MA-DRI-AKS DeS PiRAF [LILə],
KəHIS MIKA-OLaZ SA-ANIRə KA-OSiGO,
OD FI-SIS BAL-ZI-ZeRAS I-A-IDA!
NONəKA GO-HU-LIM, MIKəMA ADO-I-AN MAD,
I-A-OD BLI-ORoB,
SOBA O-O-A-ONA KəHIS LUKIF-TI-AS PERIPSOL,
DeS ABRA-ASiSA NONəKaF NETA-A-IB KA-OSiGI
OD TILaB ADə-PiHA-HaT DAM-PiLOZ,
TO-O-ATə NONəKaF aGə-MIKALəZOMA
LəRASiD TOF-GəLO
MARoB I-ARəRI IDO-IGO
OD TORoZULaP I-A-ODAF, GOHOLə:
KA-OSiGA TABA-ORoD SA-ANIRə
OD Kə-HoRIS-TE-OS I-RəPO-IL TI-OBeL,
BU-SiDI-Rə TILaB NO-AL-IRə PA-ID O-RoSi-BA
OD DO-DRoM-NI ZILəNA.
ELəZAP TILaB PARoM GI PERIPSAKS
OD TA ʋU-RəLaSTə BO-O-APIS.
Lə-NIBeM O-UKəHO SIMuP,
OD Kə-HoRIS-TE-OS AG TOLə-TORoN MI-RoK iʋə TI—OBeL
    LEL:
TONə PA-OMBeD DILaZ-MO AS PI-AN,

OD Kə-HoRIS-TE-OS AG aLə TORə-TORoN PARAKAɤ A SIMuP:
KORoD-ZIZ
DO-DePAL OD FI-FALaZ Lə-SiMuNAD,
OD FARəGaT BAMuS OMA-O-AS:
KO-NIS-BeRA OD A-VA-VOKS TO-NUGə:
O-RoSKA-TəBeL NO-ASMI TAB-GES LE-VITə-HəMONuG.
UN-Kə-HI OMuP TILaB ORoS.
BAGLE? MO-O-O-Aɤ OLə KORoD-ZIZ.
aLə KAPI-MA-O IKSO-MAKSIP
OD KA-KOKASiB GOSA-A:
BAGLENə PI-I TI-ANəTA A BA-BA-LONuD,
OD FA-ORəGaT TELOKə VO VIM.
MA-DRI-I-AKS TORoZU:
O-A-DRI-AKS OROKəHA ABO-A-PiRI.
TABA-ORI PRI-AZ AR-TABAS:
ADeRoPAN KO-RoSTA DOBIKS.
I-OLəKAM PRI-AZI ARKO-AZI-ORə,
OD ɤU-ASiB ɤəTINuG.
RIPIRə PA-A-OKSiT SAGA-KO-Rə:
UMuL OD PRoDZARə KAKaRoG A-O-IVE-A-E KO-RoMPiT.
TORoZU, ZAKAR,
OD ZAMəRAN ASPiTə SIBəSI BU-TəMONA,
DeS SURəZAS TI-A BALTAN.
ODO KIKLE ɤA-A:
OD OZA-ZeMA PiLA-PiLI I-AD-NA-MADə.

vi
## THE THIRTY AYRES

| | | | |
|---|---|---|---|
| 1 | LILə | 16 | LE-A |
| 2 | ARoN | 17 | TANə |
| 3 | ZO-Mə | 18 | ZENə |
| 4 | PAZ | 19 | PO-Pə |
| 5 | LITə | 20 | KəHoRə |
| 6 | MAZ | 21 | ASiP |
| 7 | DE-O | 22 | LINə |
| 8 | ZIDə | 23 | TO-Rə |
| 9 | ZIPə | 24 | NI-A |
| 10 | ZAKSə | 25 | U-TI |
| 11 | IKaʁ | 26 | DESə |
| 12 | LO-E | 27 | ZA-A |
| 13 | ZIMə | 28 | BAGə |
| 14 | U-TA | 29 | RI-I |
| 15 | OKSO | 30 | TEKSə |

vii

## LIBER SCIENTIAE COLUMN III

1  OKə-KODONə
2  PASiKOMuB
3  VALəGARoS
4  DONə-GəNIS
5  PA-KASiNA
6  DI-ALO-I-A
7  SAMA-PiHA
8  VI-RO-OLI
9  ANə-DISəPI
10  TəHO-TANuP
11  AKSiKS-I-ARoG
12  POTə-HəNIRə
13  LA-ZəDIKSI
14  NO-KA-MALə
15  TI-ARə-PAKS
16  SAKS-TOMuP
17  VA-VA-AMuP
18  ZIRə-ZIRoD
19  OPiMA-KAS
20  GENA-DOLə
21  ASəPI-A-ONə
22  ZAMuF-RES
23  TOD-NA-ONə
24  PRISiTAK
25  ODə-DI-ORoG
26  KəRALə-PIRə
27  DO-ANuZ-INə
28  LEKSARəPiⱬ
29  KOMA-NANə
30  TA-BI-TOMə

31  MOLaP-ANuD
32  USiNARə-DA
33  PO-NO-DOLə
34  TA-PA-MALə
35  GE-DO-ONuS
36  AM-BRI-OLə
37  GE-KA-ONuD
38  LA-PA-RINə
39  DO-KE-PAKS
40  TE-DO-ONuD
41  VI-VI-POS
42  VO-A-NAMuB
43  TA-HAMəDO
44  NOTI-ABI
45  TASiTOZO
46  KUKaN-RoPTə
47  LA-VA-KONə
48  SO-KəHI-AL
49  SIGaM-ORoF
50  A-I-DeROPiT
51  TO-KARə-ZI
52  NABA-O-MI
53  ZAFA-SA-I

54  I-ALə-PAMuB
55  TO-RəZOKSI
56  A-BRI-ONuD
57  O-MAGə-RAP
58  ZIL-DəRON
59  PARəZIBA
60  TO-TO-KANə

61  KəHI-RoZePA
62  TO-AN-TOMə
63  VIKSiPALaG
64  O-SI-DA-I-A
65  PA-O-A-O-ANə
	(LAKSə-DIZI)*
66  KAL-ZIRoG
67  RO-NO-OMuB
68  ONI-ZIMuP
69  ZAKSA-NINə
70  O-RANuK-IRə
71  KəHAS-LəPO
72  SO-AGE-ELə
73  MIRə-ZINuD
74  OBəVA-ORoS
75  RANə-GəLAMə
76  PO-PiHANuD
77  NI-GRA-NA
78  LAZəHI-IMə
79  SAZI-AMI
80  MATə-HU-LA
81  KəRoP-A-NIB
82  PABə-NIKSiP
83  PO-KISəNI
84  OKS-LOPARə
85  VASə-TəRIMə
86  ODəRAKS-TI
87  GaMuT-ZI-AMə
88  TA-A-OGəBA
89  GEMə-NIMuB
90  ADə-VO-RoPTə
91  DOKSiMA-ELə

* See Note B, *De Rebus Enochianis 2.*

### viii
### LIBER SCIENTIAE COLUMN VIII

| | |
|---|---|
| Nos. 1, 7, 24, 27, 30, 43, 51, 83 | ZARƏ-ZILaG |
| Nos. 2, 15, 21, 28, 57, 69, 72 | ZINƏ-GƏGENƏ |
| Nos. 3, 8, 14, 29, 39, 41, 53, 60 | ALƏPU-DUSƏ |
| Nos. 4, 19, 67, 70, 73, 80, 86, 89 | ZAR-NA-Aʏ |
| Nos. 5, 6, 36, 46, 49, 74, 79 | ZI-RA-KAʏ |
| Nos. 9, 10, 11, 26, 31, 37, 44, 68, 71, 82 | LA-VA-VOTƏ |
| Nos. 12, 17, 42, 45, 48, 54, 55, 61, 64, 66, 75, 76, 78, 87, 88 | AR-FA-OLaG |
| Nos. 13, 23, 38, 50, 65 | OL-PA-GED |
| Nos. 16, 18, 22, 40, 52, 58, 81 | GEBA-BALƏ |
| Nos. 20, 25, 33, 47, 59, 85, 90 | HO-NO-NOLƏ |
| Nos. 32, 34, 63, 84, 91 | ZURƏ-KƏHOLƏ |
| Nos. 35, 56, 62, 77 | KADA-AMuP |

### ix
### SPIRIT NAMES

EKSARoP
HƏKOMA
NA-NƏTA
BI-TOMƏ

### x
### ARCHANGELIC NAMES*

LEKSARƏPiʏ
KOMA-NANƏ
TA-BI-TOMƏ
PA-O-A-O-ANƏ

* Being Nos. 28,29,30, and 65, of Column III Liber Scientiae.

*APPENDIX* B

**Form of Invocation and Dismissal of Elementals**

**Invocation and Dismissal of Elementals of Air**
**Invocation and Dismissal of Elementals of Water**
**Invocation and Dismissal of Elementals of Earth**
**Invocation and Dismissal of Elementals of Fire**

## INVOCATION OF THE AIR ELEMENTALS

*(Battery: 1)*

From the East, the place of Morning Light, cometh the rushing of the wind wherein the Spirits of Air do dwell.

*(Hebrew)*

In the Glorious Name AHIH *(trace invoking ⊕ pentagram as name is vibrated),*and in the Wonderful Name YHVH *(trace invoking △ pentagram as name is vibrated),* I summon you, Dwellers in the Astral Light.
In the name of RUACHIEL, Archangel of Air, and by the power of the Man-Kerub *(trace ≈ ),* I summon you, Dwellers in the Astral Light. Come in peace and come in quietness, but come in your multitudes!

*(Greek)*

In the Glorious Name ATHANATOS *(trace invoking ⊕ pentagram as name is vibrated),* and in the Wonderful Name SELAE GENETES *(trace invoking △ pentagram as name is vibrated),* I summon you, Dwellers in the Astral Light.
In the name of SOTER, Archon of Air, and by the power of the Man-Kerub *(trace ≈ ),* I summon you, Dwellers in the Astral Light . Come in peace and come in quietness, but come in your multitudes!

*Trace a large equal-armed cross in the air before you:— first the horizontal from left to right, then the vertical downwards from the top. This done, intone:—*

In the Names ORO IBAɤ A-OZƏPI,* the Names which govern the Invisible even as the Visible, which are displayed upon the Banners of the East, I summon you, Dwellers in the Astral Light.

In the Divine and Angelical Name BATA-IVAɤ *(trace ͻ in the centre of the cross as name is vibrated),* I summon you, Dwellers in the Astral Light.

* See Appendix C.

415

ET IN CIRCUITU SEDIS SEDILIA VIGINTI QUATUOR: ET SUPER THRONOS VIGINTI QUATUOR SENIORES SEDENTES, CIRCUMAMICTI VESTIMENTIS ALBIS, ET IN CAPITIBUS EORUM CORONAE AUREAE.†

*Raise right hand, or Burin if this be employed:−*

Children of the Realms of Elemental Air, be present and attend upon this ceremony, and in your proper office participate in the Work. Dwellers in the Astral Light, thus by my potent art do I invite and invoke you!

*NOTE: This invocation, like the three which follow, is to be made facing the appropriate quarter.*

† **Vulgate,** *Apocalypsis IV, 4.*

### THE LICENSE TO DEPART
#### Dismissal of the Air Elementals

*(Battery: 1)*

Spirits of Air, be there peace between us. Dwellers in the Astral Light, with the Blessing of the All-Highest return to your abodes, and with gladness come again when you are called.

| *(Hebrew)* | *(Greek)* |
|---|---|
| Spirits of Air, Children of this world's innocence, go now in the Name AHIH *(trace banishing ⊛ pentagram as name is vibrated)*, and in the Name YHVH *(trace banishing △ pentagram as name is vibrated)*. | Spirits of Air, Children of this world's innocence, go now in the Name ATHANATOS *(trace banishing ⊛ pentagram as name is vibrated)*, and in the Name SELAE GENETES *(trace banishing △ pentagram as name is vibrated)*. |

*NOTE: This banishing, like the three which follow, is to be accomplished facing the same quarter as its corresponding invocation.*

## INVOCATION OF THE WATER ELEMENTALS

*(Battery: 1)*
        From the West, the place of Twilight, cometh the sound of the
moving waters wherein the Spirits of Water do dwell.

| *(Hebrew)* | *(Greek)* |
|---|---|
| In the Glorious Name AGLA *(trace invoking ⊛ pentagram as name is vibrated)*, and in the Wonderful Name AL *(trace invoking ▽ pentagram as name is vibrated)*, I summon you, Dwellers in the Astral Light. | In the Glorious Name ISCHYROS *(trace invoking ⊛ pentagram as name is vibrated)*, and in the Wonderful Name PANKRATES *(trace invoking ▽ pentagram as name is vibrated)*, I summon you, Dwellers in the Astral Light. |
| In the name of MIEL, Archangel of Water, and by the power of the Eagle-Kerub (trace ♏), I summon you, Dwellers in the Astral Light. Come in peace and come in quietness, but come in your multitudes! | In the name of ASPHALEIOS, Archon of Water, and by the power of the Eagle-Kerub *(trace* ♏ ), I summon you, Dwellers in the Astral Light. Come in peace and come in quietness, but come in your multitudes! |

*Trace a large equal-armed cross in the air before you:— first the horizontal from left to right, then the vertical downwards from the top. This done, intone:—*

In the Names eM∂Piẋ ARoSiL GA-I-OL∂, the Names which govern the Invisible even as the Visible, which are displayed upon the Banners of the West, I summon you, Dwellers in the Astral Light.

In the Divine and Angelical Name RA-AGI-OSiL *(trace ◌ in the centre of the cross as name is vibrated)*, I summon you, Dwellers in the Astral Light.

ET IN CIRCUITU SEDIS SEDILIA VIGINTI QUATUOR: ET SUPER THRONOS VIGINTI QUATUOR SENIORES SEDENTES, CIRCUMAMICTI VESTIMENTIS ALBIS, ET IN CAPITIBUS EORUM CORONAE AUREAE.

*Raise right hand, or Cup if this be employed:—*

Children of the Realms of Elemental Water, be present and attend upon this ceremony, and in your proper office participate in the Work. Dwellers in the Astral Light, thus by my potent art do I invite and invoke you!

## THE LICENCE TO DEPART
### Dismissal of the Water Elementals

*(Battery: 1)*

Spirits of Water, be there peace between us. Dwellers in the Astral Light, with the Blessing of the All-Highest return to your abodes, and with gladness come again when you are called.

<table>
<tr><td>(Hebrew)</td><td>(Greek)</td></tr>
<tr><td>Spirits of Water, Children of this world's innocence, go now in the Name AGLA (trace banishing ⊛ pentagram as name is vibrated), and in the Name AL (trace banishing ▽ pentagram as name is vibrated).</td><td>Spirits of Water, Children of this world's innocence, go now in the Name ISCHYROS (trace banishing ⊛pentagram as name is vibrated), and in the Name PANKRATES (trace banishing ▽ pentagram as name is vibrated).</td></tr>
</table>

## INVOCATION OF THE EARTH ELEMENTALS

*(Battery: 1)*

From the North, the place of Fertile Earth, cometh the strength of the mountain wherein the Spirits of Earth do dwell.

### (Hebrew)

In the Glorious Name AGLA *(trace invoking ⊕ pentagram as name is vibrated)*, and in the Wonderful Name ADNI *(trace invoking ▽ pentagram as name is vibrated)*, I summon you, Dwellers in the Astral Light.

In the name of AUPHIRIEL, Archangel of Earth, and by the power of the Ox-Kerub *(trace ♉)*, I summon you, Dwellers in the Astral Light. Come in peace and come in quietness, but come in your multitudes!

### (Greek)

In the Glorious Name ISCHYROS *(trace invoking ⊕ pentagram as name is vibrated)*, and in the Wonderful Name KYRIOS *(trace invoking ▽ pentagram as name is vibrated)*, I summon you, Dwellers in the Astral Light.

In the name of AMYNTOR, Archon of Earth, and by the power of the Ox-Kerub *(trace ♉)*, I summon you, Dwellers in the Astral Light. Come in peace and come in quietness, but come in your multitudes!

*Trace a large equal-armed cross in the air before you:— first the horizontal from left to right, then the vertical downwards from the top. This done, intone:—*

In the Names MO-Rə DI-AL HəKaTəGA, the Names which govern the Invisible even as the Visible, which are displayed upon the Banners of the North, I summon you, Dwellers in the Astral Light.

In the Divine and Angelical Name IKə-ZəHIHAL *(trace ⌒ in the centre of the cross as name is vibrated)*, I summon you, Dwellers in the Astral Light.

ET IN CIRCUITU SEDIS SEDILIA VIGINTI QUATUOR: ET
SUPER THRONOS VIGINTI QUATUOR SENIORES SEDENTES,
CIRCUMAMICTI VESTIMENTIS ALBIS, ET IN CAPITIBUS EORUM
CORONAE AUREAE.


*Raise right hand, or Disc if this be employed:—*
   Children of the Realms of Elemental Earth, be present and attend
upon this ceremony, and in your proper office participate in the Work.
Dwellers in the Astral Light, thus by my potent art do I invite and
invoke you!

## THE LICENSE TO DEPART
### Dismissal of the Earth Elementals

*(Battery: 1)*

Spirits of Earth, be there peace between us. Dwellers in the Astral Light, with the Blessing of the All-Highest return to your abodes, and with gladness come again when you are called.

| (Hebrew) | (Greek) |
|---|---|
| Spirits of Earth, Children of this world's innocence, go now in the Name AGLA *(trace banishing ⊕ pentagram as name is vibrated)*, and in the Name ADNI *(trace banishing ▽ pentagram as name is vibrated)*. | Spirits of Earth, Children of this world's innocence, go now in the Name ISCHYROS *(trace banishing ⊕ pentagram as name is vibrated)*, and in the Name KYRIOS *(trace banishing ▽ pentagram as name is vibrated)*. |

## INVOCATION OF THE FIRE ELEMENTALS

*(Battery: 1)*
From  the South, the place of Flashing Flame, cometh the heart of
the radiance wherein the Spirits of Fire do dwell.

| *(Hebrew)* | *(Greek)* |
|---|---|
| In the Glorious Name AHIH *(trace invoking ⊕ pentagram as name is vibrated)*, and in the Wonderful Name ALHIM *(trace invoking △ pentagram as name is vibrated)*, I summon you, Dwellers in the Astral Light. In the name of ASHIEL, Archangel of Fire, and by the power of the Lion-Kerub *(trace ♌)*, I summon you, Dwellers in the Astral Light. Come in peace and come in quietness, but come in your multitudes! | In the Glorious Name ATHANATOS *(trace invoking ⊕ pentagram as name is vibrated)*, and in the Wonderful Name THEOS *(trace invoking △ pentagram as name is vibrated)*, I summon you, Dwellers in the Astral Light. In the name of ALASTOR, Archon of Fire, and by the power of the Lion-Kerub *(trace ♌)*, I summon you, Dwellers in the Astral Light. Come in peace and come in quietness, but come in your multitudes! |

*Trace a large equal-armed cross in the air before you:— first the horizontal from left to right, then the vertical downwards from the top. This done, intone:—*

In the Names O-IPꝺ TE-A-A PiDOKE, the Names which govern the Invisible even as the Visible, which are displayed upon the Banners of the South, I summon you, Dwellers in the Astral Light.

In the Divine and Angelical Name EDeL-PiRoNA-A *(trace ꙩ in the centre of the cross as name is vibrated)*, I summon you, Dwellers in the Astral Light.

ET IN CIRCUITU SEDIS SEDILIA VIGINTI QUATUOR: ET SUPER THRONOS VIGINTI QUATUOR SENIORES SEDENTES, CIRCUMAMICTI VESTIMENTIS ALBIS, ET IN CAPITIBUS EORUM CORONAE AUREAE.

*Raise right hand, or Elemental Wand if this be employed:—*

Children of the Realms of Elemental Fire, be present and attend upon this ceremony, and in your proper office participate in the Work. Dwellers in the Astral Light, thus by my potent art do I invite and invoke you!

## THE LICENSE TO DEPART
### Dismissal of the Fire Elementals

**(Battery: 1)**

Spirits of Fire, be there peace between us. Dwellers in the Astral Light, with the Blessing of the All-Highest return to your abodes, and with gladness come again when you are called.

| (Hebrew) | (Greek) |
|---|---|
| Spirits of Fire, Children of this world's innocence, go now in the Name AHIH *(trace banishing ⊕ pentagram as name is vibrated)*, and in the Name ALHIM *(trace banishing △ pentagram as name is vibrated)*. | Spirits of Fire, Children of this world's innocence, go now in the Name ATHANATOS *(trace banishing ⊕ pentagram as name is vibrated)*, and in the Name THEOS *(trace banishing △ pentagram as name is vibrated)*. |

# ORDER LLEWELLYN BOOKS TODAY!

*Llewellyn publishes hundreds of books on your favorite subjects! To get these exciting books, including the ones on the following pages, check your local bookstore or order them directly from Llewellyn.*

## Order Online:
Visit our website at www.llewellyn.com, select your books, and order them on our secure server.

## Order by Phone:
- Call toll-free within the U.S. at 1-877-NEW-WRLD (1-877-639-9753)
  Call toll-free within Canada at 1-866-NEW-WRLD (1-866-639-9753)
- We accept VISA, MasterCard, and American Express

## Order by Mail:
Send the full price of your order (MN residents add 7% sales tax) in U.S. funds, plus postage & handling to:

> **Llewellyn Worldwide**
> **P.O. Box 64383, Dept. 0-7387-0169-6**
> **St. Paul, MN 55164-0383, U.S.A.**

## Postage & Handling:
**Standard** (U.S., Mexico, & Canada). If your order is:
> Up to $25.00, add $3.50
> $25.01 - $48.99, add $4.00
> $49.00 and over, FREE STANDARD SHIPPING

(Continental U.S. orders ship UPS. AK, HI, PR, & P.O. Boxes ship USPS 1st class. Mex. & Can. ship PMB.)

**International Orders:**
**Surface Mail:** For orders of $20.00 or less, add $5 plus $1 per item ordered. For orders of $20.01 and over, add $6 plus $1 per item ordered.

**Air Mail:**
*Books:* Postage & Handling is equal to the total retail price of all books in the order.
*Non-book items:* Add $5 for each item.

*Orders are processed within 2 business days. Please allow for normal shipping time. Postage and handling rates subject to change.*

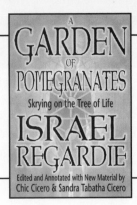

# A Garden of Pomegranates

*Skrying on the Tree of Life*

ISRAEL REGARDIE,
EDITED AND ANNOTATED WITH NEW MATERIAL
BY CHIC CICERO AND SANDRA TABATHA CICERO

When Israel Regardie wrote *A Garden of Pomegranates* in 1932, he designed it to be a simple yet comprehensive guidebook outlining the complex system of the Qabalah and providing a key to its symbolism. Since then it has achieved the status of a classic among texts on the Hermetic Qabalah. It stands as the best single introductory guide for magicians on this complex system, with an emphasis on direct experience through meditation on the twenty-two paths.

Now, Chic Cicero and Sandra Tabatha Cicero—Golden Dawn adepts and personal friends of the late Regardie—have made the book even more useful for today's occult students with full annotations, critical commentary, and explanatory notes. They've added practical material in the form of pathworkings, suggested exercises, and daily affirmations—one for each Sephirah and each path. Brief rituals, meditations, and Qabalistic mantras complement Regardie's section on gematria and other forms of numerical Qabalah.

1-56718-141-4
552 pp., 6 x 9                                                     $17.95

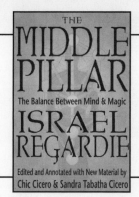

## The Middle Pillar
### *The Balance Between Mind & Magic*

ISRAEL REGARDIE
EDITED AND ANNOTATED WITH NEW MATERIAL BY
CHIC CICERO AND SANDRA TABATHA CICERO

Break the barrier between the conscious and unconscious mind through the Middle Pillar exercise, a technique that serves as a bridge into magic, chakra work, and psychology. This classic work introduces a psychological perspective on magic and occultism while giving clear directions on how to perform the Qabalistic Cross, The Lesser Banishing Ritual of the Pentagram, the Middle Pillar exercise, along with its accompanying methods of circulating the light, the Vibratory Formula, and the building up of the Tree of Life in the aura.

The Ciceros, who knew Regardie personally, have made his book much more accessible by adding an extensive and useful set of notes, along with chapters that explain Regardie's work in depth. They expand upon it by carrying it into a realm of new techniques that are directly related to Regardie's core material. Especially valuable is the chapter on psychology, which provides a solid frame of reference for Regardie's numerous remarks on this subject.

1-56718-140-6
312 pp., 6 x 9, illus.                                          $14.95

**To order, call 1-877-NEW-WRLD**
Prices subject to change without notice

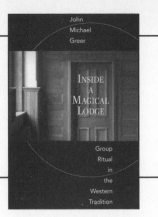

# Inside a Magical Lodge
## *Group Ritual in the Western Tradition*

### JOHN MICHAEL GREER

For centuries, magical lodges have been one of the most important and least understood parts of the Western esoteric traditions. The traditional secrecy of lodge organizations has made it next to impossible for modern students of magic to learn what magical lodges do, and how their powerful and effective traditions of ritual, symbolism, and organization can be put to work.

This is the first book to reveal the foundations of lodge work on all levels—from the framework of group structure that allows lodges to efficiently handle the practical needs of a working magical group, through the subtle approaches to symbolism and ritual developed within lodge circles, to the potent magical methods that lodges use in their initiations and other ceremonial workings.

It is a must-read for members of existing lodges, for students of magical traditions such as the Golden Dawn, for practitioners of other kinds of group magical work, and for all those who have wondered about the hidden world behind lodge doors.

1-56718-314-X
360 pp., 6 x 9                                                                   $17.95

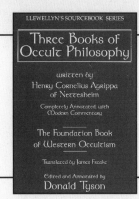

# The Three Books of Occult Philosophy

## HENRY CORNELIUS AGRIPPA
### EDITED AND ANNOTATED BY DONALD TYSON

Agrippa's *Three Books of Occult Philosophy* is the single most important text in the history of Western occultism. Occultists have drawn upon it for five centuries, although they rarely give it credit. First published in Latin in 1531 and translated into English in 1651, it has never been reprinted in its entirety since. Photocopies are hard to find and very expensive. Now, for the first time in five hundred years, *Three Books of Occult Philosophy* is presented as Agrippa intended. There were many errors in the original translation, but occult author Donald Tyson has made the corrections and has clarified the more obscure material with copious notes.

This is a necessary reference tool not only for all magicians, but also for scholars of the Renaissance, Neoplatonism, the Western Kabbalah, the history of ideas and sciences, and the occult tradition. It is as practical today as it was five hundred years ago.

0-87542-832-0
1,024 pp., 7 x 10                                                   $39.95

## Practical Guide to Astral Projection
### *The Out-of-Body Experience*

#### DENNING & PHILLIPS

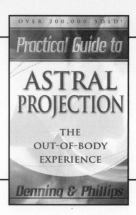

Yes, your consciousness can be sent forth, out of the body, with full awareness, and return with full memory. You can travel through time and space, converse with nonphysical entities, obtain knowledge by nonmaterial means, and experience higher dimensions.

Is there life after death? Are we forever shackled by time and space? The ability to go forth by means of the astral body, or body of light, gives personal assurance of consciousness (and life) beyond the limitations of the physical body. No other answer to these ageless questions is as meaningful as experienced reality.

The reader is led through the essential stages for inner growth and development that will culminate in fully conscious projection and return. Not only are the requisite practices set forth in step-by-step procedures, augmented with photographs and visualization aids, but the vital reasons for undertaking them are clearly explained. Beyond this, the great benefits from the various practices themselves are demonstrated in renewed physical and emotional health, mental discipline, spiritual attainment, and the development of extra faculties.

0-87542-181-4
216 pp., 5³⁄₁₆ x 8, photos                                        $9.95

## Practical Guide to Creative Visualization

*Manifest Your Desires*

### DENNING & PHILLIPS

All things you want must have their start in your mind. The average person uses very little of the full creative power that is potentially his or hers. It's like the power locked in the atom—it's all there, but you have to learn to release it and apply it constructively.

If you can see it . . . in your mind's eye . . . you will have it! It's true: you can have whatever you want, but there are "laws" to mental creation that must be followed. The power of the mind is not limited to, nor limited by, the material world. Creative Visualization enables humans to reach beyond, into the invisible world of astral and spiritual forces.

Through an easy series of step-by-step, progressive exercises, your mind is applied to bring desire into realization! Wealth, power, success, happiness, even psychic powers . . . even what we call magickal power and spiritual attainment . . . all can be yours. You can easily develop this completely natural power and correctly apply it for your immediate and practical benefit.

0-87542-183-0
240 pp. 5³⁄₁₆ x 8                                            $9.95

## Practical Guide to Psychic Powers
### *Awaken Your Sixth Sense*

DENNING & PHILLIPS

Who has not dreamed of possessing powers to move objects without physically touching them, to see at a distance or into the future, to know another's thoughts, to read the past of an object or person, or to find water or mineral wealth by dowsing?

This book is a complete course—teaching you step-by-step how to develop the powers that actually have been yours since birth. Psychic powers are a natural part of your mind; by expanding your mind in this way, you will gain health and vitality, emotional strength, greater success in your daily pursuits, and a new understanding of your inner self.

You'll learn to play with these new skills, working with groups of friends to accomplish things you never would have believed possible. The text shows you how to make the equipment, do the exercises—many of them at any time, anywhere—and how to use your abilities to change your life and the lives of those close to you.

0-87542-191-1
216 pp., 5³⁄₁₆ x 8, illus.

$9.95

**To order, call 1-877-NEW-WRLD**
Prices subject to change without notice